personal
Jesus

Engaging Culture

WILLIAM A. DYRNESS
AND ROBERT K. JOHNSTON,
SERIES EDITORS

The Engaging Culture series is designed to help Christians respond with theological discernment to our contemporary culture. Each volume explores particular cultural expressions, seeking to discover God's presence in the world and to involve readers in sympathetic dialogue and active discipleship. These books encourage neither an uninformed rejection nor an uncritical embrace of culture, but active engagement informed by theological reflection.

personal
Jesus

how popular music shapes our souls

Clive Marsh & Vaughan S. Roberts

Baker Academic
a division of Baker Publishing Group
Grand Rapids, Michigan

Published by Baker Academic
a division of Baker Publishing Group
P.O. Box 6287, Grand Rapids, MI 49516-6287
www.bakeracademic.com

Printed in the United States of America

Library of Congress Cataloging-in-Publication Data

Marsh, Clive.
    Personal Jesus : how popular music shapes our souls / Clive Marsh & Vaughn S. Roberts.
        p.   cm. — (Engaging culture)
    Includes bibliographical references and index.
    ISBN 978-0-8010-3909-6 (pbk.)
    1. Popular music—Religious aspects. 2. Popular music—Social aspects. I. Roberts, Vaughn.
II. Title.
ML3921.8.P67M27 2013
306.4′8423—dc23   2012026623

Scripture quotations are from the Holy Bible, New International Version®. NIV®. Copyright © 1973, 1978, 1984, 2011 by Biblica, Inc.™ Used by permission of Zondervan. All rights reserved worldwide. www.zondervan.com

The internet addresses, email addresses, and phone numbers in this book are accurate at the time of publication. They are provided as a resource. Baker Publishing Group does not endorse them or vouch for their content or permanence.

12   13   14   15   16   17   18   7   6   5   4   3   2   1

For Philip and Hannah,
who keep Clive in touch and don't hold back with their opinions;
and for Paul,
who didn't need to share his extensive record collection
and sound system with his younger brother,
but did—generously.

For Mandy, Becky, and Jon
and our shared love of music of all kinds.

contents

Foreword by Tom Beaudoin   ix

Acknowledgments   xi

Introduction   xiii

Part 1   Music and Religion

1. Music in Context: Contemporary Discussion about Religion and Popular Culture   3

2. Explorations in Affective Space: The Magisteria-Ibiza Spectrum   15

3. Acknowledging a Theological Interest: Popular Music from Sin to Sacramentality   29

Part 2   Living by Pop Music

4. Pop Music in the Marketplace   41

5. Pop Music and the Body   57

6. The Tingle Factor: Popular Music and Transcendence Today   77

7. Pop Music, Ritual, and Worship   91

8. What's on Your iPod? Classics, Canons, and the Question of What Matters   109

Part 3   Pop Music and Theology

9. The Discipline of Listening: How (and Why) What We're Doing with Music Matters Ultimately   123

10. Three Steps to Heaven? On Negotiating Meaning between Popular Music and Christian Theology   139

11. Embodied Social Rituals: Revisiting Theology through Popular Music   163

A Programmatic Postscript: Practical Consequences for Church, Academy, and Daily Living   183

Notes   191

Bibliography   211

Subject Index   225

Music Index   233

foreword

One of the most fundamental experiences of human life in almost any culture is music's power to structure personal and social identity and relationships. There are special reasons for this to be true in contemporary technological societies, where musical invention and enjoyment is notably diffuse and influential in everyday life. This is so on a micro level, when people can personalize their favorite music electronically, listening in privacy throughout their day. It is also true on a macro level, with the profusion of concert and festival culture, from public minstrels on street corners and in subway stations, to larger concerts and multiday festivals, all of which show every sign of increasing their place in the soundscape that arranges everyday life for a majority of the world's privileged people.

Music, especially that music disseminated "popularly" through electronic media platforms of internet, film, and television, is a fundamental palette for contemporary sensing, for negotiating what is real. Popular music is that color wheel in relation to which people identify those claiming powers around which they orient their lives. The experience of those who enjoy music, inadequately called (and sometimes dismissed as) "fans," is a significant frame for holding whatever people come to call religious or spiritual.

Clive Marsh and Vaughan Roberts are on the leading edge of research that makes theological sense of popular music. With *Personal Jesus*, they show how important it is for theologically minded people to take seriously the concerns of fans, as those active listeners experience the music that they love, that they incorporate into their bodily dispositions and their thinking, and that they ritualize. They show how religious studies is not an optional discourse for comprehending popular music's function in everyday life, but an important partner in an interdisciplinary exploration. They do all this while balancing respect for the impact of music on listeners and the active meanings that fans make of it, on the one hand, and the theological tradition that provides basic concepts for organizing experience, for those related to—but not stuck within—religious communities, on the other.

Much theological research to date in popular culture studies has treated pop culture as a set of "texts" waiting to be read, like minor bibles awaiting postmodern interpreters. I am not the only theologian who has resisted working from the experience and practice of others, having often preferred my own practice instead, but cloaked in and defended by normative-sounding, systematic-theological-aspiring, concepts. Marsh and Roberts rightly criticize my and others' work, or rather resituate it in its promise and limits, and help change the conversation. If popular music matters, they argue, that mattering has to do with its uses. Even more so, if it matters theologically, that mattering has to do with music's effect on human beings. In so proceeding, Marsh and Roberts prepare the way for a new style of making theological sense of popular culture. The continued decline of the influence of religious traditions makes this kind of theological study even more imperative. In this situation, Marsh and Roberts show us why studying the lived experience of popular music is an imperative if we want to find out where religion cohabitates with ordinary stuff, more or less openly, today: in the spaces of meaning communicated by music in everyday life.

Tom Beaudoin
Fordham University, New York City

acknowledgments

A book like this takes a long time to put together. Cowritten, long in gestation, a labor of love as well as both an academic project and a contribution to a faith tradition, a project borne of passion to which many other fans of popular music have contributed; it is the result of countless conversations and debates in addition to the hours spent before a screen, poring over books or, yes, just listening. Trying to list all those who should be thanked will prove impossible. But try we must because the material here has been thrashed out formally and informally in many places and contexts.

Chapter 2 began life as the Fernley-Hartley Lecture for 2010. Clive is very grateful for the invitation to deliver that lecture and for the continued support from the Fernley-Hartley Trust as the lecture (first published in *Epworth Review* 37/3, 2010) now finds its way into book form. He has delivered other sections, early drafts of the material presented here, or studies related to it, in many places, including the *Theologische Hochschule*, Reutlingen (Germany); the Conference of the Austrian Methodist Church (Vienna, June 2010); the Institute for Theology, Imagination and the Arts at the University of St. Andrew's, Scotland; the Leicester Cathedral theological discussion group; the 2011 Christian Congregational Music conference at Ripon College, Cuddesdon, Oxford; the Society for the Study of Theology (SST) Theology and Arts Seminar (York 2012); and Hinde Street Methodist Church (one of the Hugh Price Hughes Lectures for 2012). He is grateful to Michael Nausner, Gavin Hopps, David Monteith, Monique Ingalls, Ben Quash, and Sue Keegan Von Allmen for their initiative and support in making such opportunities possible.

Vaughan has delivered early drafts of ideas and material presented here at the British Sociological Association Sociology of Religion Study Group; the Institute for Theology, Imagination and the Arts at the University of St. Andrew's, Scotland; and with churches in the Warwick Team Ministry. He is grateful to Timothy, Beth, and Isabel Hart-Andersen for sharing their road trip across twelve states (and five national parks) of the USA in 2009 when we first tried out our music survey.

We have both presented at the Music and Religion consultation of the American Academy of Religion and at the UK-based international Religion and Popular Culture Network, both groups being important channels of support for our work and reflection.

No less significant are long-suffering local groups and congregations who have been willing to endure musical experimentation at various times. Clive wishes to thank churches in the Rotherham and Leicester Trinity Circuits of the Methodist Church, and the community at the Queen's Foundation Birmingham for their forbearance and participation. Vaughan wishes to thank the Parish of St. Thomas on the Bourne, Farnham; the University of Bath and Christ Church, Bath; the Benefice of Chewton Mendip, Litton and Ston Easton; the Collegiate Church of St. Mary and the Warwick Team Ministry; the Dioceses of Guildford, Bath and Wells, and Coventry.

More informally, though just as vitally, we have each enjoyed sometimes long-standing, often intense, discussions with friends and relatives far and near about music, religion, meaning, theology, and daily life—all of which have fed into the pages that follow. In no other order than alphabetical, we thank: John and Mary Adams; Terry Babbage; Simon Ball; Christopher Booker; Emma Carney; Barry Chapman; Elain Crewe; Rachel Eddyshaw; Ken Garrett; Ian and Rachel Gaubert; Chris and Nicky Gladstone; Ali Harris and Nick Pilkington; Nick and Ros Henwood; Chris and Jan Herbert; Andrew and Sarah Hindmarsh; Eleanor Jackson; Jonathan Kerry; Chris Leyton; Hannah, Jill, and Philip Marsh; the May family; Doreen Mills; Keith and Susan Mobberley; Michael Nausner; Andrew Northcott; Ellen and Steve Price; Becky, Jon, and Mandy Roberts; Cait, Francis, and Timothy Roberts; Penny and Chris Roles; Chris Shannahan; Alison and David Sims; Alison Skinner; Chris Smaling; Nicky Sorsby; Gina Southey; Graham Sparkes; Caroline and William Waldegrave; Sophie Waring; Martin Wellings; Chris and Trevor Wheatley; Hazel and Nick Whitehead; Jakob Wolfes; Isobel Woodliffe; and Catherine Wright. Vaughan would also like to record his abiding gratitude to Eira Roberts who encouraged him in his early years to listen to The Beatles, the Dave Clarke Five, and other bands, and who retained an abiding love of popular music until her death during the writing of this book.

On a practical note, Clive also thanks Michelle Bennett, Kathy Springthorpe, John Tompkins, and Lindsey Ball for help with processing some of the software and paperwork behind the book. We both also express our sincere gratitude to Rob Johnston and Bill Dyrness, as series editors, and to Bob Hosack and the team at Baker for taking our manuscript on and seeing it through to publication.

introduction

This book is a theological exploration of the contemporary cultural significance of popular music. It examines what popular music does *to* people and what people do *with* popular music through the kinds of music they listen to and the way they listen. It offers interpretations of what is going on and concludes with some suggestions regarding how music illustrates what popular culture generally is doing in Western society today.

The book is designed to be used by those who teach and study at college, seminary, or university to think about and explore how and why music is used as it is today. But we hope it will not be confined to classroom use. It can be used in the living room too—by any lover of music who wants to enjoy even more the music they listen to, by thinking about just *how* important it is to them (and why). It contains the fruits of some original research undertaken in North America and the United Kingdom (UK), where we surveyed people about their musical listening habits.

The book is written by two music lovers, neither of whom is a professional musician or has anything to do with the music industry. When it comes to music itself, we are amateurs. Our professional competencies are in education and religion. But our professional and personal experience of music and engagement with music over many decades have shown us that we cannot understand who we are, who we relate to, and what is happening in our fields of work and study without understanding popular culture and music's place within it. Whenever we have found people speaking of personal development, human growth, emotional intelligence, spirituality, coping strategies, meaning-making, experiences of transcendence, or sheer enjoyment of life, then music has not been far away. If we were not music lovers, we might not have chosen to write a book. But we would still need to wrestle with music's contemporary role because it is simply *there*, provoking and inspiring people, turning people on, providing emotional satisfaction, giving words to use on important occasions, structuring people's diaries, supporting political campaigns, helping people pass the time, accompanying people in their domestic tasks, filling in the potentially embarrassing silences in restaurants, and driving people to despair in supermarkets and department stores.

Our focus is on the active use of music: Why do people *choose* to listen to particular music? Why do they *choose* to listen to it in particular ways? We have not neglected to consider evidence of what music may be doing to people without their knowing it, and we have consulted the results of research conducted in such fields. But our purpose is to tease out what people are doing with their *conscious practice*—whether or not they are fully aware of the significance of their action or of the multiple ways in which their practice can be analyzed and illuminated through such analysis.

In order to understand better what popular music is doing, we had to dip our toes into many disciplines: sociology, psychology, cultural studies, media and communication studies, musicology, and anthropology. The primary discipline from which we come, however, is religion, within which we have received training in biblical, theological, literary, historical, and pastoral studies. It could be said that we are submerged in the study of religion (from insider and outsider perspectives) while we are only toe-dipping in others, and we need to accept this. But we must quickly add that to write this book we have had to surface and get out of the water (of the study of religion) in order to take a dip in other pools. We have moved well beyond our comfort zones. Others will need to judge whether we have become multidisciplinary enough to do justice to our subject matter. But even though we have adopted a multidisciplinary approach, we have to come clean too: we are interested throughout in what, if anything, contemporary popular music and its reception has to do with religion today. Our purpose is not simply to use (i.e., abuse) other disciplines to enable us to say what we want to say anyway. We have been listening to music, its recipients/users, and people from many different perspectives who, like us (though from different disciplinary perspectives), are trying to work out what's going on. That said, we are looking for a theological return here. If music is really as important as music fans suggest—in the statements they make and the behavior they display—then theology as a discipline needs to be interested.

We accept that the users of this book are quite likely to be studying courses in religion or theology, and possibly primarily in Christian seminaries/colleges or taking Christian theology courses. Yet our sincere hope is that anyone interested in the interface between religion and popular culture might find this book helpful. It is designed to give the reader plenty of material to work with and react to. You need not be identified as "religious" to use or benefit from it. Our hope is that the book will stimulate you to think through your music-listening habits to see (if you *are* religious) how your music habits do or do not mesh with your religious practice, or (if you are *not* religious) whether you have any religion-like music-listening habits on which it might be interesting to reflect further.

First let us state what we are *not* doing in this book, then what we *are* doing. We are not focusing on *religious* music in general or Christian music in particular. We are not focusing on what religious people are doing with music generally. Nor are we making a claim that, in what we explore in the book, we are uncovering a form of implicit or vicarious religion. We do make comparisons between music-listening habits and religious practice, and suggest where lyrics or the way music is performed, sold, or used might have religious allusions; when we do so, our claim is that we are using a lens to interpret what is happening more generally in society. We are not saying that such music *is* religion, or that its listeners *are* engaging in religious practice without knowing it.

The purpose of the book is thus to explore music-listening habits in the widest range possible, ensuring that a religious studies perspective is part of the mix. Let us state our basic contention: *Ensuring the critical study of religion in relation to how people listen to contemporary popular music will foster appropriate understanding of the music itself. It will help us understand how religions do (and must) work in society today. More fully exploring the function of music as a form of popular culture will be good for society as a whole.*

Whether or not you use the book in conjunction with a formal course of study, we want to encourage you, the reader, to think critically (i.e., analytically and creatively) about your music-listening habits. What do you listen to? When? For what purpose? How?—on an MP3, a computer, a sound system? Who do you listen with? How much live music do you experience? Do you play music yourself?

We are not intending to explain away your enjoyment of music or make it any less enjoyable. Our purpose is not to kill an enjoyable pastime through unnecessary analysis or overanalysis! On the contrary, our intention and hope is that you will enjoy your music listening all the more. By understanding more about your music habits and the context in which they occur, you may find that you are opened up to more and different music, prepared to think in a fresh way about how you discover or construct the beliefs you have or commitments you hold. That is what this book aims to achieve and why it is also a work of theology. Whether or not you participate in any religious practices or hold to any theistic philosophical viewpoint, this book will at least encourage you to think about the values or narratives that you live by and how those scripts interact with the way you consume music as part of popular culture.

part 1

music and religion

music in context

Contemporary Discussion about
Religion and Popular Culture

We all used to listen to a preacher every Sunday; the human need for that kind
of storytelling does not go away. It's up to writers and journalists to fill the gap.

Malcolm Gladwell, writer[1]

It is a nice thought that you might be able to listen to lots of popular music and
call it "work." That is what popular music critics do for a living. Of course, they
would quickly point out that they must listen to a lot of dross in the process
of discovering the next big hit or an emergent new band or genre. It is a nice
thought, too, that you might listen to popular music while knowing that it contributes positively to the shape of your life. Perhaps popular music develops or
supports your spirituality even while giving you a good time. Perhaps it influences your politics or at least gives a way of proclaiming publicly the political
views you have. Perhaps it somehow gives meaning to your life or helps you
figure out what, if any, meaning you think life has.

Yet popular music may do none of these things. Some philosophers, theologians, and religion scholars—especially those trying to be fashionable and
in tune—and even some cultural critics might want to *think* that it does such
things. But perhaps popular music really is just for fun. Perhaps people consume
popular music in the same way that they buy socks. Perhaps buying a CD or
downloading an album is a feel-good action that has a temporary effect and no

3

more. Through their choice of music, consumers may simply be consciously escaping everyday life or managing their moods.

There's a Lot of It Around

The scale on which people listen to music across the Western world deserves attention. As Adrian North and David Hargreaves have tellingly observed, "The UK spends more annually on music than on water supply."[2] Daniel Levitin similarly reports of North America: "Americans spend more money on music than they do on prescription drugs or sex, and the average American hears more than five hours of music per day."[3]

This mass consumption pertains to many different kinds of music. But only if all music is deemed mindless escapism can this large-scale consumption be considered wastefulness or avoidance of life. Without making any assumptions or judgments about good music or bad music, high or low culture, it is clear that such consumption might well be doing something to and for people, even if this is only keeping people happy. That may be no bad thing. But it is worth exploring *how* music is doing this and what other functions it has. Here is where this present book fits.

"Music has always had an association with the numinous and has been commonly put to ritual use."[4] "With regard to mood management it goes almost without saying that, like everyone else, adolescents will use music to achieve or alleviate particular moods."[5] Such scholarly statements stand alongside the many anthologized quotations from great and good people reminding us of music's importance. We can head back to the Reformation and hear Martin Luther's placing music alongside theology as a gift from God: "I have no pleasure in any man who despises music." The atheist Aldous Huxley declares, "After silence that which comes nearest to expressing the inexpressible is music." We may agree with jazz saxophonist Charlie Parker that "music is your own experience, your thoughts, your wisdom. If you don't live it, it won't come out of your horn." There is plenty of floating testimony to the function and significance of music. Luther and Huxley did not have post-1950s popular music in mind; hence one of the matters we need to address in this book is whether such positive statements about music can potentially apply to any type of music. Our simple opening observations are these: (1) There is a lot of music around. (2) People use music for lots of reasons and gain much from it. Yet there is also a question: Can popular music possibly have a function similar to the religious or classical forms more readily associated with being cultured, being educated, or fostering personal and spiritual development?

The practice of listening to popular music takes its place within a whole range of contemporary activities that cluster under the umbrella of "popular culture." Along with watching television and films, playing video games, and doing and watching sports, listening to popular music is something a lot of people spend a great deal of their time doing. All of these practices merit close scrutiny. As for music, whether listening is a conscious and active practice (choosing to turn on a radio or MP3 player, listen to a CD, or attend a live concert), or a more incidental activity (background music while shopping or eating in public), listening to music is an everyday occurrence. As such, it falls within the purview of what scholars of religion and culture need to address if we are to understand how religions function today. Moreover, if religions are in decline in the West, then (in so-called secularized times) it is important to scrutinize any practice that can seem religion-like to see if it is functioning *as* religion or *in place of* religion. If so, a further question remains: What has happened to metaphysics and to God? To demonstrate that social practices are religion-like merely shows that such practices are *functioning* as religion functions. It says nothing about the belief structures upon which specific religious traditions depend.

In using contemporary practices of music listening as an extended case study, this book contributes to the growing literature on the relationship between popular culture and religion and assesses the significance of its findings for Christianity and for Christian theology (see part 3). We focus on Christian theology because of our interests as authors and because speaking of religion in general terms only is impossible. After all, religions are specific, even if they change and are changeable to some degree. But we must undertake some general inquiry too. We dare not draw specific conclusions too hastily if we are to let contemporary practices speak to us. We need to ask what contemporary Western citizens *actually* do. Before that, however, we need to be clear about what work has already been done in religion/theology and popular culture (specifically regarding music). We need to delve into many other disciplines in search of material that will inform and illuminate—even explain—what we find. But for the moment we need to see what is around in religious studies, theology, and the sociology of religion, explorations within which our own study can find its proper place.

Bread, Circuses, and Popular Songs

The first recorded use of the phrase "bread and circuses" is attributed to the Roman satirist Juvenal (ca. 50–ca. 128 CE), who referred to the way the general populace can be easily bought off, or become preoccupied, with simple pastimes, as a way of being distracted from more important matters.[6] Juvenal was concerned that politicians were offering bribes—like giving candy to children—to deflect the people's interests from politics. The recipients, caught up in mindless activities, would thus neglect their public responsibilities. Switch to the present, and we hear echoes of the same concern as observers declare that popular culture numbs people; it lures them away from life's monotony. In the same way that Karl Marx called religion "the opium of the people," popular culture is a drug that draws people away from the task of changing the world. Rather than being a helpful escape, all it does is feed an addiction—to more and more of the same—inviting people to step onto the path to hedonistic self-interest. Popular culture is produced at the instigation of wealthy, devious impresarios, or big businesses, who make money off unsuspecting victims by feeding them lazy, cheap thrills that seem to satisfy but do so only temporarily and not in any really meaningful way. So some say.

Such opposition to popular culture and its dangerous impact has deep and influential scholarly roots in the modern period. Theodor Adorno (1903–69) is perhaps the writer cited most often with regard to such a line of thinking. In a series of essays written throughout the 1930s and 1940s, Adorno launched a fierce attack on popular music and on "the culture industry" for promoting mass standardization under the guise of fostering individuality.[7] Rather than encouraging listeners toward independent enjoyment of music and its potential depths, popular music merely lured people into vacuous repetition of standard formulas. It numbed them into mass groupings and stifled individual creativity.

To the "hypnotizing effect of mass culture" and the stifling of individual creativity, Kelton Cobb adds three further features of the Frankfurt School's opposition to popular culture: "the affinity for kitsch," the commendation of the avant-garde, and the preference for folk art over mass culture.[8] Kitsch as "garish, pretentious, or sentimental art," and "sugary trash," in Adorno's words,[9] demands too little of the viewer or listener and numbs the imagination. Avant-garde art, by contrast, wakes people up. And folk art carries with it an authenticity that cannot be reflected in the technological productions of mass culture. With respect to popular music, these views led Adorno to reject any form of music that is blatant in its sentimentality or nostalgia, is too easy to understand, or fails to demonstrate a raw authenticity.

Adorno presents an important line of argument. Though ultimately concluding that there is a "surplus of condescension" in the Frankfurt School's approach to popular culture, Cobb recognizes the dangers of too hastily dismissing their views as "shrill and elitist."[10] This is reflected in music studies too. In 1990, Richard Middleton observed that there are flaws in Adorno's approach but that interpreters need to understand both his method of understanding music and his historical location rather than simply dismissing him "as an embittered elitist pessimist."[11]

We agree with Cobb and Middleton. Whatever may be said about the context out of which Adorno and his Frankfurt colleagues wrote (opposition to Nazism), or of the privileged intellectual milieu out of which their thinking emerged, their critique remains potent. Having to work at music can be much more rewarding than being presented with wholly undemanding listening, which becomes tedious after multiple auditions. Furthermore, technology has had a huge impact on music by facilitating its mass production and distancing hearers from the original creators. Authenticity can too easily be compromised when the skill and creativity of those who compose and create music is filtered through multiple layers of technological processing to serve the desired market-driven needs of financial backers. These critical observations should not be overlooked.

That said, Adorno's criticisms do not always hit the mark with how much popular music (indeed much music) actually works. For one thing, repetition is an important feature in all music, within a single piece, in the act of playing (practicing) and in the act of listening. To be critical of popular music's repetitiveness fails to respect this feature of music per se and by extension disrespects ritualistic dimensions of human life more generally. Middleton's point about understanding Adorno's "immanent method" for understanding music ("the 'truth' of a work is to be found within the work itself")[12] is also well made. But as Middleton explains, though Adorno's criticisms may hit the mark with Tin Pan Alley music of the 1930s and 1940s, they do not really do justice to the complexity and diversity of "the entire musical production-consumption process" as it has developed. As we shall see, the move to a greater respect for the participative nature of music consumption—according to which a contemporary listener (of all forms of music) is not to be regarded as merely a passive, numb consumer—substantially qualifies Adorno's critique. Furthermore, we need to consider the *positive* impact of technology upon music, both in terms of the music created (e.g., by electronic means) and technology's role in disseminating music.

It is clear, then, that within current academic discussion of the interplay between theology or religion and popular culture, substantial criticisms of popular culture are possible and perhaps necessary. At the same time, we should not permit those criticisms to have the last word. Whatever the dangers of popular culture, there has been such a shift—in the way popular culture works, in the way popular arts and media are produced and consumed, and in the context where reception of such arts and media happens—that it is vital for these to be respected within theology/religion and popular culture discussions.

From Mass Culture to Pop Culture

Three important conceptual developments that affect our understanding of the relationship between religion/theology and popular culture form frameworks that take us beyond Adorno and the critical assessments of his work.

The first of these is the shift from mass culture to pop culture. Middleton logs "three 'moments' of radical situational change" in the development of Western music history over the past two hundred years: the "bourgeois revolution," the onset of mass culture, and the emergence of pop culture.[13] It is the shift from the second to the third moment that we must note here, while Adorno's critique of popular music applied largely to Middleton's second moment. This means that we are in a different place from Adorno when looking at popular music's relationship to theology and religion. By "mass culture" Middleton means "the development of monopoly-capitalist structures" and "an emerging American hegemony" as music became internationalized and its consumption more standardized across the West.[14] In the third moment—the emergence of pop culture—Middleton observes that while the global reach of the music business continues, "the existing monopolistic cultural formation both confirms itself and, at another level, becomes noticeably fissured, through the development of an assortment of transient subcultures."[15] These developments are allied to changes in technology and production, as well as linked to groups' identity formation, especially the emergent youth market. In other words, widespread expansion of music consumption happened in the 1950s and 1960s, with global aspirations on the part of the music business, while the seeds of diversification in music taste and styles were sown, which came to fruition later. In the 1950s, pop music culture may have appeared to be largely about rock 'n' roll. Yet by the end of the twentieth century, rock, folk, punk, heavy metal, hip-hop, garage, country, and many other types of music all had their market niches.

Middleton acknowledges that the moments he identifies are economically driven. But he cautions against making easy assumptions about causal links between economic factors and musical developments. In other words, one cannot control how music is understood and received simply by demonstrating how it is produced and marketed. The economic factors must not be overlooked, for at times they may account for why so many people know, and can get hold of, particular music in the first place. But they cannot of themselves always explain how and why music works.

For this book, we must look at what was happening in the world of religion (and in Christianity in particular) during this time in the West. The shift from mass culture to pop culture in popular music occurs alongside a major leap in the longer, more gradual process of secularization, which has been happening over two to three hundred years.[16] As now widely recognized, though the Enlightenment was not itself a movement hostile to religion, it did set in motion a process of "turning to the subject" and toward the dominance of rationality in academic inquiry. Human experience, and the capacity of human reason to understand that experience, became central to intellectual endeavors. In the long term, this could not do anything but undermine the established authorities in intellectual and cultural life, especially the authority of the Christian church.

Move forward to the period after World War II and the rise of pop culture just sketched, and we find secularization accelerating across Western culture. Many scholars have mapped this and theorized about it, and some continue to support a version of the secularization theory, which says that religion will continue declining until it is no longer a major part of Western cultures or needed by them.[17] Whatever we make of these reasons and projections, for our purposes it is undeniable that Christianity underwent a major challenge to its intellectual credibility and cultural significance across the West in the second half of the twentieth century. In this context Middleton, a musicologist, observes:

> The thrust of modernization—involving the breakdown of traditional frameworks of meaning, the growing crisis of traditional socializing institutions (family, church, school), the secularization and deritualization of life—has resulted in an increasing stress on the sphere of culture, and especially popular culture, as a primary site for the interpellation of subjects.[18]

In and through popular culture, Middleton observes that people are questioning meaning and explanation. However, popular culture is tangled up with commerce and entertainment, so we cannot always easily see how this is happening, what value systems are being adopted, what moral choices are being made. But it is essential when human inquisitiveness occurs in a new place—displaced from institutional settings such as the religious—that all disciplines contribute to working out what is going on. Our task is not to identify the obviously religious in secular sources. Nor is it to claim in any simple way the religion-likeness of secular practices in the world of popular music.[19] Our point is simply to notice the cultural displacement of meaning-making from identifiable religion. Religions continue to do their work but have no monopoly on meaning-making or truth-seeking. Our task is to examine what we are to do when folk culture and entertainment (which in the past would have been more clearly identified as religious practice) are more clearly detached from religion, while sometimes serving a similar function. This is our context. Pop culture is that important.

From a Transmission View to a Ritual View of Communication

Understanding the relationship between religion/theology and popular culture must address the second of the three important developments: the shift that has occurred in understanding how communication works. The shorthand version of this shift states that we have moved from a transmission view of communication to a ritual view. A transmission view suggests that communication is about imparting, sending, passing on information to others.[20] As James Carey states, "The center of this idea of communication is the transmission of signals or messages over distance for the purpose of control."[21] When applied to religion, such a view focuses on beliefs as held by individuals: the convictions held, and to be held, by people who come within a message's reach. It becomes important for communicators to get the message across and for recipients to show that they have heard by demonstrating their belief in what they have been told. When related to the world of music, such a view of communication puts great emphasis on a composer or lyricist. The assumption at work here is that a songwriter wants to get something across to a listener. In the case of popular music, the application of a transmission view of communication inevitably places emphasis on lyrics alone. Thus, despite the fact that we are dealing with music, lyricists are seen only as poets, and it is through words that they communicate their message.

This surely is not the case for songwriters past and present. In the case of songs, words matter. But they do not matter equally for all songwriters. Some songwriters seek to be poets; many do not. As Barry Taylor rightly says, "With pop music, the meaning of a song is not found exclusively in the lyrics; it is also found in the emotional arc the song creates."[22] In addition, instrumental music may not have any clear message to communicate. Focusing wholly or primarily on a composer's or songwriter's intentions may be a mistake when it comes to understanding how music works.

The transmission view of communication, then, though dominant in Western culture, does not tell the whole story. A ritual view of communication is also needed. As Carey explains, "In a ritual definition, communication is linked to terms such as 'sharing,' 'participation,' 'association,' 'fellowship,' and 'the possession of a common faith.'"[23] Mention of "faith" in that definition already indicates how this view is applied to religion. Carey continues: "This definition exploits the ancient identity and common roots of the terms 'commonness,' 'communion,' 'community,' and 'communication.' A ritual view of communication is directed not toward the extension of messages in space but toward the maintenance of society in time; not the act of imparting information but the representation of shared beliefs."[24] Strikingly, Carey counts the ritual view as older than the transmission view. Thus, though the transmission view may now be dominant in the West, it is a modern view, riding on the back of technological developments in the field of communication, the increased capacity to send messages farther and more effectively. The ritual view focuses more on the relationship between communication and the culture of a *gathered* community. Much greater emphasis is placed on embodiment and body language, drama, visual elements, and use of space and time. Not surprisingly, this ritual view of communication, when applied to religion, merely highlights what has long been going on in worship and liturgy.

To speak in any unqualified sense of moving *from* a transmission view of communication *to* a ritual view is misleading on two fronts. First, before the modern period, the ritual view was already predominant as a practice.[25] To imply that the ritual view is something new is unhelpful. Second, as Carey points out, though the ritual view needs to be rediscovered, we cannot have one view without the other.[26] Hence, while Carey clearly favors the ritual view and stresses the significance of understanding communication as culture through this lens, he is not neglecting the transmission element, which is still present.

When applied to religion and to understanding any form of Christianity in the present, the move from a transmission view to a ritual view of communication means there is a shift away from the *content* of what is believed to *how beliefs are shaped* within religious communities. What people believe seems to matter less than the fact that a believer is a community member and an active participant in that community's ritual practices. Believers receive communication by virtue of their participation. This shift recognizes (again) the importance of religious *practice*, as opposed to simply religious *belief*. Its drawback is that the content of belief (orthodoxy) could disappear from view in a damaging way.

Such a concern lies beyond the direct focus of this book, though it is worthy of note here. This book's interest in popular music's use, in the light of a new emphasis on a ritual view of communication, means that paying attention to the reception of music will entail looking at the communal contexts in which music is heard, listened to, and used. We shall inevitably need to notice the roles played by concerts, fan clubs and fan sites, and festivals; these are examples of settings in which a ritual view of communication enables us to make more sense of music consumption, rather than using a transmission view, which overemphasizes lyrics.

From Production to Reception

The third important development in the task of understanding the relationship between religion/theology and popular culture is the shift from production to reception. Again the heading is shorthand. What we mean here is a shift of focus that has taken place across the humanities and arts, in many different academic disciplines, in understanding how the creation and consumption of works of arts and media products occur and are best to be studied. In the study of literature, for example, there has been a shift of focus from author, to text, and more recently, to reader. It is recognized that a written text, especially a work of fiction or a poem, may not mean simply what its author intended. Great works of written art become significant precisely because they are used and prove to be helpful and inspiring in fresh ways and new contexts. The text, therefore, has a life of its own and works beyond what an author intended. The reader plays a role in seeing what a text might say in one's context. Although a text cannot be made to mean anything a reader intends, the interplay between text and reader is where creative things happen.

Likewise in the study of film, where once the focus was on the director (What did the director *intend*?), there has been a shift over many years to the film *as a film* (What is on the screen? How does a film work as a kind of visual text?), and then in turn to the viewer.[27] How much does the viewer need to bring to a film for a film to mean anything? Isn't it true that in the choices a person makes about which films to watch, and through the intentions one brings to the watching, the viewer contributes to what a film achieves in the viewer's life?

It is easy to see how these developments have an impact on understanding the reception of any art form, music included. If we accept that it may be wrong to focus only on lyrics in popular music, then the lyricist has already decreased in significance to some degree. And when a work is listened to, what form of a song/work are we talking about? There can be a world of difference between a CD/downloaded version of a studio recording and a live performance itself. Popular songs increasingly lack definitive form. For example, though there is the version of Arcade Fire's "Rebellion" on the album *Funeral*, keen fans of the band may quickly claim that you have not really heard the track until you have experienced it live.

The shift from production to reception—a shorthand version of what Middleton calls "the entire musical production-consumption process"—has had a major impact on attempts to grasp how popular music works and what it is doing in Western culture. Discussions of theology/religion and popular culture have described this shift in different ways. In exploring popular music, musicology favors a "textual" approach (the music in itself: Adorno's "immanent method"); cultural studies, however, "have gravitated toward forms of 'consumptionism,' which want to locate the textual moment, the moment of meaning production, overwhelmingly in acts of use."[28] The shift is seen in discussions of popular music, where the primary focus is now on use. As with the two views on communication, the point is not that one approach replaces another (author-text-reader and composer-music-listener are always present and worthy of investigation). We must simply recognize that cultural studies approaches are currently dominant in the attempt to understand popular music: what are people actually doing with music, and why?

The tripartite approach to the study of popular culture and its reception appears in many ways in the field of theology/religion. Three examples will suffice. Gordon Lynch uses the approach to especially good effect in his 2005 work *Understanding Theology and Popular Culture*. Lynch adopts an "author-focused approach" to reading Eminem, a "text-based approach" to interpreting *The Simpsons*, and an "ethnographic approach" to understanding club culture.[29] In this way, Lynch demonstrates how the threefold approach works with different forms of popular culture: music, television, dance. In *Participation and Mediation: A Practical Theology for the Liquid Church*, Pete Ward takes up Brian Longhurst's version of the production-text-audience continuum, breaking down the three moments of the continuum into a five-stage process: (1) the context and methods of production; (2) production of music itself; (3) music as text; (4) identifying audiences; (5) examining patterns of consumption.[30] In choosing to apply Longhurst's approach to an example of modern Christian (worship) music, Ward demonstrates that an interpretative framework devised for popular culture generally works equally well for Christian resources. Christian popular culture is thus shown to be not different in kind, but merely one form of popular culture. Finally, Kevin Vanhoozer adapts the same "author-text-reader schema" to enable the contributions to the essay collection *Everyday Theology: How to Read Cultural Texts and Interpret Trends* to be located within a clear interpretative framework.[31] In our view, Vanhoozer rather underplays the significance of audience and receiver in his use of the schema. Yet it is refreshing to see the tripartite approach being used across the theological spectrum to good effect.

There is widespread recognition of the need for more empirical data—evidence of what actual audiences (be it of film, television, music) are doing, thinking, and believing.[32] In this book we cannot yet provide the full findings even of our own research in this area. We shall, however, be in a position to draw on, in a limited way, the music-reception research we have done, as well as ensuring that we draw on the empirical work of others.[33] In exploring how music works, we shall thus be respecting all three "moments" of the production-text-listener continuum.

To Whom Are We Speaking?

In locating this work within the shifts of focus just identified in patterns of interpretation in the arts, we are indicating what kind of contribution we hope to make to theology/religion and popular culture discussion. The fact that we speak of a "theology/religion and popular culture discussion" at all signifies our primary readership: those in the academy who are also contributors to this discussion, and those in ecclesial communities who make use of the fruits of related research and writing. However, because our focus is on actual reception and use of popular music, though without disregarding composition and production, we have other readers in mind. Reception and use cannot be studied without undertaking interdisciplinary work. We therefore write also for those in other disciplines and for everyday users of popular music. If the claim we make is accurate—that much more occurs in the midst of music consumption than meets the eye—then such an argument cannot be left for consideration by theologians, religion scholars, or ministry practitioners alone. The insights that religious studies and theology can bring to the task of analyzing what music consumption is doing in society then become publicly important. These insights cannot be confined to the religious realm.

explorations in affective space

The Magisteria-Ibiza Spectrum

Religion and Popular Culture as an Interdisciplinary Endeavor

In their discussion[1] of the music used at the funeral of Diana Spencer, Princess of Wales, on September 6, 1997, psychologists Eric Clarke, Nicola Dibben, and Stephanie Pitts comment that the many ways in which the music functioned at that event "raises significant challenges for the researcher who may need to acquire knowledge and expertise in a potentially bewildering range of disciplines."[2] They mention psychology, sociology, anthropology, and neuroscience, but they do not refer to the discipline of religious studies, which is puzzling because they are critically studying a religious ritual. Perhaps they deem religious studies not scientific enough, or they consider religious studies to be subsumed within the psychology, sociology, and anthropology of *religion*, rendering further study superfluous. Be that as it may, their conclusion that the study of how music is used requires multiple disciplines mirrors our own. In a study of the reception of U2's music, we observed:

> In moving beyond our own comfort zones, . . . we have needed to draw on: (1) sociology, both in relation to the study of reflexivity (Archer) and the habits of daily music usage (DeNora); (2) social psychology and the functions of music in daily life (North and Hargreaves); (3) popular music and cultural studies (Longhurst, Middleton, Negus, Frith, Lynch); (4) media studies and the phenomenon

of fandom (Hills, Gray); (5) musicology, particularly with respect to the affective dimension of music reception (Juslin and Sloboda); and (6) anthropology, insofar as it influences liturgical studies (Bradshaw, Davies).[3]

This conclusion remains true of this present text. Though we are not experts in these various fields of study, we need to venture into them in order to do justice to the material we are considering, in particular the way music is received and consumed. We have long known that to explore adequately, appropriately, and critically what is happening in religion, and the functions that popular culture and the arts are currently playing, religious or theological studies and cultural studies *alone* will not do. To be able to speak with integrity to all potential readers, however, we have eavesdropped on, and have done our best to contribute to, many different scholarly conversations. This chapter reports on one main conclusion from those conversations and offers one direct contribution. It forms the framework for much of what follows in the book as a whole.

Defining Affective Space

We must first introduce the concept of "affective space."[4] By this term we mean any practice or activity that entails significant emotional engagement, through which a person can be shown to be doing more than just enjoying the moment. Such a practice could therefore be listening to a piece of music, going to a concert, watching a film, attending a major sporting event, watching a television program, or attending a religious act of worship. None of these activities may require additional cognitive work for the activity to be enjoyed, be deemed significant, or be held to have meaning. Furthermore, such activities may be undertaken formally or informally. But they prove to be meaningful through the emotional commitment devoted to them or required by participation in them.

To put such activities and practices more broadly in context entails exploring what goes on *in and around* the experience of listening, watching, or participating. The exploration of what occurs in such affective space thus becomes an exercise in examining what film, media, cultural, sociological, and music studies contribute to our collective understanding of how arts and culture work: how people use them and how people are influenced by them in processing their emotional engagement in artistic and cultural activities and practices. We need to remember that though we use the term "space," this is an overused word with which we must take care. This space is far from empty. Speaking of a space is more a way of talking about a site, a location, where things happen. So we are exploring locations within public life where significant *affective* events happen, in and through which much more happens than may be acknowledged at the time.

We must also stress that we are not necessarily speaking of engagement with proven, lasting, classic forms of art. Exploring fully what goes on in such affective space would naturally need to include attending to how such art forms as fine art, classical music, and opera are currently being accessed and used. But it is crucial to acknowledge that people's participation in affective space is not restricted to interaction with what is defined as high culture. It is vital not to make prior or even later judgments about any popular culture or art's intrinsic worth or purpose. *Here we are examining what people actually do with products of art and culture, whether high or low.* It is not possible to attach a value to what is done with an artistic or cultural product by virtue of some aesthetic or ethical judgment of a product itself. To put this another way: profound things could happen to a person in interaction with a television melodrama or a (musically) poor pop song. But what matters most is the activity in the affective space at that point and in the process of reception.

Introducing the Magisteria-Ibiza Spectrum

In asking what happens in and around the affective space in which such emotional engagement with the arts and culture occurs, it is necessary to construct a framework for understanding and interpreting the experience of the participant. At this point we introduce what we call the Magisteria-Ibiza Spectrum (see fig. 2.1 below).[5] This spectrum is a relatively simple and playful diagram, but for the purposes of this book, it proves to be extremely useful for mapping how the consumption of music takes place. Though this spectrum has uses beyond music, with respect to many forms of the arts and popular culture, it is illuminating for our purposes in that it locates the experience of music listening within a range of influences and forces, and of conscious and unconscious factors, so that we can better understand that experience. In particular, we can use this spectrum to observe where and how religions, faith, and spirituality fit into the picture we are seeking to describe; to pinpoint similarities and differences; and yet to reveal the relationship between religious practice and affective engagement with the arts and popular culture.

"Magisterium" is the term used for the teaching authority in the Roman Catholic Church. Here we use the term in a more general (and original classical/Latin) sense to mean "a group of authoritative official leaders." Of late, the scientific world has also explored the notion of magisterium as a means of defining the relationship between science and religion. Following a number of encounters with the Catholic Church and professional scientists who were also Catholic priests, the biologist Stephen Jay Gould (1941–2002) took this concept and applied it to the relationship between science and religion with his concept of nonoverlapping magisteria. He understands magisterium as "a domain where one form of teaching holds the appropriate tools for meaningful discourse and resolution."[6] In his original proposal Gould argues: "The net of science covers the empirical universe: what the universe is made of (fact) and why does it work this way (theory). The net of religion extends over questions of moral meaning and value. The two magisteria do not overlap, nor do they encompass all inquiry (consider, for starters, the magisterium of art and the meaning of beauty)."[7]

There is clearly common ground between Gould's use of magisterium and ours in that we identify various domains of meaningful discourse that have degrees of authority and help to define our affective space. However, Gould's firm distinction between the magisteria has been criticized as unsustainable. For example, John Polkinghorne observes: "The most cursory acquaintance with the intellectual history of the last four centuries makes clear that there has been a degree of mutual influence flowing between science and religion, rendering quite untenable the supposition that they can be isolated from each other in watertight compartments."[8] This instantly raises questions: Can magisteria be quite so watertight as Gould claims? What is the significance of overlapping? How can we live with multiple, interweaving, potentially conflicting magisteria in the course of daily life? Our Magisteria-Ibiza Spectrum allows for the openness and mutual influence between magisteria and other factors that Polkinghorne advocates, and we shall return to the way they interweave in due course.

Ibiza is a picturesque Balearic island off the coast of Spain, a popular holiday destination. Here it is used symbolically to refer to a rather extreme form of individual freedom.[9] Its use in this way slots into a tradition of use, being emblematic of the rise of leisure culture in the late twentieth century as different waves of movie stars, hippies, and musicians washed up on its beaches and seafronts. Film stars such as Errol Flynn, Ursula Andress, Denholm Elliott, Goldie Hawn, and Roman Polanski came to Ibiza to relax. As hippie culture discovered the isle in the 1960s, it made an impact on some progressive rock music later in that decade (e.g., the film *More* was shot there, and the Pink Floyd album *Soundtrack for the Film More* (1969) includes the song "Ibiza Bar," which recounts the first-person-singular experience of an actor making a film). Another song from this era influenced by Ibiza is "Tales of Brave Ulysses," by Cream from *Disraeli Gears* (1967). Out of the tolerant 1960s grew a 1970s disco culture and then the 1980s dance scene, which fed into pop music in North America and the UK.

In this respect "Ibiza" is shorthand for a culture characterized by diversity and tribalism but also by the importance of the individual and of personalized autonomy. Within this tribal context there can be clear distinctions, even rivalry between the different groups. Lee Gilmore's study of the Burning Man arts festival in the Black Rock Desert in Nevada provides an intriguing link with our reference to Ibiza here. Gilmore observes how the rising profile of that gathering as a party spot drew attendees who were perceived not to be of the same tribe: "In 2002 my colleague Mark Van Proyan—who typically spends several summer weeks traveling around Europe and thus waiting on train platforms with many of those headed to and from Ibiza and other glamorous locales—reported that he was beginning to see more and more apparently young, wealthy, and fashionably attired individuals at Burning Man who looked like members of what he dubbed 'the Ibiza set.'"[10] Gilmore goes on to describe Ibiza in terms of a "commercial tourist spectacle" akin to Disneyland.[11] The significance of this for our understanding of the Magisteria-Ibiza Spectrum is that even on parts of the spectrum characterized by nonhierarchical, antiauthoritarian, and pick-and-choose approaches, there still appear to be some (inchoate?) criteria at work for making judgments about the cultural bricolage occurring and about how affective space is being defined and used.

Figure 2.1. The Magisteria-Ibiza Spectrum

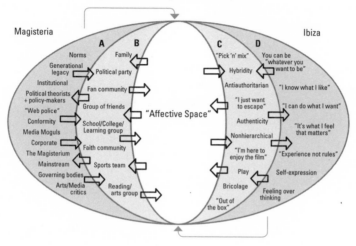

Working with the Magisteria-Ibiza Spectrum

By using this spectrum, then, we seek to map where individuals (listeners, watchers, participants) are located on a range of a number of social factors—some welcome, some perhaps not—and the assumption or hope that despite these social factors, they can nevertheless exercise considerable freedom in what they listen to, participate in, or watch.

Having identified what we consider to be in the affective space, we now need to build up the diagram further in order to use it more effectively. Participation in culture is never just an individual matter. Why do we end up participating in some events rather than others? Why are we interested in certain music or art or films? And when we have seen or listened to films or music, with whom do we talk or think through our experiences? At this point, the many groups listed in section B in figure 2.1 come into play. These are obvious types of groups to list as important; yet as a representative list, it is not meant to be complete. There are two-way influences between the groups and our participation in affective space. The groups in which we participate directly affect us in the affective spaces we inhabit (e.g., in the choices of what to listen to or watch). But we also make choices about which groups can help us process our experiences. By doing so, we grant them authority. For example, as a music fan, I may choose to belong to a fan community (perhaps an online community). Yet I am also likely to belong to informal groups of friends, whose opinions and judgments I respect, with whom I also reflect on my music-listening experiences. But these friends may not be fans of a musician or band that I like. I am making different kinds of authoritative alliances all the time.

But that is only one context within which to understand what goes on in the affective spaces that we inhabit. There is a broader framework still, which pushes in individual and social directions. Move further in the Ibiza direction, and there is more of a sense that individual choice and individual freedom are important (section C in fig. 2.1). The extent to which we have the freedom to "pick 'n' mix," in sheer celebration of the many ways we can combine features of what we choose to allow to influence us, is paramount. This produces a mixing of styles and tastes often referred to as *bricolage* or *hybridity*. Go a stage further, and the sense of not being bound by any human structure and there being nothing objective to which we can appeal can be extended so far that only what an individual feels really matters (section D). Indeed, it often appears as if we have moved so far in this direction that what we feel individually is so crucial that everything that happens on the left side of the diagram, or any appeal to rationality, is not worth much.

The fact that we term the central shape "affective space" shows how seriously we want to take the emotions. We are not arguing in favor of a dry rationality that can somehow correct the waywardness of our feelings. We do, though, want to explore how we can be more than either reason-based or feelings-based as we process our life experience in healthy ways.

Now let us turn to the far left of the Magisteria-Ibiza Spectrum to see where authority structures take effect. Beyond the social contexts in which, and in relation to which, we enjoy our participations in affective space, there are also social structures that affect, even control, what happens in the affective space we inhabit when we listen to music, watch television, go to films, participate in faith communities or family life, or participate in or support a sports team. Section A highlights how this happens, compelling us to identify who is pulling the strings and to note the kinds of concepts at work (e.g., norms, conformity, corporateness). Sometimes we are happy to know and accept the role of such factors and groups. At other times we might want to resist. Consider our music-listening example: not only might I be a member of an online fan community and participate in discussions about my favorite music; I might also eavesdrop on the words of established music critics. I might accept that they are deeply knowledgeable about what they are discussing and are influential, even while

I might not like what they say. But the fact that I have paid attention *at all* is significant.

We can, of course, apply this insight to all the groups we might be able to identify in our own personal versions of section B. Behind and around the groups in which we participate as we consume the arts and culture, we are also being influenced all the time by, and sometimes actively choosing to respect the authority of, those who affect the groups of which we are a part. In the case of faith communities, the doctrine that is carried in practical ways in section B derives in some way from (and is continually monitored by) a magisterium in section A.

To see this process as a spectrum implies that the two extremes have little relation. It looks as though there are authority structures to be respected in section A, and then totally free individual choice in section D, and they do not have much to do with each other. Yet things are more complicated than that. If I am listening to music in Ibiza, having the time of my life, expressing my individual freedom, I am also subject to the choices and fashions in music that have created this world (section A). These fashions are subject to commercial decisions made by those in section A. And I may even be there as part of a group of friends (section B). So we need to acknowledge that the affective space in which all of us consume arts and culture brings all this together in one confusing, sometimes overwhelming, configuration.

We may sum up the contribution made by the Magisteria-Ibiza Spectrum as follows:

- Every form of participation in the affective space occurs in multiple social contexts.
- Some of the social contexts we choose, some we do not.
- We can never be quite as individualistic as we think we can.
- Authority structures (often as hidden factors) are always at work.
- We actively make some choice about who we want to exert authority over us, whose authority we respect.
- All of this happens even while we might well be having a good time!

Listening to Music as a Human Practice: The Contribution of Daniel Levitin

If attention to affective space locates the realm of human practice within which important, enjoyable human practices take place, and the Magisteria-Ibiza Spectrum helps us identify more about what goes on there, we must turn next to music itself. In asking what popular music, as a specific form of popular culture, is achieving in Western culture today, we must prepare ourselves to be able to assess what we might find. In keeping with the tenor of this chapter so far, we must look outside of religion and theology in search of a framework within which we can then assess the material to be presented in part 2. As part of our extensive reading across many disciplines, we have opted to use the work of neuroscientist and anthropologist Daniel Levitin as an aid to our inquiry. In his *The World in Six Songs*, Levitin argues that the evolution of a particular brain mechanism located in the prefrontal cortex has enabled humans to develop language and art. This neural mechanism developed these three cognitive abilities: (1) perspective taking—an understanding that others have different ideas; (2) representation—being able to think about things that are not directly in front of us; and (3) rearrangement—an ability to order the world and our experience of it.[12] Levitin explains: "The combination of these three faculties gave early humans the ability to create their own depictions of the world—paintings, drawings, and sculpture—that preserved the essential features of things. . . . These three abilities, alone and in combination, are the common foundation of language and art."[13]

Throughout his book Levitin highlights the evolutionary advantages of music. For example, he suggests that early musicians "may have been better able to forge closer bonds with those around them; they may have been better able to communicate emotionally, diffuse confrontation, and ease interpersonal tensions."[14] In addition, because songs are easily memorized, the humans who developed music may have been better at encoding important survival information. However, the significance of lyrics and poetry extended beyond basic shared knowledge to become (using poetry critic Helen Vendler's phrase) "hypothetical sites of speculation" that enabled individuals and communities to explore feelings and interpretations of events.[15] According to Levitin, these songs, or "abstractions of reality," give us "a multilayered, multidimensional context, in the form of harmony, melody, and timbre. We can experience them in many different modes of enjoyment—as background music, as aesthetic *objets d'art* independent of their meaning, as music to sing with friends or sing along with in the shower or car; they can alter our moods and minds."[16]

He argues that six of these song forms have been particularly influential in the process of human evolution: friendship, joy, comfort, knowledge, religion, and love.

Levitin believes *friendship* songs, or what he describes as "synchronous, co-ordinated song and movement," enabled the earliest humans or protohumans to create bonds of community and "society."[17] Thus the shared experience of singing and dancing brought about the development of shared group behavior and cohesion. We can see the continued effect of this in the role that music plays in national identity (national anthems) and social bonding (ceremonial and sports events). Levitin draws a distinction between these songs and religious songs, which may include this element but not as their main raison d'être.

The important role of *joy* songs in contemporary society indicates to Levitin the equally important role for them during human evolution: "The group member who could make others feel good, either through grooming, sexual activity, providing more food, and so on, was one who became valued and could ascend to the position of group leader. . . . Communication by sound allowed a potential leader to spread his influence around to many more at a time than could be done by one-to-one grooming."[18] Levitin employs terms that (from a sociological perspective) could be described as the language of enchantment. Thus as he tries to analyze the mental and physical impact songs of joy have on us, he speaks about music's "magic," its "ineffable power," its ability to bring "healing."[19] He summarizes the value of these songs for this fusion of body and mind: "We have joy songs because moving around, dancing, exercising our bodies and minds is something that was adaptive in evolutionary history. Stretching, jumping, and using sound to communicate felt good because our brains—through natural selection—developed rewards for those behaviors. Joy songs today give us a jolt of good brain chemistry as a biological echo of the importance they held over thousands of years of evolution."[20]

In his short chapter on *comfort* songs, Levitin identifies various examples of such music: lullabies that mothers sing to children, songs for the disaffected or disenfranchised, songs to calm us in the face of a threat, and songs to reassure us when we are seeking a sense that we are understood or not alone. He observes that we might expect people who are sad to seek out happy music, but some research suggests that a tranquilizing hormone is released when we are sad. This may help us in times of stress to conserve energy and reorient future priorities, and the desire for sad music may assist in the release of this hormone. There could also be a psychological aspect to these songs because when people are depressed, they can feel that no one understands them, but listening to sad songs can provide a sense that someone has not only shared that experience but also recovered enough to reflect and sing about it.

As Levitin has already suggested in his chapter on friendship, he believes that one of the fundamental functions of music is the passing on of *knowledge*: "Music, especially rhythmic, patterned music of the kind we typically associate with songs, provides a more powerful mnemonic force for encoding knowledge, vital and shared information that entire societies need to know, teachings that are handed down by parents to their children and that children can easily memorize."[21] Or as Ian Cross (as quoted in Levitin's *The World in Six Songs*) puts it, music is "optimally adapted for the management of social uncertainty."[22] Since humans are *motivated* to share and learn certain observations, interests, and experiences, Levitin regards knowledge as "emotion" and science as an "emotional judgment." Thus "scientists are motivated by intense curiosity and a desire to interpret and represent reality in terms of higher truths—to take collections of observations and formulate them into a coherent whole that we call a theory. Of course artists do the same thing, taking *their* observations and trying to formulate *them* into a coherent whole that we call the painting, the symphony, the song, the sculpture, the ballet, and so on."[23] Then in a startling conclusion, Levitin remarks: "Knowledge songs are perhaps the crowning triumph of art, science, culture, and mind, encoding important life lessons in an artistic form that is ideally adapted to the structure and function of the human brain."[24]

At this point Levitin is perhaps in danger of substantially qualifying his persistent emphasis on the importance of chemical processes in the body and on the emotions that relate to them. The extent of this cognitive focus (people actually learn things, even gather data, through music) comes close to suggesting that people may gain a worldview through music. In his defense, Levitin might argue that gaining knowledge via musical cultural stories or myths and thereby learning *how* to do something does not necessarily mean that what one learns is true. But this form of song does at least highlight that *what* one learns through music cannot be downplayed.[25]

For Levitin, *religion* fulfills an evolutionary function and has contributed to human survival. He argues that songs associated with religion, ritual, and belief "served a necessary function in creating early human social systems and societies. Music helped to infuse ritual practices with meaning, to make them memorable, and to share with our friends, family, and living groups, facilitating social order. This yearning for meaning lies at the foundation of what makes us human."[26] Religious rituals are visual displays of a shared worldview, and Levitin identifies eleven characteristics common to such practices: (1) actions are divorced from their usual goals; (2) the activity is undertaken to achieve an end; (3) rituals are regarded as compulsory; (4) often no explanation is given; (5) participants engage in behaviors with more uniformity than in regular lives; (6) objects are infused with special meaning; (7) the environment is delimited in a special way; (8) there is a strong emotional drive to perform the ritualized activity; (9) actions, gestures, or words are repeated; (10) there is a strong emotional drive to perform the ritual in a particular way; (11) rituals involve music of rhythmic pitch-intoned chanting.[27] He follows the anthropologist Roy Rappaport (1926–97) in holding that human society could not have come into existence without the religious beliefs that "trained us and taught us to accept society-building."[28] The ability to believe things that are not readily apparent remains a cornerstone even in modern technological society; thus "the fundamental human ability to form societies based on trust, and to feel good about doing so (via judicious bursts of oxytocin and dopamine), is intimately linked to our religious past and spiritual present," and music has played a crucial part of that process of bonding and memory.[29]

In his final chapter, on songs of *love*, Levitin draws on various research evidence to contend that natural selection "acted to select for altruism, fidelity, bonding, and those qualities that are all part and parcel of mature love."[30] Within this process Levitin follows Noam Chomsky (b. 1928) in making a distinction between the forms of language for "conveyance" and forms for "computation."

Conveyance is a basic form of language that expresses concepts and emotions; computation language arose later, when the human brain had developed sufficiently to be able to analyze hierarchies and rearrange utterances. Levitin sees animal song and mating patterns as an example of conveyance and human song as an example of computation. This computational aspect enables human beings to plan how we want to use music in achieving a particular aim. Thus

> human music has hierarchical structure and complex syntax, and we compose within that constraint. Music, like language and religion, contains elements shared with other species and also elements unique to humans. Only humans compose a song for a particular purpose, made up of elements found in other songs. Only humans have the vast repertoire of songs (the average American can readily identify more than one thousand different songs). Only humans have a cultural history of songs that fall within six distinct forms.[31]

Assessing Levitin's Work: Initial Reflections

We want to make critical use of Levitin's six-song argument in part 3 of this present book, and there we will have more to say both about its usefulness and its limitations. It will clearly be valuable as a heuristic device: we shall use Levitin's six songs as a lens through which to read what we find in the world of contemporary popular music, and what a diet of listening might produce. Even at this stage, however, we must register a few points of reservation. First, for all his academic credentials and undoubted credibility, much of his argument remains dependent on anecdote and hunch. This raises the suspicion that his conclusions are rather too neat. Second, he merges the different vocabularies of "disenchantment" (data, science) with "enchantment" ("natural selection can work its magic")[32] without providing an explanation for how these forms of language fit together. Much more needs to be said about how enchantment, disenchantment, and—as is being said quite often at present—the tendency toward reenchantment are to be understood in relation to how humans do meaning-making and try to find and tell truth. Third, Levitin fails to set out clearly both what he means by "meaning" in his discussion of religious songs and how music provides meaning in this instance. Meaning may be defined in a very functional way (e.g., humans use music to get through the day or to cope with their emotions). Perhaps Levitin really means no more than this. Or it could be claimed that attempts to make meaning are also more than coping strategies and constitute efforts to venture metaphysical claims. For example, when I say I am "taken out of myself" while listening to certain pieces of music, I mean that I am put in touch with an ultimate reality that lies beyond me, but that I somehow feel/know is "there" and is "true." Levitin leaves these distinctions hanging. Fourth, his reference to gnosticism as "friendly" to the material world is a common modern misinterpretation of this phenomenon, not borne out by historical evidence and puzzling to say the least.[33] Given Levitin's own chapter on religion and our own interests throughout this book, we will come back to where Levitin's discussion of gnosticism might lead and how it might in due course be corrected.

All of that said, Levitin's approach will certainly prove useful when we begin to assess what contemporary popular music is doing today.

Acknowledging Religion's Displacement, Affirming Meaning-Making

In much more detail with respect to contemporary popular music, part 2 of this book will explore what is occurring in the affective space we have identified, when understood by use of the Spectrum. By the time we get to part 3, we shall be taking stock of that exploration as we pursue contemporary understanding of religion and theology. Even at this point, however, we need to notice how religious motifs, symbols, ideas, and beliefs are wrapped up explicitly in culture, high and low, even in supposedly nonreligious forms of culture. We must not assume from the Spectrum that theological and religious ideas and beliefs are present only in religious groups. Conrad Ostwalt speaks for many contemporary cultural observers: "We find popular culture functioning in some of the same ways as institutionalized religious ritual, so that popular culture is the entity that provides the context for understanding values, belief systems, and myths."[34]

It is much too simple, of course, to conclude simply that the arts and popular culture have *replaced* religion (without remainder), or that they have *distracted* people from religion. The latter could be true and is worth examining. But the evidence of the actual reception and use of popular culture and the arts should catch Western societies up short insofar as exploration of the human practice of meaning-making is concerned: whether to be labeled as religion or correlated with religion or not, meaning-making happens because it is a facet of what it means to be human.[35] Meaning-making occurs as a dimension of what people do when they are engaged in things they do regularly and enjoy doing. Our study of what music is doing will show this. We have already noticed how Levitin has seen this to be so, even if we question the way in which religion becomes just one out of his six categories.

The interweaving (and sometimes hiddenness) of religious themes in so-called secular culture is as problematic for religious groups, however, as it is confusing for those who are enjoying themselves in the affective spaces created by entertainment. People are sometimes unwilling to admit that they are doing anything more than escaping or being entertained by popular culture and the arts; and religious groups are frequently reluctant to acknowledge the extent to which their practices, and their members, are caught up in the media world. Stewart M. Hoover, professor of media studies, says, "The realms of 'religion' and 'media' can no longer easily be separated. . . . They occupy the same spaces, serve many of the same purposes, and invigorate the same practices in late modernity."[36]

Whether or not we feel that Hoover's statement can be substantiated fully, his conclusion can be broadened to incorporate all media-related activities, including consumption of the arts and popular culture. Those who argue for the importance of faith must therefore accept that their beliefs are tangled up, in ways they may not wish, with a whole range of cultural texts and practices. And those who wish there were no religions at all need to accept that what people are doing with their consumption of arts and culture may be closer to religious practice than they may wish to admit.

Yet we must not be too hasty to conclude that everything looking like religion or seeming to function like it (from the perspective of a scholar of religion) really is operating as religion for the participant. With respect to the function of film viewing in Western culture, Gordon Lynch has rightly said that while recognizing how films contribute to religious meaning-making, "we need to be equally attentive to the ways in which films do *not* function in this way if we are to have a nuanced sense of the real significance of film watching in people's lives."[37] Religion, it could thus be argued, is but one participant in the affective space; it creates one set of communities and authorities in sections B and A respectively of the Spectrum. There may be no need to correlate its workings with other activities and practices that occur in the same space.

That said, there are common human explorations occurring within the affective space: explorations of forgiveness, redemption, meaning, self-understanding, identity, and so on. Whether or not these explorations have religious roots or can be set within religious frameworks, religions will want to have their say as to what such terms mean and how such concepts are best understood. Perhaps they *need* to have their say, even if they lack an a priori claim to have particular, immediate truth in what they do. In a postmodern, pluralistic world, religious authorities cannot expect immediate respect beyond their own communities. Public respect must be won through open argument. But in a postmodern, pluralistic world, religion does at least have a chance to be heard once more.

Fun and Beyond

In a media-saturated, attention-overloading context, our claim is simple: in the everyday world, and in the everyday life of listeners to music, whether those listeners be religious or not, it is in the affective space they inhabit in their listening where their explorations of such issues and questions are in part (perhaps large part) being worked out. Even if it does seem that "I'm just listening for enjoyment, for fun," it is far from clear that this is all that is going on. And it seems that at least *some* listeners are themselves fully aware of this. In part 2, we present our detailed case study of the way in which popular music now functions in affective space and is to be understood with respect to the Magisteria-Ibiza Spectrum. Before we get there, however, we need to acknowledge the *theological* interest that also shapes our work. Having located this book within the field of religion/theology and popular culture (chap. 1) and having stepped outside of religion and theology to ask about the multidisciplinary way in which the consumption of the arts and popular culture is to be understood (chap. 2, here), we must now (in chap. 3) identify questions that contemporary Christian theology will want us to address when we reach part 3. To that we now turn.

acknowledging a
theological interest

Popular Music from Sin to
Sacramentality

The Shock of the New: Recent Responses to Popular Music

The phenomenal scale of the development of popular music in Western culture
in the second half of the twentieth century was a shock to most social systems.
Always allied to the general increase in disposable wealth (many people with
more money and thus the means to buy new musical products created as a result
of technological developments in sound recording), the availability of many
and varied types of music and the social practices that accompanied the private
and public playing and performances of such music (parties, dances, concerts,
gigs, festivals) caused major disruption to conventional social practices across
the Western world. We do not need to reach a firm conclusion as to whether it
was the 1950s, the 1960s, or the 1970s that contained the most disruption. We
do not even need to worry about decades at all. But we do need to recognize
that churches struggled to know what to do with such rapid developments.
We must also notice that it was not only churches (or religious groups) that
struggled, and we shall consider this further in our next chapter (4). Accepting the fact that through the 1950s and 1960s Christianity in particular still
shaped Western culture to a considerable extent, it is nevertheless clear that

the concerns about the impact of popular music upon society were not being expressed solely by the explicitly religious.

Christian concerns are, however, easy to document. Widely cited is the claim made by the (Anglican) Bishop of Woolwich in the UK that rhythm might have a "maddening effect" on young people and reduce their capacity to control themselves.[1] And in the same way that the film industry was said to be allied with the works of the devil from its inception, so also rock 'n' roll was readily linked to "the devil, lawlessness and immorality."[2] These UK examples are echoed by reactions elsewhere. The reaction of the churches and the wider public square to the rising popularity of Elvis Presley included preparations for charging him with "impairing the morals of minors" if his shows were not moderated, plus prayer meetings and sermons against the emerging phenomenon of rock and roll.[3] Presley's image was contrasted by critics (including the churches) with his clean-cut Christian rival Pat Boone, although this ignored Presley's own religious background. As we have seen, tensions between conventional churches and rebellious rock music continued in subsequent decades. Thus Eileen Luhr has observed, "When musician Larry Norman recorded the song 'Why Should the Devil Have All the Good Music?' in 1972, he captured the spirit of a youth movement unwilling to cede any terrain to secular culture."[4]

Popular Music in Social Context

These instances from both sides of the Atlantic can be seen as part of a much broader process of social change. Charles Taylor describes how many developments emerge in society not through "intellectual reasoning" but through "the relief of revolt," which allows tensions within individual and communal faith perspectives to be resolved through a "flip-over," a dramatic change of understanding in the search for personal significance and social sense-making.[5]

Quaint and misguided though these reactions appear with the benefit of hindsight, and especially with respect to the theological assessments we shall consider in this chapter, it might have seemed understandable to many that the arrival of mass-scale popular music in the age of rock 'n' roll should not be welcomed. It is difficult to disentangle popular music's late twentieth-century role in society from many other concurrent developments, not least the changing sexual mores, Western culture's decline of support for organized religion (especially Christianity), major political changes (from support for left-wing causes to the apparent triumph of capitalism in market-led democracies), and widespread unrest about military interventions (e.g., Vietnam, Northern Ireland, Iraq). Wherever music played a role in what is commonly regarded as the quest for individual autonomy and freedom, particularly through the 1960s and 1970s, it can be regarded as both a positive force in contributing to that quest and a negative influence in bringing people under unwelcome spheres of influence (e.g., drug culture). The fact that it *can* be both shows how difficult it is to draw conclusions about causes. Yet it was not music *of itself* that caused young people to take drugs, though some did so "because The Beatles did." The function of celebrity culture should not be underplayed. Although it is clear that some of the negative reactions to both popular music and the practices with which it was associated were quite unreasonable and extreme, and very much borne of social conservatism, we must not underestimate the temporal distance needed to have a chance to see this. Popular music by itself could rarely be said to be dangerous. But the society in which it was being performed and listened to was clearly not ready for the social and political consequences of its appearance.[6] Put in theological terms: such music may not have been sinful in itself, but it was quite understandable that, in response to the shock of rock 'n' roll, Christians would be among those who could not easily welcome it with open arms.

Stephen Wright tellingly (and rightly) states, however, that much of the reporting of Christian opposition to popular music in the 1960s comes from secular reporters latching on to the words of outspoken Christian leaders. In other words, the caution with which popular music needed to be handled led to blatant condemnation by those from whom public pronouncement might be expected. Below the radar of such pronouncements and of public media, however, ordinary Christians were getting on with their lives and often enjoying the new forms of music, either not asking questions about whether it was compatible with their faith, or simply ignoring the advice of those who encouraged them to steer clear of it. Jill Marsh, wife of one of the authors, reports how, at an address she gave in the UK in 2002 to a group of Methodist women in their 50s and 60s, on mention of one or two Beatles songs, some of the women spontaneously burst into song. Others quickly joined in. Some said it was the first time they recalled singing Beatles songs in church. They knew all the words after forty years (having no doubt sung them many times elsewhere). The songs had been fun (even if not churchy) and life-enhancing. In other words, for them not to be seen as of the church or connected to their faith, indeed perhaps at some distance from church and faith, meant sadly that at times the church might have been viewed as *not* fun and *not* life-enhancing. As we shall see, the dangers of maintaining such a sharp distinction between church and world would in due course need to be challenged theologically.

Popular Music and Christian Theology

All Western theologians and church leaders working in the past fifty years have grown up in a context in which they have needed to make sense of the popular music all around them and adopt a response to it. Whether or not a basically positive or negative view is adopted will not, as we saw, have simply to do with the music itself. But unlike previous generations, where it may have been possible to claim that "church and society" or "church and world" could be kept quite separate, maintaining such a sharp distinction now is much more difficult. In the case of music, a crucial ever-present aspect of popular culture, many contemporary theologians know that they must now address the existence of popular music as they offer accounts of how theology is to be undertaken and what its content should be.

In the remainder of this chapter, as a way of orienting ourselves theologically for the task of critically scrutinizing what popular music is doing in Western society today, we take up the work of three contemporary Western theologians from different Christian traditions. Each is a contributor to the debate about how to make sense theologically of popular culture; two (Brown and Beaudoin) quite specifically interact with examples of popular music as they do so. The writings of all three could be regarded as the self-justification for their personal practices, since they are all fans of popular culture in their own ways and are thus defending their theological engagement with it. We review their work because they represent a major and theologically significant shift in the way popular music has been and must be regarded in Western Christian theology. Popular music, we shall suggest, *must* be seen as a resource for theology since people are listening to it, singing it, and performing it, including people of faith. And as our three writers show, there is an important theological case to be made for why popular music as a phenomenon (even if not every popular song) is to be seen as the work of God. Not until part 3 shall we judge whether the way in which our three writers present their cases is the most appropriate theological defense of what popular music achieves. But let us listen to them first.

Contemporary Theological Encounters I: David Brown

David Brown has written one of the most expansive theological studies of the interaction between Christian tradition and human experience ever published. Across five lengthy volumes, and in particular in his trilogy—*God and Enchantment of Place: Reclaiming Human Experience* (2004), *God and Grace of Body: Sacrament in Ordinary* (2007), and *God and Mystery in Words: Experience through Metaphor and Drama* (2008)—Brown has sought to acknowledge and heed the implications of a "God active outside the control of the Church."[7] To undertake his task, Brown trawls through Western forms of human culture searching for resources with which he deems theology must engage in order to do its work. His search takes him to nature, fine art, significant places, buildings, gardens, and to sport (*God and Enchantment of Place*). It finds him exploring dance, food and drink, the ugliness and beauty of the human body, and music in its many forms, including pop, rock, blues, and musicals (*God and Grace of Body*), before turning back to ecclesiastical culture itself in observing how words, the visual, and the theatrical all play a role in the drama of liturgical life (*God and Mystery in Words*). The sweep of the inquiry is breathtaking. The insights presented rarely disappoint.

For our purposes, we notice the primary theological basis on which Brown conducts his research. From the start, Brown's intent is clear: "So far from the sacramental being seen as essentially ecclesiastical or narrowly Christian, it should be viewed as a major, and perhaps even the primary, way of exploring God's relationship to our world."[8] Brown wishes to make a theology of sacrament, or a kind of "sacramental principle," central to his task. We must understand "sacramental" here to mean, in most general terms, that "something of the god becomes, as it were, embodied."[9] Brown is observing that even from outside of the Christian tradition, here with respect to classical Greek culture, it is possible to perceive across times and cultures how the embeddedness of the divine in human culture has been assumed or claimed. God/the divine is not to be seen simply as the spiritual or immaterial within the material. Indeed, it is precisely the Christian conviction about the incarnation of God in Christ that enables the commitment of God to the material world to receive fullest respect. Hence, while the sacramental principle may be discernible most clearly in the sacraments of Holy Communion (i.e., in bread and wine) or baptism (through water), it is vital that the presence of God in and through the material is not to be confined to the sacraments themselves. In Brown's words: "Earthy reality is present not just in the bread and wine but also through the whole humanity of Christ being once more available, however transformed it has become through entering a new type of existence."[10]

To adopt a sacramental approach to the material world and to human culture means, then, to take the example of God's incarnation as celebrated in the theology and practice of sacraments and apply it to the rest of life. Because of the incarnation, and steered by the way in which the incarnation is celebrated in the practice of participation in sacramental worship, according to Brown, we should not be in the least surprised to encounter the reality of God in all sorts of places, spiritual and material. That is the premise of his theological project. His work invites us to consider popular music firmly as a potential channel through which the self-revelation of God in the world may be considered. He states that popular music is often assumed to "lie at the opposite extreme from true religious experience since the superficiality of music and lyrics alike deprives it of all depth."[11] Brown challenges this assumption. Even if he adopts a cautious approach, we welcome his willingness to bring his sacramental emphasis to bear on the task of interpreting popular music theologically.

Brown writes as a High Anglican/Episcopalian who values the liturgical tradition of the church. His theological persuasion and favored style of worship may not be to all readers' tastes. Thus we need to look in other directions to see how human experience and the material world are currently being examined from a theological perspective.

Contemporary Theological Encounters II: Tom Beaudoin

Tom Beaudoin (b. 1969) is an American Roman Catholic theologian, currently working as an associate professor of practical theology in New York. He is also a rock musician and host of the blogsite "Rock and Theology." Beaudoin is the author of three major works: *Virtual Faith: The Irreverent Spiritual Quest of Generation X* (1998), *Consuming Faith: Integrating Who We Are with What We Buy* (2003), and *Witness to Dispossession: The Vocation of a Postmodern Theologian* (2008). Though he has engaged theologically and philosophically with many topics germane to our current study, for our present purposes we wish simply to review, as with Brown, the primary theological basis on which Beaudoin undertakes his work. From *Virtual Faith* on, Beaudoin has been working hard to ensure that theologians operate in full awareness of the extent to which Western people are "formed by pop culture."[12] In 1998, he identified four main themes characterizing the "lived theology" of Generation X[13]: deep suspicion of religious institutions, the sacred nature of experience, the religious dimension of suffering, and an exploration of faith and ambiguity.[14]

In exploring the second of these themes—the crucial role played by experience—it is striking that Beaudoin makes use of theological emphases similar to Brown's. Hence Beaudoin recognizes the recourse to "sacramentals" in popular culture: symbols and experiences that are like sacraments, and have a similar function, yet that are in the end simulations of actual sacraments. These often take bodily form and may include tattoos, piercings, or expressions of sexuality.[15] Nevertheless these symbols and experiences can still manage to convey that which is really of God even though they are not themselves sacraments: God can be encountered through the most common of experiences, even if there has been something of a shift to human control of the experiences that are being described.

Striking too is the christological basis on which such attention to sacramentals becomes possible. The experience of incarnation ("finding the divine in human form"[16]) is being explored, in Beaudoin's view, by Generation Xers' emphasis on sensuality, bodily experience, and sacramentality. He is then able to conclude: "Xers live a theology revolving around *incarnation*—the experience of the human in the context of the divine, and the divine mediated by the human. Thus, Xers express religiosity with *sacramentals*, which can evoke the religious depth of the most common objects or experiences."[17]

Brown and Beaudoin are thus similar in their theological emphases. Christology and sacraments are theological foundations on which the valuing of popular culture, and thus the revelatory significance of popular music, becomes possible. God's commitment to human form means that many channels of God's self-communication through the human/material are feasible. Yet both Beaudoin and Brown remain cautious. Brown is cautiously bearing in mind the theologians and philosophers for whom he writes, many of whom, while knowing the fine artists and classical composers he cites, may not be familiar with the popular music examples he uses (e.g., Nick Cave, Jay-Z). Beaudoin wishes to be more consistently positive about the value of a broader range of popular culture, of which music is only one aspect. But he stresses the dangers of assuming that the simulations (as imitations) are the real thing.[18] In traditional Roman Catholic theology, sacramentals are not the same as sacraments, even while being channels of divine grace. The distinction is important for Beaudoin even as he stresses, positively, how Generation Xers approach faith finding.[19]

In Beaudoin the practical theologian, then, we can see a deep appreciation of the importance of popular culture today. Popular music finds its place within the broad context in which people are "formed." Theologically speaking, it is not a matter of opposing "religion" and "culture." People are formed within culture anyway, and popular culture is a crucial aspect of that mix. God incarnate must be seen as part of that blend too. At issue is what religious practice and theological insight might contribute to the task of interpreting the rich mix in a way that prevents the simulation's being mistaken for that which is explicitly religious, while acknowledging the possibility of God's being revealed through nonreligious phenomena, events, and practices.

Contemporary Theological Encounters III: James K. A. Smith

James K. A. Smith takes us a step further in our efforts to locate this present study within contemporary Western theological approaches to popular culture. Writing from a Christian Reformed perspective and highly conscious of the potentially controversial nature of his positive stance toward popular culture, Smith is a third theologian who argues for the importance of a sacramental approach. Smith's *Desiring the Kingdom: Worship, Worldview, and Cultural Formation* is the first volume of his Cultural Liturgies work. Smith intends this trilogy to be a comprehensive theology of culture. In his first volume he sees the need to clarify how people are formed in contemporary culture. He shares a concern (similar to Beaudoin's) that it will not do to offer a theology of any kind, even a theological reading of culture, without understanding first both the context of reception and the framework within which any citizen, religious or not, is being shaped. His eventual focus, even in this first volume, is the education of the Christian person. For our immediate purposes, however, part 1 of *Desiring the Kingdom* is relevant. Here Smith expounds a view of the human being as "liturgical animal" (*homo liturgicus*).[20]

This is not, it should be stressed, a direct argument for the implicit religiosity of all humans. Rather, Smith shows how all humans are formed. In contrast to a worldview approach that would too easily place emphasis on *cognitive* elements of human formation (ideas, beliefs), Smith shows how ideas and beliefs are but part of many aspects of what it means to be human. It is *desire* that drives us, and therefore our emotions, our guts, and our heart are what primarily steer us. This being so, Smith argues, the practices we engage in and the way we participate in those practices (be they sport, shopping, listening to or watching· forms of popular culture) are what shape us. "Because our hearts are oriented primarily by desire, by what we love, and because those desires are shaped and molded by the habit-forming practices in which we participate, it is the rituals and practices of the mall—the liturgies of mall and market—that shape our imaginations and how we orient ourselves to the world."[21] For this reason human beings are fundamentally *homo liturgicus*.[22]

The result of this change of emphasis (from worldview acquisition to personal formation) is that theology itself undergoes a shift. Though it remains a cognitive discipline, it is not trading *only* in ideas and beliefs. If theology as a discipline is to do justice to how religion works, and if religion relates to the whole embodied human person, then it will need to respect the many facets of what it means to be human. As Smith recognizes, religion does not specifically or primarily shape many contemporary Western citizens. Nevertheless, the many dimensions of what it means to be human (cares, concerns, motivations, desires, as well as ideas and beliefs) remain active. A contemporary theology of culture (and a contemporary theological engagement with popular music) will therefore inevitably have to address these many dimensions. To be highly practical, following Smith, a trawling of lyrics in search of explicitly or implicitly religious themes will not be sufficient. It is necessary to pay attention to how a pattern of consumption of popular music contributes to a person's formation.

Smith uses his insights of *homo liturgicus* specifically in relation to Christian formation. This is not our main concern at this stage. Yet it is vital that we notice the theological arguments Smith uses to develop his reflections on humans as liturgical animals when relating them to Christian practice, for they dovetail nicely with those of Brown and Beaudoin. Smith develops an argument for "the sacramental imagination."[23] Working back from the practice of Christian worship, Smith observes "how earthy, material, and mundane it is."[24] It is profoundly embodied ("lungs to sing, knees to kneel, legs to stand, arms to raise, eyes to weep, nose to smell, tongues to taste, ears to hear, hands to hold and raise"). Regular Christian practice involves water, bread, and wine. "This liturgical affirmation of materiality," Smith observes, "is commonly described as a sacramental understanding of the world—that the physical, material stuff of creation and embodiment is the means by which God's grace meets us and gets hold of us."[25] He knows, however, that he quickly needs to reassure his (largely Reformed or evangelical) readership and urges them to "suspend judgment for just a few pages" lest they misunderstand his emphasis on the sacramental and the liturgical. His goal, we soon discover, is to draw out the "understanding of the world implicit in Christian worship." It is a form of "theological materialism" that "both affirms the goodness of materiality but also that the material *is* only insofar as it participates in *more* than the material."[26]

We find ourselves, then, at a similar place to where Brown and Beaudoin brought us: wanting to affirm the material and the embodied on theological grounds, and doing this with reference to a theology of sacrament or a sacramental principle. In Smith's case, wanting to go on to see what such a sacramental approach to culture means for Christian education, his starting point in Christian worship leads him back to reassess what is going on in culture generally. Rather than being separate from the rest of life, the earthiness of Christian worship enables him to see how humans generally are formed. The person-forming practices that people engage in may well not be religious, but they do form us. Like Beaudoin, only perhaps more so, Smith clearly has major concerns about where our consumer-driven practices lead us. He sees the need for *homo liturgicus* to be steered into practices that are life-enhancing rather than life-destroying. He also acknowledges, however, that the church has things to learn from the liturgies, practices, and rituals that form people beyond it.[27]

From Sin to Sacramentality?

We have seen, then, that the trajectory from the mid-twentieth century to the end of the first decade of the twenty-first century can be regarded as a move from sin to sacramentality. Popular music was more likely at first to be viewed as dangerous, or at best as trivial. It could actively lead people away from God or distract them from a more serious approach to life. By contrast, fifty or sixty years later, a more nuanced view is taken. Popular music is everywhere. Most Western citizens, whether religious or not, listen to it. Some popular music may well be dangerous or trivial. But not all popular music can be labeled this way. Thus in the same way that the grace of God may be embodied in or discerned through any aspect of the material world or human culture, popular music is ripe for reassessment.

Given the approaches of Brown, Beaudoin, and Smith—coming from quite different theological backgrounds—there is common ground across the theological spectrum about the basis on which such a reassessment might be possible. In Christian understanding, a sacramental theology provides a basis for any aspect of popular culture's becoming a channel of the self-revelation of God, or of the grace of God. This therefore is a theology *for* such an approach. It does not yet tell us anything about what a theology might be that results *from* engagement with popular music. That will come later. In chapter 9, we shall use the work of Ian S. Markham to develop further the theological framework necessary for understanding what to do with popular culture. We shall also, in conversation with Kelton Cobb, reflect on what can be gained *from* popular culture. Building on both, we shall then be in a better position, in chapters 10 and 11, to ask what happens to theology if it takes a journey through popular music.

First, though, we need to listen to popular music itself. This sketch of recent decades of theological responses to popular music has, however oversimple, set the scene and suggested that part 2 will be far from fruitless. We will face some challenges. How, if at all, will popular music rise above the concern that it remains superficial (feared by Brown), that it is an imitation or a simulation of what is truly sacramental (Beaudoin), or that it may contribute to the misdirecting of our desires (Smith)? To what extent can a regular diet of popular music have any chance of forming a person in a life-enhancing way? We will address these questions in part 3.

Charles Taylor contends that unresolved issues around bodily desire remain at the heart of Western culture. This results in the periodic sidelining of the body within Christianity and across society in general.[28] In the context of Christianity, he calls this process "'excarnation,' the steady disembodying of spiritual life, so that it is less and less carried in deeply meaningful bodily forms, and lies more and more 'in the head.'"[29] Daniel Levitin's discussion of the role of music within religion gives an example: "Religious thoughts take us outside ourselves, lift us up higher, elevate us from the mundane and day-to-day to consider our role in the world, the future of the world, the very nature of existence." Levitin describes how music changes the chemistry of our brains and through that the thoughts of our minds.[30] While this is an embodied account of Christianity and music, it is entirely focused on the head. Taylor argues for a more holistic, embodied approach on the basis that "Christianity, as the faith of the Incarnate God, is denying something essential to itself as long as it remains wedded to forms which excarnate."[31] We shall argue that engagement with popular culture is an important part of reversing this process of excarnation and reengaging with the incarnation and sacramentality that is vital to Christianity.[32]

part 2

living by pop music

pop music in the marketplace

Kids now—they seem to have very little of the snobbery about music that I had, and the downside of that is that music doesn't play a kind of ideological part in their lives. It is slightly surprising to realize that something which had enormous meaning for you doesn't have so much meaning for them. The currency is devalued in some way. So what I look out for is: so what *does* that for them now? Because I assume there's always a currency through which people are communicating with one another. Though they do pass music around and they appear to love music. But what they really seem to like is the communal experiences that music can give rise to. So what they really like is going to festivals; what they really like is exchanging music on *Facebook*, not for the music but for the fact of the exchange, of the communication.

Brian Eno, musician, composer, and record producer[1]

Popular Music as Commodity

The notion of both popular music and faith as commodities is not as far-fetched as it may seem since there is more that connects the selling of religion and music than at first meets the eye. Popular music is certainly a commercial phenomenon. It makes or loses money. Whatever other motives those who make popular music may have (to entertain, to create art, to politicize listeners, to have fun, to become famous), they also want to make a living from playing, producing, or selling it. Indeed, many participants in the world of popular music would clearly like to make a lot of money from it. A few do. In beginning our exploration of what popular music is and does, we must face this key aspect. There is no avoiding popular music's alliance with moneymaking.

Our purpose in this chapter is not, however, either to be unduly critical of this aspect of popular music—as if moneymaking itself is a bad thing (we all need to make a living)—or to claim that the most popular (or commercially successful) music is inevitably the most significant, be that culturally, artistically, morally, or religiously. In later chapters we shall address ways of arguing the question of what is *worth* listening to. By beginning here we dig further into the insights presented by David Brown, Tom Beaudoin, and James K. A. Smith in the previous chapter as we begin to address the question of how and why popular music works.

We wish simply to note some of the ways in which commerce, faith, and popular music interact in Western culture and how wider cultural elements have shaped their development. In so doing, we locate popular music *and* religion within the ongoing history of capitalism and thereby argue that to see them as wholly separate entities is a mistake. Even while they relate to different sets of social practices, to view them as wholly distinct is not accurate.

First we observe some key features of the relationship between Christianity and capitalism, noting how the history of evangelical Christianity's use of music, especially in the USA, reflects this relationship. Then we use two examples from the rock band U2 in exploring the dynamics at work in commerce, religion, and popular music. We conclude by observing the way changes in technology (which we will explore further in later chapters) have a direct connection to commerce as well as to how popular music and religion develop as forms of communication.

"I Will Sing, Sing a New Song": Popular Music and Evangelical Christianity

Religion and Consumption

Study of the relationship between Christianity and capitalism goes back at least as far as the sociologist Max Weber (1864–1920), who developed the thesis of the "Protestant work ethic." Weber argued that ideas found within Calvinist strands of Christianity played a key role in the emergence of a capitalist economy. Noting the extent to which Christian faith in its Protestant form, over against its Catholic form, encouraged hard work and the methodical accumulation of wealth, Weber argued for this faith-driven element in the rise of modern capitalism. The thesis has been widely influential, though often questioned, most recently by historian Diarmaid MacCulloch, who observes: "Detailed acquaintance with the story of the Reformation and Counter-Reformation makes it dissolve into qualification and contradiction; it is an idea best avoided. Discipline and the urge to order people's lives were ecumenical qualities."[2] Nevertheless the relationship between patterns of faith and systems of economics remains a subject for study and debate.

Researchers have approached the question from various perspectives. Sociologist George Ritzer—best known for his McDonaldization theory[3]—has argued that religion can be taken as a metaphor for consumption. He calls the places where we make purchases "*cathedrals of consumption*, which points up the quasi-religious, 'enchanted' nature of these new settings. They have become locales to which we make 'pilgrimages' in order to practice our consumer religion."[4] David Lyon has explored the same image from a different angle, arguing that in contemporary society cathedrals and churches have become symbols of how the place of religion has been transformed in the marketplace: "Venerable worship edifices are still visible in all the cities of the world, both ancient and relatively modern. But in Europe and North America they frequently find their most faithful visitors are tourists. Cathedrals are under new management. Such church buildings often stand as symbolic sentinels, museums marking the sites of old practices, quaint relics of a bygone era."[5] In other words, religion and spirituality have themselves become consumer items, which reflect much deeper changes in human culture as "the basic coordinates of social life—time and space—are being reconfigured, decomposed from their modern lines and shaped into flows and fragments that will alter radically life in the twenty-first century."[6]

Thus, as Smith notes, trips to shopping malls really are like religious experiences.[7] But the deeper point to be made here is that the complex interplay of religious and economic life means that it is not possible to contrast faith and consumer practice in any simple way. If to a considerable extent we are what we consume (i.e., that which we desire, what we attach ourselves to emotionally, that to which we are committed and claim for ourselves), then we also choose to be shaped by such commitments. The choices we make in the popular music we listen to are part of this dynamic at both the production end (people make music in part to encourage us to buy it) and the point of reception (we listen to [consume, buy] what we like, if we can afford it, or if we choose to download it illegally). Smith rightly and understandably wants to inform people's desires and cultivate good practices in Christian life. But this cannot be a simple matter in a complex commercial context.[8]

Does this make listening to popular music a religion? Dell deChant follows Jacques Ellul (1912–94) in seeing politics and technology as modern cosmological religions but observes that in the light of disillusion in both these fields, consumption has become the place where Western society finds "the shared myths and rituals of our community. . . . Rather than myths of history, science, or progress, the myths that relate us to the sacred realm of the economy are the much more vital, robust narratives of our postmodern culture."[9] Where most of the roles previously undertaken by religion have been transferred to the orders and processes of the economy, deChant believes we need to analyze consumption in the same way we would scrutinize religion. To undertake a careful scrutiny of popular music in terms of its production, its content, and its reception is thus to take up deChant's challenge. More than studying an analogy of religion or seeking traces of religion in culture at large, to study popular culture as a key form of consumption is at the same time to examine the myths and practices that at least some people live by.[10]

This link between the contemporary market for entertainment and the sacred realm of myth is something that Bono, the lead singer of U2, has also observed. Writing about the biblical Psalms, he says:

> I stopped going to churches and got myself into a different kind of religion. Don't laugh, that's what being in a rock 'n' roll band is, not pseudo-religion either. . . . Show-business is Shamanism: Music is worship; whether it's worship of women or their designer, the world or its destroyer, whether it comes from that ancient place we call soul or simply the spinal cortex, whether the prayers are on fire with a dumb rage or dove-like desire, . . . the smoke goes upwards . . . to God or something you replace God with, . . . usually yourself.[11]

In recognizing the religion-like power of popular music and acknowledging that popular music may be replacing religion, Bono is also sounding an alarm: what we thought of as worship of God is in fact worship of the self/oneself. This insight echoes a persistent concern about what the centrality of consumption does to a human: "I shop (and shop and shop), therefore I am."[12]

These ways of analyzing the relationship between consumption and religion are thus far flowing in one direction in their exploration of the language, rituals, and myths of faith. They show how these aspects of faith have been poured into our contemporary capitalist context and remolded as humans have sought to reengage with the enchanted worlds of the past. At the same time, there has been another flow as the churches have sought to learn from the economic structures of McDonald's, Disney, and other corporations. Indeed, Ritzer acknowledges: "We can bring this discussion full-circle by pointing out that although the cathedrals of consumption have a quasi-religious character, religion has begun to emulate those cathedrals particularly in the form of megachurches."[13]

The link between Christianity and a consumer approach to faith is not, however, merely a recent development. It has been argued that the Second Great Awakening, a revival movement in the USA during the early nineteenth century, was "driven by consumers."[14] The moment that faith and the worlds of work and economics are brought close together, neither can remain unaffected. With good biblical precedent, Christianity has often sought to remain detached from "the world," where the world is easily seen as ungodly and sinful. The same Bible, however, reminds people of faith that creation is God's, that humans are made in God's image, and that the world is the object of God's love. Our main point here is that although many kinds of Christians have been skeptical of Christian involvement in the world of commerce, their separateness is less clear-cut than many expect.[15]

Developments in Contemporary Christian Music

Debates continued throughout the twentieth century in churches and academia about the connection between Christian faith and economic capitalism, sacred space and the market square, Christianity and culture. A significant element for developments in the late twentieth and early twenty-first centuries was the Jesus movement of the 1960s and 1970s. Out of that movement and in conjunction with other trends from the evangelical, Pentecostal, and charismatic worlds the nondenominational megachurches grew. That change has, in turn, had a significant impact on how music is used in public church worship and in the private lives of individual Christians.[16] This development in Christian music among evangelicals in the USA has been examined with particular reference to their attitudes toward popular music by Eileen Luhr. She argues that during the Reagan-Bush era major changes took place involving the suburbanization of evangelicalism and "Christianization" of popular culture. This in turn means that "the emergence of politicized evangelical youth culture ranks as one of the major achievements of 'third wave' conservatism in the late twentieth century."[17] Luhr traces a line of development in postwar, evangelical faith through the outright rejection of 1950s' and 1960s' culture in some quarters to a gradual embrace of certain aspects of mainstream life in the 1970s and 1980s. The trajectory Luhr follows encompasses numerous contradictions and is not straightforward. She argues that "conservative Christians disagreed about what constituted a 'biblical' or 'Christian' stance on rock music, yet they concurred that youth culture exerted tremendous influence over young people."[18] At the same time these shifting attitudes to youth culture provided insights "into how [conservative Christians] attempted to reenter public conversation about culture at the end of the twentieth century."[19] The roots for a later change of approach among evangelicals lay in the Jesus movement of the late 1960s and early 1970s and can be summed up in an observation from the period: "The pulpit of this generation and the next is the guitar."[20]

This insight is even more credible with the engagement of evangelical Christians in the worlds of heavy metal and punk in the 1970s and 1980s. "Whereas punk appealed to young evangelicals' tendencies toward righteous renunciation, metal's emphasis on theatrics, along with its use (or desecration) of sacred symbols, gave Christians a perfect opportunity to engage in a dialogue with popular culture."[21] Another area of influence has been the Harvest Crusade, an annual evangelical revival meeting that has played a significant role in generating a conservative Christian response to gay rights activism, abortion protests, the creation of megachurches, and a wider attempt to sacralize public space.[22]

It is striking that publicity for Harvest Crusade's 2006 rally drew on the publicity produced for U2's Vertigo Tour of 2005, thus visually underscoring a correlation between Christian faith and popular music despite the differences that exist between U2's political interests and those of the Harvest Crusade.

Music and Commerce: The Case of U2

During his conversations with Michka Assayas, Bono as U2's lead singer reflects on the early days of the band in the late 1970s, when he was elaborating his vision for the future to Chris Rowe, a mentor and key member of the evangelical community to which some of U2 belonged. Bono recalls that Chris

> was an older man. He relied on the Lord to provide them with everything they needed. They were living hand-to-mouth, this community. I guess he would have been what you would call the pastor of the church, but he'd be much too radical to wear a collar or anything like that. This was the real deal: a radical group. And I said: "Look, you shouldn't have to worry about money. We're gonna earn plenty of money. I'm in a band, and I know we'll be able to help. We're gonna make it." He just looked at me and laughed. I remember he said to me: "I wouldn't want money earned that way." And I said: "What do you mean by that?" He revealed to me that, even though he had known we were serious about being musicians, and being in a rock group, that he was only really tolerating it. He didn't really believe that our music was an integral part of who we were as religious people unless we used the music to evangelize. I knew then that he didn't really get it, and that indeed he was missing out on our blessing. Such a zealot was he, and such a fundamentalist, he didn't want a part of this rock 'n' roll thing.[23]

This tension between Christians who reject mainstream culture and commerce and those who engage with it can be found in the work of U2 as a band and in the experiences of their fans. A good example of this is the song "40" from their third album, *War*. In a number of places Bono has described how the band came to write the song:

> Years ago, lost for words and forty minutes of recording time left before the end of our studio time, we were still looking for a song to close our third album, *War*. We wanted to put something explicitly spiritual on the record to balance the politics and the romance of it; like Bob Marley or Marvin Gaye would. We thought about the psalms . . . Psalm 40. . . . There was some squirming. We were a very "white" rock group, and such plundering of the Scriptures was taboo for a white rock group unless it was in the "service of Satan." Or worse, Goth. . . . [He continues:] Psalm 40 is interesting in that it suggests a time in which grace will replace karma, and love replace the very strict laws of Moses [i.e., fulfill them]. I love that thought. David, who committed some of the most selfish as well as selfless acts, was depending on it. That the Scriptures are brim full of hustlers,

murderers, cowards, adulterers, and mercenaries used to shock me; now it is a source of great comfort.[24]

The tension between personal experience and the expectations of others—whether that means Scripture, church leaders, or parents—is reflected in comments made by fans and others who watched a video of the band performing "40." For example, Lisamarie656 on YouTube comments: "Growing up in a strict Christian household, we were taught that U2 was bad simply because they had a song entitled 'Sunday Bloody Sunday.' How naive!! My parents would have been grateful to have me singing along to Psalm 40! I missed out on them during the most formative years of my life and am more than making up for it now!! The favor of the Lord is definitely upon them."[25] And on a site dedicated to exploring the meaning of songs, mlock317 picks up a comment by jou12n3y, "I never knew this side of U2 until I heard this song today," and responds:

> Well, my dear, you have alot to learn about U2! As long as you don't expect them to be squeaky clean Bob Jones–type fundamentalists, then you won't be disappointed. They have a deep, long-lasting faith and have produced some of the most inspiring music I have come across (even counting CCM). And don't assume that just because a song's title (e.g., "The Playboy Mansion," "I Still Haven't Found What I'm Looking For") or its sound (e.g., "Mofo") doesn't sound very Christian, that U2 have lost their way. There's some great spiritual content in those songs if you really look.[26]

These cases illustrate the many tensions present in popular music's function in contemporary Western culture, and in the different ways in which religion interweaves with it. The interaction between religion and music takes place in various ways in the contemporary commercial world. As noted, some argue that consumer capitalism is functioning in a manner that is similar to the ritualized behavior of religion (Ritzer, deChant). Others argue that the influence of consumer capitalism has changed the nature of faith, particularly Western forms of Christianity (Lyon, Luhr). Along this two-way street of religion and capitalism acting on each other at a macrolevel, we see a similar two-way dynamic at work at a microlevel as faith and economics act on individuals, together with the social groups to which they belong, at the point of production, in a lyric, and at the point of reception. It is not easy to identify what a "religious song" might be. Nor is it easy to disentangle religion from commerce at each stage in the production-product-reception process. At the point of production—U2 members scratching around for material to fill their third album—they turned to a religious text because that's what they knew. But a commercial decision was being made. In terms of the text/product (i.e., the song itself), even now listeners are not always aware that the lyrics are biblical. And in relation to other songs, some of U2's own fans indicate that it is not always easy to locate religious content ("if you really look"). U2's songs are frequently ambiguous.

At the point of reception, religious control is still applied ("We were taught that U2 was bad"). To use the theological narrative introduced in chapter 3, we might say that it is not always the case that sin has given way to the possibility of sacramentality.

Some of the dynamics of commerce and faith can thus be found in the work of U2. Within evangelical Christianity on both sides of the Atlantic, people are willing to engage with musical culture, yet others strongly reject all that it stands for. Once again we can see this in terms of the dialectic between the worlds of the Magisteria and Ibiza as people's affective space is defined by what might be seen as institutional, normative, and corporate on one side, and by the creative, alternative, and nonhierarchical on the other. On the Magisteria side, religious communities (e.g., the representatives of Christianity who deem U2 to be "bad"), commercial voices (the sheer pressure of the music market), and fans ("Well, my dear, you have alot to learn about U2!") exert their respective influences. On the Ibiza side, individuals make their choices, sometimes in response to magisterial voices ("How naive!"). These are also choices about individual consumption, reflected in music purchases and perhaps concertgoing ("I . . . am more than making up for it now!").

There is, however, a further dimension to the developing relationship between commerce, consumption, religion, and technology. This, too, can be illustrated and explored with reference to U2. It concerns the development of the iPod.[27]

Selling the Beat: Popular Music in a Digital Age

On the Question of Paying for Music

On U2's 2004 single "Vertigo," Bono mixes images of commerce, finance, fashion, and religion when he sings: "I can't stand the beats / I'm asking for the cheque / The girl with crimson nails / Has Jesus round her neck."

The selling of music within the wider context of culture and faith has a long history, which extends throughout Western society and different religions. For example, the church was a great patron of music from the formulation of Gregorian chant and the rise of polyphony through to the increasingly complex musical expressions of the Renaissance; the tradition of minstrels and troubadours, who earned a living by singing for those with wealth, brought together Islamic and Christian practices; and music itself entered the life of the church from the marketplaces of Edessa.[28] During the twentieth century a music industry emerged that enabled composers and musicians to sell their work through many commercial channels—Tin Pan Alley, sheet music, concerts, recordings, movies, radio, jingles, advertising, and more. One phrase that describes the growing use of music in the selling of products is "sonic branding." North and Hargreaves define this as "the attempt to use very short periods of music and other auditory cues to convey core brand values and prime brand recognition whenever customers come into contact with a company."[29] In other words, they are the auditory equivalent of the company logo.[30]

This process of using music to "sell the beat" extends to musicians themselves. Artists sell their product. It is not merely their music that carries a commercial impact. The appearance of U2's Bono (along with the track "Vertigo") in the first commercials for Apple's iPod in 2004 is a good example of a high-profile musician being used to sell a product. This was part of a complex economic relationship that continues to develop and be debated between consumers and purveyors of music, and in which the management of U2 has taken a leading role.

In January 2008, Paul McGuiness, manager of U2, made a speech at MIDEM, the world's largest music industry trade fair. He outlined the changing nature of the music business as he saw it and said that the relationship between the musical and commercial sides of U2 has always been important: "U2 always understood that it would be pathetic to be good at the music and bad at the business, and have always been prepared to invest in their own future. We were never interested in joining that long, humiliating list of miserable artists who made lousy deals, got exploited, and ended up broke and with no control over how their life's work was used, and no say in how their names and likenesses were bought and sold."[31] However in the rapidly changing world of the music business, more people are listening to music than ever before, through many more media than ever before, but fewer people are paying for it. In McGuiness's opinion: "Part of the problem is that the record companies, through lack of foresight and poor planning, allowed an entire collection of digital industries to arise that enabled the consumer to steal with impunity the very recorded music that had previously been paid for." He concludes his speech with a litany of companies that he feels have benefited from enabling file sharers to steal from musicians: "They have built multibillion industries on the back of our content without paying for it."

Music and Technology: A User's View

We conducted a music survey in 2010 and collected a range of comments about the significance of technology. Some were very positive. One white British woman in her thirties observed how having "an MP3 player . . . has revolutionized my life." Another respondent described owning an iPod touch as "a transformational experience." Others made a distinction between types of media technology that influence their lives. One respondent stated: "I would rather listen to music than watch television. I wouldn't want to live without music. I find music can help me through emotionally difficult times."[32] Some applied technological analogies to describe their use of music. One male respondent talked about how he was able to use music for the purpose of "recharging my batteries."[33] And one man felt that technological developments can also have a negative impact on the listening experience: "I dislike music being played from other people's mobile phones/iPods."[34]

This ambiguity over technological developments expressed by consumers is reflected within the music industry as musicians appear divided over file sharing. The US music website Pitchfork reported in September 2009 that Radiohead band members were heavily criticized by Lily Allen for their own negative response to UK government proposals to cut the internet connections of file sharers.[35] It is unclear which of these approaches to file sharing and the future of music will emerge victorious or whether both will be subsumed by a further wave of technological developments; in many respects this dilemma is merely another manifestation of a fundamental dichotomy at the heart of rock and other forms of music. One cultural commentator, writing just before the digital revolution took hold, observed: "If it is the case that the rock music industry requires a stable and reproducible product, it is equally the case that this industry depends upon the periodic invasion of difference and innovation. Indeed, the rock music industry is probably the best example of the process by which contemporary capitalist culture promotes or multiplies difference in the interests of maintaining its profit-structure."[36]

Seen in this light, the debate over file sharing reveals itself to be a technological manifestation of the ongoing dialectic between stability and innovation that is found in all forms of music. As North and Hargreaves observe, classical music develops through a dynamic of "predictability" and "novelty."[37] In particular, they quote Dean Simonton's research into ratings given in record-buying guides. He argues that pieces of low originality enjoy moderate popularity, pieces of moderate originality enjoy most popularity, and pieces of high originality enjoy the least amount of popularity.[38] Elements of this same dynamic can be found in popular music. U2 described the radical departure in musical style between their fifth album, *The Joshua Tree* (1987), and its official follow-up *Achtung Baby* (1991) as "the sound of four men chopping down *The Joshua Tree*."[39] In this instance *The Joshua Tree* and *Achtung Baby* consistently remain their most popular albums, though the change of departure had to be signaled, and the change of musical direction that then continued throughout the 1990s (in their *Zooropa* and *Pop* albums) had to be worked at, even among their loyal fans.[40] Significantly, a similar dialectic between stability and innovation can be identified with respect to the way in which religious faiths handle tradition. We shall return to this point in the concluding section of this chapter.

Music, Religion, and Globalized Capitalism

This chapter demonstrates that the links between religion and economics are very complex. To explore these links adequately, we would at least need to draw on the disciplines of theology and religious studies, economics, sociology, history and media, and cultural studies.[41] Exploring how the worlds of faith and capitalism interact involves an understanding of the processes of secularization and pluralism, together with the development of civil society and international relations.[42] It is not possible to do justice here to the multifaceted nature of this topic, but when we see the enormous impact of globalized capitalism on different cultures, it is perhaps not surprising that it affects both faith and music. Nor is it surprising that it affects faith and music in similar ways, for both entail commitment through practice (devotion to a way of life or to an artist or style of music).[43]

As we are emphasizing throughout this study, the practice of being religious (praying, interacting with scriptural texts, worshiping, conducting oneself mindful of others) and of listening to music (as a regular discipline, with emotional commitment, as a fan within a fan community) have much in common. They are life-shaping practices. Despite their undoubted differences (Do we *really* choose a religion?) in an age of global capitalism, commitment to either entails consumer choices. We certainly make choices about the music we listen to. Even if we are more directly shaped by the religious influences that may have affected us since birth, we also choose whether to accept the religion we are born into. And when we do, we make choices about how to develop and practice that religious commitment. Included within this, tellingly, is the religious music we listen to, or the music we listen to that we believe supports our faith.

A key element in religion is the shaping of social identity, and we shall discuss this issue further in our chapter on music and the body.[44] As Charles Taylor notes, "Denominations are like affinity groups. They don't see their differences from (at least some) others as make-or-break, salvation-or-damnation issues. Their way is better for them, may even be seen as better *tout court*, but doesn't cut them off from other recognized denominations."[45] Taylor is arguing that here we can see the effects of the voluntarist dimension of the Great Awakening from the mid-eighteenth century, and the impact of "the second Awakening in the early nineteenth century [which] involved an even greater profusion of denominational initiatives than before."[46] As we noticed earlier in this chapter, the rise of the free market in religious ideas and of the free market in economic transactions belong together. Choosing a religion may not be the same as choosing which tracks to download or which CD to purchase, but their similarity is much closer than we might often suppose.

Although the privatization of faith may have been necessary for the rise of free-market capitalism and of nation-states, the contemporary emphasis on the individual obscures a bigger picture: civil society consists of a "community of communities" and needs to balance the demands of individuals, associations, and governments.[47] We shall discuss the tribal nature of religion and music in subsequent chapters on ritual and the body; but given our insights gained from the Magisteria-Ibiza Spectrum and the tensions between corporate/communal pressures and individual choice, a key question presents itself at this point: How can these factors find their equilibrium? As Stephen Prothero has observed: "The Vatican excommunicated, colonial Massachusetts banished, Salem hung. But the freewheeling, spiritual marketplace of the United States has had no real authority other than public opinion and individual conscience."[48]

One active ingredient not yet fully drawn out in our discussion so far, then, is the marketplace, which is a very specific and influential means for the public to voice its opinion by allocating limited resources for economic transactions. The market is not a neutral actor in this process because it also shapes opinions and individual consciences. In his analysis of global capitalism, Benjamin R. Barber describes the process and justification that producers use to manipulate consumers: "The cynical slogan behind which earnest marketers hide when faced with the tawdry, the harmful, and the meretricious proclaims, 'Don't blame us, we just give the people what they want!' Yet when the skeptics reply, 'It is you, however, who tell the people what they want!' marketers offer the ingenuous

---

"The Man Who Sold the World" by David Bowie

"The Man Who Sold the World" is the title track from David Bowie's third studio album, which has been described as the first "proper" Bowie album. The song itself has been covered by numerous artists including Nirvana, Lulu, Nine Inch Nails, The Waterboys, and others. The lyrics are open to many interpretations and some have seen in them references to God, Jesus, Satan, Adam and Eve, and other religious subjects. People with more secular perspectives have perceived allusions to Robert Heinlein's novella *The Man Who Sold the Moon* (1949), H. P. Lovecraft's writings, and the poem "Antigonish" by William Hughes Mearns which includes the lines:

> Last night I saw upon the stair
> A little man who wasn't there
> He wasn't there again today
> Oh, how I wish he'd go away

Others have seen this as a much more personal statement of David Bowie's own "becoming" but with wider implications for the development of popular music. Nick Stephenson believes a key theme throughout the album is the notion of toying with one's identity. He argues that with Bowie's playful approach to his persona, "This does not lead to the 'real' human being beneath the surface of contemporary culture but just more surfaces and further possibilities of invention."[49] This song provides the origin of a template that David Bowie imparts to future rock and pop stars as they sell their wares in the market place. What they are offering is not themselves but imagined aspects of their identities that they can discard for other facets or faces when the market requires or demands something new.

---

response, which contains a seed of truth, that 'Yes, to be sure, but the people *want* to be told what they want!'"[50]

We see the impact of the free market on a particular expression of the Christian faith in Luhr's analysis of how evangelical Christianity changed during the late twentieth and early twenty-first centuries. The willingness of some from within that tribal context to engage with changes being wrought on popular culture and the public square has led not only to new forms of church organization but also to new forms of music and to changing use of music in churches and individual lives. Just as various forms of pop music have—to use an idea found in the work of Hervieu-Léger and Davie[51]—"mutated" during this period, the same can be said of certain manifestations of the Christian faith. Some manifestations, such as the megachurch and the rise of praise and worship music, seem to be in direct response to (and even as a reflection of) consumer culture. We don't need to simply accept the realities of consumer culture (within which all faith formation and music listening happen) as if such influences are inevitably benign, or to be negatively critical of them. Instead, we must ask if we can learn from the roles that stability and innovation, as key dynamics in technological development and consumer culture, play within the worlds of music and faith. When linked with the more traditional terms "tradition and imagination," we may be able to view stability and innovation in a different light.

Stability/Innovation and Tradition/Imagination in Music and Faith: A Working Conclusion

David Brown was one of the three writers discussed in chapter 3. Before completing the three main volumes we considered, Brown produced two preparatory works, *Tradition and Imagination: Revelation and Change* (1999) and *Discipleship and Imagination: Christian Tradition and Truth* (2000). In the first of these, Brown explores how the Christian faith develops and changes over time. He believes that religious narratives "maintain their imaginative power not by staying the same but by being open to the transforming power of influences beyond themselves."[52] This premise is the foundation of the three-volume work assessing the value of human culture for theology. Brown identifies a dialectic between the resources within the narrative tradition and fresh stimulus that comes from without. Thus "the resources for change come in part at least from within the tradition itself. Sometimes this can be decisively so, as forgotten aspects of the past are recovered and reapplied in different ways, as with classical art at the Renaissance or 'primitive' in modern times. More often, however, it will be a case of the past interacting with some fresh stimulus from outside the tradition, *and responding creatively*."[53] Brown argues that what is at stake within this process of continuing to reimagine the Christian tradition is the future of Christian identity. As Christianity engages with "new social triggers," the narratives of the Christian faith "must engage the imagination, and to do this they must relate to the readers' own life situations and dilemmas, not simply to the past."[54] In his later work *God and Mystery in Words* (2008)—the third volume of his trilogy—he describes poetry as "necessarily iconoclastic" because of its "refusal of closure."[55] Brown argues that this resistance to closure and persistence of transcendence are shared characteristics of poetry and religion.[56]

Building directly on Brown, and mindful of the market-related issues we are examining in this chapter, we suggest that the refusal to move toward closure is part of a wider cultural trend rather than just being inherent in certain forms of art. Therefore film, drama, dance, music, and religion remain open works that involve "the collective enterprise of the audience."[57] Indeed Brown himself believes this fundamental shift in culture took place when the physics of Aristotle, which claimed that a body at rest was the natural condition of all things, was overturned by the insights of Galileo and Newton, which established the motion in all things. "Human identity thus lay not in an ideal static form but in self-creation, in movement from one type of being to another, in an acted drama of existence."[58] Thus in contemporary religious, musical, and economic worlds a creative dialectic exists between the stability of the existing structures and, in the words of Steven Connor, a "periodic invasion of difference,"[59] or in Brown's terms, a "refusal of closure."[60]

The quest for novelty that at one moment can appear as (and sometimes be) the insatiable thirst of the addict for constant innovation, or for persistent consumption, can at another moment equally be recognized as necessarily refusing to permit the stagnation of values and structures within which one lives. A desire for new music, and the joy in welcoming the rapid pace of musical and technological development as one listens to the ever-changing frontiers of popular music—these can indeed be viewed as the listener's response to rapacious commerce. But in this chapter we have sought to demonstrate the inevitability also of the desire for the new being tangled up in the way art and culture work. We may know what we like when it comes to music. We may or may not have examined the market forces that impinge on our music-buying habits. But having located our listening habits within the affective space identified above (chap. 2), and respecting, as we have seen in this chapter, the entanglement of market pressures and faith choices, we are able to conclude that commerce, faith, and pop are not discrete and disconnected elements in Western culture. The quotation from Brian Eno at the head of this chapter indicates the creative role that art plays in our perceptions of the world and the way in which the changing nature of that world can affect how musicians see their craft.

We examined two aspects of this interaction in more detail. First, we observed how the relationship between evangelical Christianity and popular music has changed during the late twentieth and early twenty-first centuries. Second, we saw how some of the challenges that are now facing popular music in the West are similar to those facing religious groups in the same context. Our analysis shares some common ground with Barry Taylor's discussion of postsecular soul space: he identifies a clear tension between the traditional religious sites (churches, synagogues, and mosques) and the new sites for postmodern spirituality in individual lives, cultural imagination, and the reenchantment of society.[61] Using Malcolm Waters's work on globalization, Taylor sees soul space in contemporary Western culture as changing from a treelike existence with roots to a single point of origin into that of a rhizome-like existence with a complex and interrelated network. He observes that the surface nature of this postmodern cultural existence, and its loss of solid ground, is illustrated metaphorically by the movie *Waterworld* (dir. Kevin Reynolds 1995) where the story is driven by the search for some mythical dry land. At this point Taylor is exploring theological ideas analogous to Don Cupitt's long-legged fly[62] and perceives a similar theological trajectory away from "old-fashioned Christianity" to a form of the faith that is better able to move "across the waters of these turbulent times":

> Democratized spirituality is the result of the democratization of spirit along with pretty much everything through the new globalized cultural imaginary. . . . In arguing for a move to Christian spiritualities, and a move *away* from old-fashioned Christianity, it is my desire that our imaginations be attuned to the realities of the present situation and that our missional impetus be challenged by the times.[63]

Our exploration of the affective space created by the metaphors of Magisteria and Ibiza suggests that the tension between old-fashioned Christianity and democratized spirituality (Taylor) or between tradition and imagination (Brown) runs much deeper and is part of the same pattern of stability and innovation (North and Hargreaves) that exists in popular musical culture. In this chapter we have seen how the business of pop music interacts with Western culture and patterns of faith. Within the context of this social flux, not only do pop music and religion change in response to changing circumstances; they also affect and shape one another in the process.

pop music
and the body

I blub all the time, in the most weird situations—not in the ones that should make me cry. Music makes me very emotional. I think I cried yesterday, in fact.

Toby Stephens, actor[1]

You can't compare a congregation to a crowd at a concert. A concert crowd does what they want. A congregation's got rules and regulations.

Al Green, pastor and musician[2]

Music's Multiple Embodiments

In the previous chapter we explored how music, faith, culture, and commerce interact and how their relationship is more complex than is often perceived. This chapter examines how music interacts with the body and draws out some of the implications that such interactions have for the world of faith. The quotations above point us in two helpful initial directions. Toby Stephens's reflection of how music makes him cry shows how music affects our physical bodies and produces an emotional response.

Physical Bodies

Immediately one could say that the emotions indicate something is happening deep in the inner life of the individual. Or one could account for such physical and emotional effects in terms of chemical processes in the body. Daniel Levitin, whose work we cited in chapter 2, takes the latter course: "What we call emotions are nothing more than complex neurochemical states in the brain that motivate us to act. Emotion and motivation are thus intrinsically linked to each other and to our motor centers."[3] The physical link between music and the body was expressed this way by one of our survey respondents: "Music is like a second heartbeat to me. I need to feel it, taste it, smell it, live it. Melodies and bass lines and stories and words dictate my being—they can lift me or drown me."[4] No matter how we see the interaction between ourselves and music, it will always have an irreducibly embodied component that affects us.

The quotation from Al Green describes his differing experiences of performing as a singer in front of an audience and as a pastor in front of a congregation. Each is a communal occasion created by a musical performance. At issue is the significance of *being there*, even if in quite different contexts, since people have chosen to locate their bodies in a particular place in order to experience live music. We do not necessarily need to agree with the distinction that Green draws between the two communal settings he describes in order to see that music also has a collective impact upon humans. A respondent in our music survey drew together the embodied element and the social component: "The best music is that which makes me dance or cry!"[5]

In several ways Levitin takes note of the shared characteristic of music.[6] With respect to singing, he comments: "All over the world and in disparate cultures, human singing is present in two broad styles or forms: strict synchrony and alternation."[7] Naturally, both of these singing forms involve social interaction. However, Levitin argues that the anticipatory nature of alternation (such as call and response found in gospel music and in other forms of musical response) also has an evolutionary advantage: "Those individuals who were better able to predict the behavior of others because they could 'read their minds' would have a competitive advantage within the group."[8] The matter of whether music conveys evolutionary advantage or is a mere "exquisite confection" that tickles the senses, as cognitive scientist Steven Pinker has claimed,[9] remains a contested issue. But even if that debate is resolved, it remains true that music has a significant impact upon individual human bodies, and it brings humans together in forms of embodied social interaction.

When we explore the relationship between music and the body, then, it is clear that we are dealing with a physical relationship in two senses, individual and communal: I dance to music, I sing along to music, and I attend musical events. All of these are experiences that affect my own body and have a physical bearing on my embodied existence as an individual and with respect to the social contexts in which I move.

Symbolic Bodies

The relationship between music and the body has two further dimensions to it, however. In addition to individual and communal physical experience, human bodies and music relate at a symbolic level. We use music and songs to express personal identity and tribal belonging, political views, ideas about sexuality; and to explore questions of human meaning and sense-making. We will consider two ways in which this process works, and here we move into ideas about how we use language in songs, poetry, and in everyday life. Verbal and written interaction between humans is a complex phenomenon that has long been studied. Two of the most important tools of analysis are analogy and metaphor.

At its most straightforward level, analogy is the process of describing one thing in terms of another through *similarity*, whereas metaphor is the process of describing one thing in terms of another through *dissimilarity*. Perhaps the most significant theological reflection on the nature of analogy remains David Tracy's *The Analogical Imagination* (1981). Tracy highlights how analogy tends toward similarity in his discussion of how analogy shaped meaning in early Catholicism. At one point he considers the role of the "everyday" as a carrier of meaning through analogy and especially

> through doctrine rendering certain clear, explicit, and in that sense ordinary meanings rather than the world of the extraordinary disclosed in tensive symbols; through an ordered institution rather than sect or charismatic community; through analogies which assume and employ but rarely disclose the tensions of the negative within their measured tones, their drive to harmony, even their willingness to compromise on nonessentials in order to clarify and explicate the essentials into doctrine.[10]

We shall explore how the body is used in a symbolic or analogical way by Bruce Springsteen on his album *The Rising*.

Tracy acknowledges the implicit dialectic in analogy and the tensive nature of symbol; this is overt and acknowledged when we come to metaphorical language. In their analysis of how metaphors are used to organize human experience, Lakoff and Johnson highlight three distinct types of forms this process can take: (1) orientational metaphors: our experiences and activities are structured by metaphor, such as "More is up"; (2) ontological metaphors: more abstract concepts can be viewed metaphorically as objects, such as "Time is money"; and (3) structural metaphors: our conceptual system detects metaphorical similarities, such as "Ideas are food."[11] Metaphors tend to resist the drive to harmony and closure, thus remaining open, dialectical, and playful. We shall explore how the body is used in this metaphorical way by Nick Cave on his album *Dig, Lazarus, Dig!!!*

When we speak of music and the body, therefore, we shall be exploring four dimensions: (1) the *physical* body; (2) the *social* body; (3) the *symbolic* body;

and (4) the *metaphorical* body. The first two categories might seem removed from the second two. However, as John Milbank reminds us, the process of "deriving meaning" is also one of "movement," which is just one of the ways in which ideas about symbolic and metaphorical bodies are closely linked with physical and social bodies.[12] This chapter will explore each of these notions of the body with reference to a specific song or album:

the physical body—"Bodyrock" by Moby
the social body—"Two Tribes" by Frankie Goes to Hollywood
the symbolic body—*The Rising* by Bruce Springsteen
the metaphorical body—*Dig, Lazarus, Dig!!!* by Nick Cave and the Bad Seeds

By exploring each of these dimensions to the music-body relationship with respect to a particular song, we will examine how various aspects of human embodiment impact the interaction between the body and popular music.

The Physical Body

A new study has discovered that playing your favorite records can increase your blood circulation and give you the same feel-good factor as going to the gym. (*Mail on Sunday* newspaper, April 11, 2010; info from Dr. Michael Miller, cardiologist at the University of Maryland Medical Center)

Methodists live longer because we sing so much. Singing is good for your body. (Methodist choir leader, UK, July 2010, after research results showed that Methodists "live more than seven years longer than the rest of the population")[13]

Human experience and thought is acquired in and through our embodied form. This may seem to be an obvious statement, but some belief systems (e.g., gnosticism) have distanced mind from body to such an extent that our physical side is regarded as entirely "fallen" or "evil."[14] This chapter is based on the understanding that bodily experience precedes thought, or as Mark Johnson has put it, "Propositional content is possible only by virtue of a complex web of nonpropositional schematic structures that emerge from our bodily experience."[15] In terms of music, first we hear music, and then we reflect upon it. As numerous writers have observed, the first music we hear are the sounds in the womb such as a mother's heartbeat, the rhythmic movement of blood, and familiar voices—all contributing to the "intrauterine symphony."[16] These neonatal patterns and textures, of which sound and music are an integral part, contribute to our embodied awareness, identity, and security.

The importance of individual bodily reception of music does not lessen following birth. Our experience and understanding of music continues to be shaped by such physical expressions of personhood.[17] Several of our respondents testified to this. One male respondent from the USA stated, "Music calms me down, and I like songs that I can relate to."[18] By contrast one female respondent in the same age group said, "It pumps me up to work out."[19] A British female in this age group observed: "It's definitely true that emotion and music go hand in hand. I find particular pieces of classic music are needed for stressful days, and a good rock anthem on the radio will make me more assertive when driving."[20]

The physicality of listening reminds us that the experience of it is necessarily embodied. It is also ritualistic, whether or not we own a faith. There are occasions (such as at work, out jogging, or ironing) when we always listen to music; there are habits (such as using an MP3 player, sitting in a particular room, or lying across a favorite chair) that we adopt in the way we listen. We shall explore this aspect of listening more fully in chapter 8 below. But for the moment, Don and Emily Saliers's observations are worthy: "Rituals, whether sacred or secular, always involve the body and its senses—what is heard, seen, tasted, and given bodily expression in movement and gesture."[21] They link listening as a human practice with spirituality: "Spirituality is not an idea in the brain but rather a disciplined bodily experience that grows deeper with practice. If we are to grasp why and how true spirituality takes root in human beings, we must attend to the power of sound and its impact on us as sensual, sensuous, sensitive beings."[22]

Getting Physical: "Bodyrock"

A good example of a song that has fun with and celebrates the human body is Moby's "Bodyrock," from his album *Play* (1999). The three videos of the song all focus on individual bodies dancing. The UK video has one male dancing to the track in a parking lot, with Moby looking on and acting as the special effects assistant. Another video also filmed in the UK is presented as the auditions for this role and has several males with different body shapes, forms of dress, and styles of movement, dancing on their own to the track, which all combine to highlight the individuality of our bodies. The US video features Run-DMC and involves Moby's leaving his apartment while wearing special sunglasses that turn everyone he looks at into a dancer. First he meets an older woman who is mopping the hall floor, now seen as a young, lithe dancer through the glasses; last he sees a group of younger women walking down the street who become a dance troop when viewed in this way. The US video moves from individual dancers, to pairs of dancers, to a group of dancers, and highlights both the individual and social nature of our physical bodies.

The song is thus a celebration of music, dance, and embodiment on many levels. It is a dance track, inviting listeners via its beat to get up and dance to the music, whatever their bodies are like. That it is for all types of dancers is evidenced in the video's purporting to be auditioning dancers for the "official video" (which then becomes one of the official videos). Such music is not for accomplished dancers. It is meant to be for all who simply want to dance and to celebrate their embodiedness through their dancing (however fit or unfit they may be). The "Sunglasses Version" of the video accentuates the difference between actual bodies and the dancing bodies that many dancers may aspire to be. But it does this in a playful way, even though it is Moby who wants to see people as potential dancers, and not necessarily the people themselves.

The Social Body

Social bodies have several different facets. For example, one aspect that straddles the line between the physical and social is that of an audience looking at the performance of a musician or a singer. North and Hargreaves have identified three ways in which seeing bodies in a social context has an impact on musical performance: (1) by seeing the performers' movements, audiences can better understand their "expressive intent"; (2) bodily movements enable a group of performers to coordinate "timing, dynamics, and other expressive effects"; and (3) individual musical preferences have an impact on how attractive people are to others.[23] It is not just taste in music that relates to attractiveness. As Daniel Levitin observes with respect to the creation of music, "Music making, because it involves an array of physical and mental skills, would be an overt display of health, and to the extent that someone had time to develop his musicianship, the argument goes, it would indicate resource wealth."[24] In other words, speaking in evolutionary terms, being musically proficient makes individuals more attractive to potential mates. Bodies thus attract each other to create social connections.

More Than a Memory: Beyond the Physical

As well as influencing how we view others in performance or in (potential) relationships, music also plays a significant part in our embodied social practice. The human activities of singing and dancing together, deeply ingrained across all cultures and in contemporary Western society, may now include being part of a choir, karaoke, collective singing at an act of worship or sports event, aerobics and dance classes, and more. This *embodied* social practice can extend beyond our present existence and into our world of memories. For instance, a group of women in their eighties and nineties were asked about why they liked certain hymns: "When they began to say why they loved them, they spoke of hearing their grandmother's voice, of feeling the vibrations in their mothers' breast as they leaned against her in church; of the squeak of the parlor organ when the family would gather to sing; or of church suppers, funerals, or 'dinner on the grounds' in their Southern traditions."[25]

Levitin observed the same process at work for those who have impaired memory function: "In old people's homes and convalescent hospitals, when people have lost their memory due to Alzheimer's disease, stroke, or other degenerative brain trauma, music is one of the last things to go. Old people who are otherwise unable to remember the names of their spouse, or children, or even what year it is, can be brought arrestingly back to focus by hearing the music of their youth."[26]

So on the one hand, music not only manifests memory as a process of the mind; it can also bring back embodied memory—memories that are linked to physical and social encounters from the past. Yet on the other hand, music can be seen to have a long history of shaping human social interactions. As Levitin suggests in his discussion about songs of joy, music has long been a fundamental part of social ordering: "In addition to social bonding, fundamental to the experience of early humans was communicating their emotional states to others—the expression of joy through music-dance."[27]

Signed, Sealed, Delivered: The Body and Social Order

On linking bodily experience with social contact, such memories contribute to social ordering, the way in which societies shape themselves. It is thus possible to see hymn singing not only as an element in the social ordering of US society a century ago but also as pointing to where music functions in providing similar ordering in the twenty-first century. Organized religion may no longer be the main provider of the music that contributes to such social ordering, but music still plays a key role. DeNora states that to consider music's role as a device for social ordering means understanding "how music may be employed, albeit at times unwittingly, as a means of organizing potentially disparate individuals such that their actions may appear to be intersubjective, mutually oriented, co-ordinated, entrained and aligned."[28] In other words, music is a component of daily life that facilitates human-to-human and human-to-nonhuman interaction in many different and complex ways. We can take two examples from DeNora's work.

In analyzing the means by which music can order social bodies, DeNora distinguishes two forms: (1) domestic spaces and (2) public spaces. Within domestic spaces, DeNora identifies three different forms of social ordering: partnerships, which may use music to set the scene for developing romantic encounters, new friendships, or for "sexual-political negotiation"; social settings, using mood music to create the right setting for dinners, parties, barbecues, and other group gatherings; and social relationships, a development of the first form (partnerships), where a shared enjoyment of music plays a significant role in *continuing* friendships and partnerships.[29]

In the category of public spaces, DeNora also identifies three forms: social groups that provide music to structure social interaction, such as dance classes, aerobics, and so forth; retail and consumption, which in many ways use music to encourage, shape, and manage consumer choice; and organizational settings, which employ music to create an ambiance for the workplace. From DeNora's study we can see that music is used across a wide range of embodied social interaction, as a way of structuring and shaping those collective encounters. The process whereby music helps to form people's social spaces is complex and multilayered. While this is done *to* us, we as consumers can also affect the way in which music is used or heard or ignored by choosing where we shop, dance, attend concerts, or by wearing earplugs or listening via earphones to our own MP3 device instead of what is in the public space. This reminds us that there can be tribal aspects to modern music that indicate, whether conscious or not, the social groups to which we belong or have allegiance.

My Generation: Belonging to the Tribe

Sarah Thornton does not use the word "tribe" when discussing the nature of club culture, though she makes it clear both that the musical worlds of younger people are divided into numerous subcultures and that those who observe, describe, and research such tribes are usually members of one tribe or another. Thus, when she analyzes how Simon Frith divided British mainstream subculture into "middle-class rock" and "working-class pop" (published in the early 1980s), she comments: "Frith seems to view the terrain of music crowds through the eyes of his middle-class student interviewees—the result of a 'natural' and, perhaps, not quite conscious identification."[30] Whoever looks at the tribal nature of other people's musical tastes inevitably examines such tastes from their own place within a particular tribe. Heavy-metal fans look askance at the enthusiasms of folk-music followers. Rap fans have little time for rock, and so on. Yet the intensity with which such tribal affiliations are supported merely confirms the importance of such attachments. As we have stressed through this book, such fandom merely indicates where our affective spaces are located (see chap. 2), and thus how much we invest in the musical tastes and listening practices to which we are (tribally) committed.

Don and Emily Saliers have described how the overtly tribal nature of music extends across a wide range of musical genres (chamber music, rock, folk music) and different contexts (schools, churches, on the street). Yet there is more to this process of social definition than music. For example, "membership in a specific musical tribe—often one shaped also by ethnicity or economic class—becomes a badge of belonging."[31] Nevertheless, by proclaiming our taste in music, we are in effect saying which tribe (or tribes) we belong to. At issue is how much we are able to choose the tribes to which we belong: this both links back to our discussion about the role of choice in popular music as a commodity (chap. 4) and looks ahead to our future discussion about pop music and ritual. The issues of embodiment and tribalism are brought together in a unique way by the Liverpool band Frankie Goes to Hollywood, to which we now turn as a case study.

Switch Off and Feel: Frankie and Social Bodies

Frankie Goes to Hollywood provides an interesting example of the interplay between popular music and its wider social and semiotic fields, including the visual elements of marketing and dissemination (music videos), embodiment, and tribal loyalty. In particular, we see this interplay in the content of and responses to the band's first three singles, released in 1983–84, which were consecutive number one singles in the UK. Because the band members came from Liverpool and had a string of top hits, there were casual comparisons at the time to The Beatles; but with the demise of the band after two albums, these no longer bear scrutiny.[32] Yet the band remains a phenomenon in its own right, and the success and influence of the first three singles deserve close attention, especially with regard to the subject matter of this chapter. "Relax" (1983) is about the physical body (sex), "Two Tribes" (1984) is about the social body (global politics), and "The Power of Love" (1984) is a love song; the video of this song shows images of symbolic bodies with a specific theological incarnation (the body of Christ).

The videos for all three tracks play a significant role in embodying the songs. Numerous videos for "Relax" are available on the internet and include the band's first television appearance singing a rough version of the song and videos for the original single and later remixes. A common theme in these videos is an emphasis on the human body as a site of sexuality and decadence—the exception being a rather traditional presentation of the band's playing the song against a background of laser beams. The song was highly controversial because of its lyrics, celebrating orgasm, and because people assumed it promoted promiscuity. As is often the case with popular music's celebration of the human body and sexuality, however (Lady Gaga being a more recent example), lyrics and visuals together remain at best ambiguous.

The most well-known video for the band's second single, "Two Tribes," is the wrestling bout between actors representing then-US President Ronald Reagan and then-Soviet leader Konstantin Chernenko, surrounded by band members and world leaders placing bets. The depiction of the two tribes (Western capitalism versus Eastern communism) embodied by their two leaders is played out against the backdrop of that era's concern over the arsenals of nuclear weapons on both sides and the danger of a nuclear war. A twelve-inch remix (a longer version) includes audio clips from a broadcast of Richard Nixon and impressionist Chris Barrie, speaking as Ronald Reagan. If we listen to this while keeping in mind our Magisteria-Ibiza Spectrum, we can see affective space being shaped as institutional and governmental elements (from the left-hand side of our Spectrum) are playfully morphed with nonhierarchical and antiauthoritarian elements (from the right-hand side).

"The Power of Love" was released in November 1984 in time for the Christmas market, and its video was initially a very straightforward retelling of the traditional nativity story about the birth of Christ. A border (frame) featuring the embodied band members was later added and appears at various points in the Christmas narrative. This addition was apparently at the request of the record company, to ensure that viewers knew the song was by Frankie Goes to Hollywood. The twelve-inch remix of the third single has Chris Barrie curiously reprising his impression of Ronald Reagan's quoting Jesus's teaching about prayer—which involves removing one's body from public view in order to pray (Matt. 6:6), followed by the opening petitions of the Lord's Prayer (6:9–10). The embodied theme is further underscored by the original cover for the single, which shows Titian's depiction of the Virgin Mary's bodily assumption into heaven from the Frari Basilica in Venice.

Frankie Goes to Hollywood signed with the label ZTT, set up by musician and producer Trevor Horn in collaboration with music journalist Paul Morley and others. Warner comments: "From its inception, ZTT was a highly image-conscious company intent on selling a complete pop product, . . . realizing from the outset that, as a cultural phenomenon within the mass media, pop was now firmly established as a mixed art form relying on music, image, dance, poetry, etc. Unsurprisingly, many of the artists signed to ZTT are associated with strong, highly defined and complex images."[33] The complex images and sonic creations of Frankie Goes to Hollywood, combining elements of sexuality and religion, were played out against the backdrop of geopolitical uncertainty on the world stage and a bitter battle between striking miners and the Conservative government of Margaret Thatcher in the UK. The group's phenomenal success was not repeated after 1984. But Warner is probably right in his claim that for a particular tribe of people, Frankie Goes to Hollywood has become as iconic as 1967 and the "Summer of Love" has for another tribe.[34] Other observers see the rise of this band as a manifestation of the "circuses" that appear in times of social and economic unrest. Unlike the critique made of imperial Rome by Juvenal, however, the circuses are not provided by the state. Simon Frith argues that the "new pop" championed by Paul Morley and others and represented by bands like Frankie Goes to Hollywood and the duo George Michael and Andrew Ridgeley's Wham! were "not just a matter of cultural manipulation—rulers laying on circuses when there is no bread. 'Escape' from hard times is a cultural necessity, and the harder the times the more fantastic and precarious and desperate a business it becomes."[35] For Frith, the marriage of music, politics, and social change during this period marked a significant departure in Western culture and a distinct move toward postmodernity: "New pop was a postmodern form generally—in its cut-up of styles and media, its genre cross-references, its use of pastiche and parody, its dressing up of mass cultural forms with high cultural claims and *vice versa*."[36]

One paradoxical aspect of Frankie Goes to Hollywood was that although the band provided a uniform by appropriating Katherine Hamnett's message T-shirt for their fans to drape over their physical bodies ("Frankie says . . .") and sang about the tribal nature of humanity's social body, the band itself was not part of a tribe. It was a response to the increasing culture of economic individualism and choice at that period of time, and they forged elements of common social capital (sexuality, politics, and religion) into products (songs, videos, clothes) that sold well in the marketplace. At the start of "Two Tribes," lead singer Holly Johnson asks, "Are we living in a land where sex and horror are the new gods?" Perhaps the better question to have asked at the time was, "Are we living in a land where *selling* sex and horror is the new god?" Nevertheless, in the varied use of social bodies, Frankie Goes to Hollywood point us toward two further embodied forms: the symbolic and metaphorical bodies.

The Symbolic Body

The album-listening experience is cumulative and greater than the sum of its single-track components. Over the course of its 45, 50 minutes, you are transported into a band/artist's soundworld, over an arc of moods and ideas bound by a cohesive and engaging musical vision. (David Stubbs, "Prog[ressive] Rockers Strike a Blow for All Musical Artists," *The Independent* newspaper, March 12, 2010)

In our discussion of physical and social bodies, we recognized how pop music produces physical reactions in our bodies, shapes social interaction, and encodes memory. As Levitin states when discussing songs of love, "A song like the national anthem or 'Happy Birthday' can certainly trigger memories, but a song you haven't heard since you were fourteen years old is more likely to trigger deep, buried memories."[37] A significant part of this process of memory recall is the song's words, which provide the basis for two other embodied forms of song. As we outlined at the beginning of this chapter, the symbolic body describes songs where the body is used as an analogy or to describe something else in terms of similarity, while the metaphorical body describes something else in terms of dissimilarity. We will illustrate these different bodies with reference to Bruce Springsteen's *The Rising* (symbolic body) and Nick Cave's *Dig, Lazarus, Dig!!!* (metaphorical body).

Spirit's Above and Beyond Me: Springsteen's Absent Bodies

American rock star Bruce Springsteen and French philosopher and social theorist Michel de Certeau seem far removed from each other. However, besides their Catholic backgrounds, they also have an interest in stories generated by the experience of urban life. In his celebrated text *The Practice of Everyday Life*, de Certeau begins his chapter "Walking in the City" by discussing the view from the World Trade Center and how this is akin to "looking down like a god," but more ordinary city dwellers need to live down below, in the paths on the streets.

He pursues this idea and concludes by arguing that a person's journey through a modern urban landscape begins with oneself and, in particular, with one's childhood. Thus "the childhood experience that determines spatial practices later develops its effects, proliferates, floods private and public spaces, undoes their readable surfaces, and creates within the planned city a 'metaphorical' or mobile city, like the one Kandinsky dreamed of: 'a great city built according to all the rules of architecture and then suddenly shaken by a force that defies all calculation.'"[38] In these post 9/11 times, that image of architecture shaken by a force that defies all calculation brings us back sharply to the World Trade Center and the destruction wrought by forces that we still struggle to analyze and comprehend. We are also brought to some of the real and symbolic connections between de Certeau and Springsteen because not only do these insights strike a chord with our earlier discussion about neonatal origins of musical sensibility for our physical bodies, they also provide a doorway into a symbolic use of the body in popular music.

Our case study for this is the musical journey of Bruce Springsteen as he travels through the urban landscapes of the USA, in particular his album *The Rising* (2002), offered as a response to the events of 9/11, when physical and social architecture was "suddenly shaken by a force that defies all calculation." Into the lyrical mix born from reflections on those tumultuous events is added Springsteen's own childhood reflections and his willingness to draw upon the symbolic language of his Catholic upbringing in shaping the poetic spaces inhabited by his songs. As Jim Cullen has observed, *The Rising* "is a profoundly religious document."[39] Springsteen himself has described the album as "secular stations of the cross."[40] In addition to Springsteen's regular use of religious terms, *The Rising* frequently employs the image of the absent body as a symbol for the effects of 9/11 and signifying the impact that moment had on individuals and communities. At this point in Springsteen's own development, then, the performer's experience, world affairs, and a background framework of religious belief feed into the writing of contemporary popular music. A listener encounters this convergence and has the opportunity to participate in the symbolic world created in the process of listening and enjoying the music.

We shall here bring *The Rising* into conversation with ideas from the French Jesuit and philosopher Michel de Certeau, with whose quotation this section began. The constructed dialogue will not be a simple one-to-one process whereby a song by Springsteen is mapped to a point made by de Certeau. Rather, we shall notice how the symbolic fields of Catholic-raised singer/songwriter and Catholic philosopher share common ground in faith and liturgy and inform the symbolic bodies they each inhabit as they reflect upon the nature of everyday life in Western culture. We briefly explore three instances in which Springsteen and de Certeau have a shared field of symbolic production: (1) cities, (2) homes, and (3) stories. All three aspects of life are important loci for both men in understanding the dynamics of the contemporary world, and the body and/or absent body play an important role in each of these three fields.

THE CITY AND THE ABSENT BODY

De Certeau argues that the city is defined by a threefold operation: (1) production of its own space; (2) substitution of "nowhen" for traditions; and (3) the creation of a universal and anonymous subject, which is the city itself.[41] By this de Certeau is pointing out how city life often crushes the patterns of meaning that people need to live their lives. In coming to be, as large physical spaces, cities risk stifling the sense of time within which people live. The sense of personal, individual identity is also lost due to the sheer mass of people who live alongside one another. Often in de Certeau's thinking, then, the city is a place of forgetting and anonymity for individuals and the symbolic institutions that shape urban life. One of the tasks he embarks on is to rediscover that symbolic life (tradition) in the city's space.

The urban dialectics of presence/absence, losing/searching, cityscape/spiritual site find resonance across much of Springsteen's *The Rising*, when viewed as a whole album. It begins with *embodied* reflections on *loneliness* ("Once I thought I knew everything I needed to know about you—Your sweet whisper, your tender touch") as the opening song "Lonesome Day" explores feelings of loss and possible bereavement. This contrast between embodied themes and absence of body is developed over several tracks (e.g., "Into the Fire," "Nothing Man," "Countin' on a Miracle"). "Empty Sky" speaks about "an empty impression in the bed where you used to be," and this sense of absence reaches a culmination in "You're Missing" as Springsteen lists all the domestic details that remain in place following a bereavement. The sense of a body's absence is heightened by the opening stanza referencing the shirts and shoes left in the closet. Springsteen's reflections on the loss of bodies from city streets come to a conclusion in one person's home, which is another theme that de Certeau explores.

THE HOME AND THE ABSENT BODY

De Certeau argues that in the symbolic desert of the city, one of the primary settings for finding meaning is the domestic environment. "Only the cave of the home remains believable, still open for a certain time to legends, still full of shadows. . . . It is through the opportunity they offer to store up rich silences and wordless stories, or rather through their capacity to create cellars and garrets everywhere, that local legends permit exits, ways of going out and coming back in, and thus habitable spaces."[42] Although Springsteen opens a number of windows onto various household environments (or "caves," to use de Certeau's term), such domestic settings have always played a much more ambiguous role in his songs. Frequently the home is something that his characters are seeking to escape from, so the theme of home and absent body is one that runs throughout Springsteen's work. On *The Rising* this familiar theme is given a new perspective not only through an extended exploration of bereavement but also in different ways, such as "Further On (Up the Road)," where the symbolism of the absent body is not an expression of wanderlust but of hope that the song's characters will be reunited after death "further on up the road."

STORIES OF THE ABSENT BODY

Springsteen's songs are often in the form of narratives, short stories, or parables about modern, everyday American life, and here we find another link with the work of de Certeau. For de Certeau, stories not only provide the narrative container for everyday life in the city; they also shape everyday practices, and this collection of verbal "relics" provides the landscape of memory.[43] The songs on *The Rising* give a narrative shape to the absent bodies of 9/11 and the feelings of bereavement felt by the immediate families and friends who lost loved ones, as well as loss being felt more widely in the USA and across the world.

Sky of Fullness: The Rising *and Symbolic Meaning*

This process of engaging with an artist's lyrics and seeking to understand their deeper meaning is an activity that fans engage in on a regular basis. In his pre–*The Rising* discussion of how Springsteen's fans approached his body of work, Daniel Cavicchi observes: "Fans are not necessarily thinking about where they stand in an abstract, larger social order or how their fandom can change that order; rather they are concerned with how to get through each day and how their participation in performance helps them to understand the fluctuating and contradictory experience of daily life and to make connections with other people around them."[44] We can find examples of this phenomenon in fan sites dedicated to particular artists and websites that focus on the meaning of particular songs. For example, the SongMeanings site includes debate about the meaning of the title track on *The Rising*, during which one contributor states:

> I'd say you're overthinking this. *The Rising* is pretty clearly a literal story of a firefighter making a sacrifice in the face of great danger and evil. There's nothing "corny" or "embarrassing" about that. He CERTAINLY isn't singing about what the towers "represented," at least as far as American capitalism is concerned. He's using the story of the firefighter to tell the story of what he hopes for the country. He does this sort of thing repeatedly throughout *The Rising* and, in fact, throughout his career. He'll take a power[ful] story, give it a literal meaning, and make it a statement about something much more broad. Here he's talking about faith, redemption, sacrifice, hope, and forgiveness. On a song like "Born in the U.S.A.," for example, he tells the story of a Vietnam vet rather than stand on a soapbox and say, "Hey, some of these policies are unfair and un-American." The real corniness would have come if he'd spent the album grandstanding. Instead, he tells powerful stories for everyday people. It's rock and roll, it's brilliant, and

it's not . . . just about the imagery and characters he uses, whether it be the story of a firefighter or biblical allusions.[45]

The way this observer describes Springsteen's lyrical composition—"He'll take a power[ful] story, give it a literal meaning, and make it a statement about something much more broad"—is analogical (making imaginative comparisons through similarity). In this section we have suggested that by looking at the way Springsteen has used the analogy of the body in this album and bringing that into conversation with the ideas of de Certeau, a new level of meaning is provided. That is not to say this is *the* meaning of these lyrics or the *only* meaning for them, but that the process of seeking meaning in lyrics is an important activity for some of those who listen to popular music, and it is important to understand the ways in which it works. One alternative approach is to explore how songwriters use metaphor (or the process of making imaginative comparisons through dissimilarity) in their work. The image of the body can also be used in this way; to this end we turn to a case study of how a metaphorical understanding of the body might shape an interpretation of *Dig, Lazarus, Dig!!!* by Nick Cave and the Bad Seeds.

The Metaphorical Body

In his discussion of the "Eucharistic Body," David Brown explores the theological significance of bodies as beautiful, sexual, and ugly, which he says are "three key ways of integrating body and mind." Thus the beautiful body offers a genuine reflection upon divine grace and beauty as "sheer gift"; the sexual body is a metaphor that "draws us into new ways of relating to our surroundings, as well as to other people," particularly when it avoids selfishness; the ugly body "can give us a deep affective life that enables our emotions and hearts to play as large a role in our religious life as our intellects."[46]

Feasting on Lovely Bodies: Nick Cave, Metaphor, and Story

Analogy and metaphor are closely related since they describe one thing in terms of another but in different ways—through similarity (analogy) and difference (metaphor). In his detailed exploration of the place that the "ugly" body has within Christianity, Brown examines how embodied images of Jesus's suffering and tears were used as a means of involving observers in the events of Jesus's life.[47] Within this context Brown notes the storytelling skills in Mark's Gospel as the author draws us into the narrative with such devices as his use of the present tense and participles: "Such strategies parallel the resources employed by [visual] artists to the same effect. Our involvement is secured."[48] As described by Brown, the process uses embodied images of Jesus analogously, enabling viewers to enter into that experience, and something similar is taking place in the work of Nick Cave.

Cave is also a great fan of the second evangelist. Not only did he write the introduction for *The Gospel According to Mark* in Canongate's published series of individual books of the Bible, but also Cave has said that one of his own novels, *The Death of Bunny Munro*, is shaped by the same immediacy found in Mark's Gospel.[49] The connection is mentioned on the publisher's website in an interview with Cave. The interviewer observes: "There is something Christlike about the survival of Bunny Munro's son, just as there is in Cormac McCarthy's *The Road.* . . . But it was the literary template of Mark's Gospel that was a direct influence." The interviewer quotes Cave: "Mark just wants to get to the death. It's done with such urgency."[50] For Cave, this notion of using artistic means to effect an immediacy with aspects of Jesus's life clearly extends beyond the second evangelist to other Gospel stories; thus we can see him moving beyond the symbolic or analogous use of the body to a more playful and metaphorical use.

In Cave's own reflections about the song "Dig, Lazarus, Dig!!!" he articulates his ambiguous feelings regarding the story of Jesus's raising the physical body of Lazarus from the dead (John 11:1–44), which is the basis for the track. On his website Cave explains some of the background to the lyrics: "Ever since I can remember hearing the Lazarus story, when I was a kid, you know, back in church, I was disturbed and worried by it. Traumatized, actually. We are all, of course, in awe of the greatest of Christ's miracles—raising a man from the dead—but I couldn't help but wonder how Lazarus felt about it. As a child it gave me the creeps, to be honest. I've taken Lazarus and stuck him in New York City, in order to give the song a hip, contemporary feel."[51] In this track we appear to be taken into the mind of Lazarus and are being asked to imagine what it must feel like to be on the point of being raised from the dead. This embodied artistic encounter with Jesus is playful and ambiguous in that at this point Lazarus can be regarded as being on the edge of having and not having a body, and the sense of contradiction extends further into Cave's use of metaphors from the world of carnival.

Chants and Incantations: Carnival Images

As we explore Nick Cave's use of carnival, we should continue to keep in mind Brown's discussion about Jesus's "ugly" body: "As a religion Christianity sometimes comes across as taking an almost perverted delight in suffering, whether it be of Christ or of his saints."[52] It is the metaphorical tension within carnival that Cave is drawing upon to heighten the garish, grotesque, and gaudy atmosphere of "Dig, Lazarus, Dig!!!" Not only is this use of the ugly and the grotesque a well-established part of Western artistic tradition; it also has a well-established place in the canon of Cave's songs. For instance, in a sympathetic discussion of Cave's body of work, Robert Cousland has described it as an

"Thriller" by Michael Jackson

On the face of it Michael Jackson's "Thriller" is about the world of horror movies, and his lyrics draw heavily upon that genre. The award winning, fourteen-minute video for the track was groundbreaking for its time and remains highly regarded. However, it is hard to discuss Jackson's work without getting drawn into the many controversial aspects of the star's life or his premature death at the age of fifty, as is illustrated by the contributions to the SongMeanings website discussion thread for this track. There are numerous comments regarding allegations about Jackson's life and character but comparatively little about how this song might be understood. One of the more interesting contributions is from a listener named ringfingers, who makes political parallels between the dark imagery of the song and the social changes introduced by the Republican administrations of Ronald Reagan and George W. Bush. At the other end of our affective spectrum, listener crimeofpassion states: "I love this song. It's not deep and meaningful or anything like that. I just love the song. It's catchy and I'd give anything to learn the dance."[53]

It is, however, possible to look beyond the horror motifs, the political speculation, and the fact that the song is a good example of why Jackson earned the title "the prince of pop." "Thriller"—and in particular Jackson's embodied performances in the video and live shows—suggests deeper levels of meaning both in relation to the lyrics and with respect to Jackson's treatment of his own body. The words use horror movie tropes that are underscored by the video interpretation as Jackson's body mutates into a were-creature and a zombie. In keeping with this theme, during some live performances Jackson wore a mask as he sang "Thriller" and so continued to play with his own identity and the embodied identity of the central character in the song. On the HIStory tour (1996–97) in addition to the mask, the embodied nature of the track was emphasized by the dancing and, especially toward the end, by the illusion of Jackson being dragged, protesting and resisting, into a closet and run through with spikes.[54]

Another track written and recorded during the "Thriller" sessions but released only posthumously in 2011 was the song "Behind the Mask," which has subsequently become a project in which Jackson's fans can contribute their own embodied "lip-sync" performances of the track to a video for it.[55] Jackson's work in "Thriller" and "Behind the Mask" is similar to the commercial trajectory established by David Bowie with "The Man Who Sold the World" and his character Ziggy Stardust. One of the significant changes in Jackson's persona is that, while Bowie altered his body with makeup and could switch into another role (e.g., the Thin White Duke), Jackson altered his body and especially his face (his mask) through surgery, making the nature of his embodied performances more tangible, physical, and corporeal.

"aesthetic of the grotesque,"[56] with particular reference to "its fusion of the sacred and profane."[57] That characteristic mixing of apparent opposites continues on the track "Dig, Lazarus, Dig!!!" and on the album more generally. Furthermore, on this album Cave has acknowledged a number of references to dreams and dreamlike experience[58] and has observed: "What I fell into through the writing of this record was that the characters seemed to be in a state of inactivity or intense apathy; they were kind of comatose, repeating endlessly the same kind of movement without any effect. They're completely absent from the event in some way, and that seems to me to echo a genuine malaise in the Western world."[59] Yet despite these frequent references to out-of-body experiences, the references are almost always located within an embodied context.[60] The metaphorical tensions between such out-of-body and embodied existence, and the person of Lazarus in the Palestine of Jesus's time and the person of Lazarus in New York of our own time provide much of the lyrical impetus for the song.

Some listeners to this track are working through the meaning-making process of the metaphorical body in conversation with others. One online commentator wrote: "At first the 'something going on upstairs' seems to be literal: Lazarus is lying in his tomb, hearing what's going on above him—his mother grieving for him and 'some guy' who is presumably Jesus praying for him. But at the end Cave is talking about what happens to the dead, and the line turns into a vague declaration of faith. Very clever little twist!"[61] It is worth repeating that, as with the symbolic body, this approach to sense-making with song lyrics does not close off further interpretation. The ideas outlined here are not the only way to understand "Dig, Lazarus, Dig!!!," but exploring how metaphors stretch and twist the process of seeking meaning in lyrics helps us to understand how some of those who listen to popular music embark on the process of seeking meaning in and through song.

Conclusion: Meaning in Bodies, Embodied Meaning

Not only is the body a complex biological organism; it is also a multifaceted social and symbolic phenomenon. We have explored some of that complexity and its relationship to music and faith. Sociologist John O'Neill has written widely on the body from a philosophical and sociological perspective; he argues that the embodied experience of humans is fundamental to all social experience and speaks of "that visceral body whose capacity for language and society is the foundation for all other institutions."[62] This embodied insight extends into the world of religions, yet the metaphor that God has a body or a number of bodies in the Hebrew and Christian Scriptures is not frequently discussed[63] nor are its theological and ecclesiological implications fully worked through.[64] We begin to get an indication of this complexity from Sommer's observation about the difference between divine and human bodies: "The divine body, like the divine self, can be fragmented yet somehow remain unified. Any one body was part of the god, but did not exhaust the god's fullness, just as god's self was not confined to one person. In short, gods' bodies paralleled gods' selves. Similarly, a human's body paralleled a human's self in that both human bodies and human selves lack this sort of fluidity."[65] However, once we move from speaking about physical human bodies to reflecting upon symbolic and metaphorical bodies, then human embodiment can take on characteristics similar to the dispersed divine embodiment that Sommer describes.

In this chapter we have sought to examine how the visceral body, language, and social institutions interact in the specific areas of music and faith. We have considered these matters in terms of (1) an individual physical relationship; (2) a communal physical experience; (3) symbolic or analogical use of the body in lyrics; (4) metaphorical application of the body to sense-making in songs. In other words we have analyzed the physical body, the social body, the symbolic body, and the metaphorical body. At this point it is worth returning to one of the quotations with which we started, from Al Green: "You can't compare a congregation to a crowd at a concert. A concert crowd does what they want. A congregation's got rules and regulations." In some respects he is defining our Magisteria-Ibiza Spectrum, placing the congregational experience on the left of the Spectrum and the concert crowd, due to its unruliness, on the right.

However, we have already seen how the world of the music business operates within similar tensions to those of the world of faith, in terms of stability and innovation, tradition and imagination. Now we can begin to see that the embodied nature of music and faith share a good deal of common ground as well. The affective space of musical and spiritual practice is inhabited by individuals-in-relationships, and both those individuals and their social contexts utilize embodied symbols and metaphors of faith in creating and listening to popular music. We now turn to the experience of transcendence and examine how music's ability to transport people out of everyday life fits into this developing picture of the links between pop music and faith.

the tingle factor

Popular Music and Transcendence Today

> I wouldn't describe myself as particularly spiritual, but something happens when loads of people do the same thing, whatever that thing is.
>
> Guy Garvey, singer/guitarist for the band Elbow[1]

The British Broadcasting Corporation (BBC) broadcast a radio show during the 1990s called *The Tingle Factor*. The host invited celebrities to choose a selection of music that made their spines tingle. The program was therefore about guests' favorite music, but rather than invite them to select pieces that were important at particular stages of their life, or that they just happened to like, these had to be pieces of music that moved them. In many cases guests spoke of music as "transporting them to another place," being "lost in the music," or being "taken out of themselves." Such descriptions of human experience are common both in how people report the effects that music can have on them, and in how people record what are often labeled "religious experiences."[2] It is therefore not surprising that music and religion are brought close together at this point. Nor is it surprising that those who wish to argue the contrary position—that religious experiences have no real content to them and are not really "about" anything, are psychological or chemical states only and do not enable the one having the experience to get in touch with anything "out there"—can claim that music is a life experience showing that religion is "only human." That is, they say music is but a part of life, has a physical dimension to it, does arouse powerful emotions, but is just about life here and now.

This chapter cannot address or answer all of the questions that arise from such debates. But we must look at what the tingle factor amounts to, especially when reported as occurring when listening to popular music. To what extent do people think that such a physical experience is merely physical or merely psychologically caused? How much do people refer to "transcendence" or to something similar, and what do they mean by it? Is it only people who are already religious or claim to "have a spirituality" who use such a term? What content do such claims have, if any?

Music, Ecstasy, and Escape

There is little doubt that listening to music can produce some remarkable experiences. When exploring the category of "transcendent ecstasy," Marghanita Laski discovered that music "was the most frequently mentioned trigger among the arts" for evoking such experiences.[3] The research was published in 1961, and the music referred to was classical.[4] It has thus been heavily challenged regarding its cultural assumptions, for assuming in advance which particular arts would be likely to evoke experiences of "transcendence," and for focusing too heavily on the middle class.[5] We need newer studies to establish that forms of popular music function similarly, to ask what precisely is being claimed for such transcendent ecstatic experiences, and to allow for major shifts in thinking about what constitutes the arts and who consumes them.[6] Nevertheless, there is clear evidence that the (transcendent, ecstatic) feelings of loss, of gaining something, of ineffability, and of quasi-physical feeling (e.g., of light or heat, of calm or peace)—the four categories into which Laski subdivided the experiences of "transcendent ecstasy"—are aroused with similar intensity by many forms of popular music. Although the arousal of such strong emotions might also need to take account of other factors, which are considered elsewhere in part 2 of this book (e.g., in communal gatherings, in interactions with fans, in the context of dance activity),[7] yet the intensity remains. Here are just a few recent accounts to confirm this.

In our own music survey we asked, "What words or phrases best describe your emotional experience of music?" Respondents' replies include the following:

- Extacy [sic], spiritual.
- Ecstatic (in the etymological sense: going out of myself).
- Music can . . . transport me—a sort of out-of-body feeling akin to touching one's soul.
- Delighting, consoling, exploring, taking out of oneself.
- The gamut of emotions, from sadness to ecstasy, from joy to depression, from seriousness of meaning to silly humor. The gamut.

- Escapist, moving, transcendental, a shared experience (at a gig).
- Energy, escape, experience, feeling.
- Contemplative, escape, cultural identity, stimulating.
- Escape from everyday life.
- Joy. Transcendent.

To these we can add two more analytic comments from contemporary interpreters of the popular music scene (one is a deeply influential contributor to it):

The essence of rock . . . is fun, a concept strangely neglected by sociologists. . . . [Fun has to do with] . . . sensuality, . . . grace, . . . joy, . . . energy, . . . vigour, . . . exhilaration.[8]

Gospel music is never pessimistic. Gospel music is always about the possibility of transcendence—of things suddenly getting better. And the other thing it's about is the loss of ego, the idea of [sic] somehow, the way you're going to do this, the way you're going to get through, or, as they say in Gospel music, "get over," is to do with losing yourself and becoming part of something bigger.[9]

These quotations give us plenty to work with. Transcendence has yet to be more closely defined. Does it equate to "things suddenly getting better," as Eno suggests? How are "exhilaration" or "escape" and "escapism" to be connected with transcendence or differentiated from it? What does "going out of oneself" amount to? Is it mistaken to be exploring the concept of transcendence in too close alliance with subjective human experience, and with the emotions in particular? In this chapter we shall explore four examples of what popular music does in this regard, and we shall probe how people's reports of its workings are to be understood. Then we shall offer a working definition of transcendence at the end of our inquiry.

Four Forms of Transport

Creating an Experience of Wonder

Our first example of popular music's capacity to transport people out of themselves is the ethereal music of the Icelandic band Sigur Rós, who came to prominence with the release of their 2005 album *Takk*. Though the band formed in the mid-1990s, it took some time for their brand of meditative postrock to catch on. Their first North American tour took place early in 2001. They specialize in combinations of minimalism, sound experimentation, and sweeping, soaring anthems. The resulting sound has been termed "otherworldly soundscapes."[10] A particular feature is their playfulness with lyrics. They use what may be called "cod old Icelandic," implying profundity, yet the band makes no great claims for any deep metaphysical substance and signals the playfulness directly by titling one of their tracks "Gobbledigook."[11] The reception of their music clearly indicates how otherness may be evoked without particular attention to words and their meanings. Though the human voice is used for its sound qualities, the combination of vocal sound and instrumentation creates sounds capable of "taking people out of themselves." Their music works (as popular music) in a way similar to ethereal religious classical music: people (who do not necessarily have any religious conviction) profess to be "transported to a different place." Sigur Rós thus clearly demonstrates both the highly relative function of lyrics and the capacity of popular music to create an affective space into which people can escape from normal life. The context of listening becomes a safe space within which listeners can be exposed, in a state of enjoyment, to the rawness of their own thoughts and circumstances. There is no need to conclude that some particular ecstatic state is being, or needs to be, reached in response to the music. It is enough to recognize that enjoyment and participation occur in the affective space created. Since no listener's first language is the playful, invented Icelandic used by the band (which they have termed "Hopelandic"),[12] there are no verbal distractions. The *sounds* create the space. Tracks such as "Heysatan" (from *Takk*) and "Fljotavik" and "Straumnes" (from *Med Sud I Eyrum Vid Spilum Endalaust*) do this especially through their (near Eastern Orthodox liturgy-style) minimalism. "Hoppipolla," by contrast, is more anthemic in style.

The creation of space for wonder, for undertaking inner work or some kind of inner journey, or for being transported to an ineffable zone by music does not, of course, mean that one is transported anywhere. What is happening may be all in the head. The sensations that occur are chemical and physical. They are also psychological. Though wordlessly evoked, they are not, however, cognitively empty experiences. The suggestiveness of the juxtaposition of "Hoppipolla" and attentiveness to the natural world does not necessarily lead to an expression of gratitude for creation, and to a creator, even while awe and wonder may be the dominant human emotions that the music evokes. As Craig Detweiler and Barry Taylor recognize, "Listeners get involved in the moods created by the music. Interpretations begin from feeling, not thinking. This approach makes the recipient the sole interpreter of the material, and each listener brings a different interpretation to each song."[13] The lack of explicit content in the lyrics and in the experience shaped by the soundscapes created, *until* the listener fills in the gap, means that the music is not to be linked easily with any particular worldview or philosophy.[14] This opening example of the function of Sigur Rós's music does, however, demonstrate that one of the functions popular music can have is *the creation of an experience of wonder* within the affective space that listeners inhabit as they undertake their listening. It shows that opening up room for emotions to begin working may not be accomplished only with emotional work or with attention to feelings that are evoked. There is more to be explored with respect

"Hoppipolla" by Sigur Rós

The Icelandic band Sigur Rós is an excellent example of a band that evokes an atmosphere through the creation of compelling sound. Though most of its songs do contain words, it is not because of the words that their music is best known, responded to, or used. The band members recognize this themselves, acknowledging that few people around the world know Icelandic. They therefore use a playful form of Icelandic ("Hopelandic"), the words of which do sometimes carry meaning, though not always. The words are used more to contribute to the sound produced.

"Hoppipolla" ("hopping into puddles") has lyrics not yet translated into English on the band's official website, despite being long promised. Since the track's release in 2005 on the album *Takk* and its re-release in 2006 (when the song began to be used extensively in the UK and beyond as uplifting background music), the track has gained popularity as an anthem of exhilaration. One telling use of the track was in the UK natural history program *Planet Earth* (BBC); as a result the song became synonymous with wonder, energy, awe, and dynamism. The ease of association between the musical buildup and the visual imagery displayed led to the song being used as a celebration of creativity and natural power. Some soccer teams now use it as a source of inspiration.

The track is a prime example of the limitations of seeking only the composer's intention when interpreting a song. Though the composers are still alive and could comment on their intentions, the soundscape created is most meaningful in the way it is *used*. It cannot be interpreted in unlimited ways, as there are constraints created by the shape and flow of the music. But the varieties of use in a media-saturated age (when multiple uses quickly proliferate) demonstrate that the uses themselves begin to shape the meanings attached to and gained from the music.

---

to how such affective space is used and what listeners bring to and expect from their experiences of escape or being taken out of themselves.

The Communal Dimension

A second example of escape/escapism, being taken out of oneself, of release, of exhilaration, of ecstasy—which once more questions the primary or direct significance of lyrics in popular music—is that of the sing-along anthem in the context of live performance.[15] In the next chapter we shall further explore some dimensions of communal gatherings at which popular music is heard. Here we must recognize how *the communal dimension in experiencing music* contributes directly to the sense of being transported. The respondent in our own survey who spoke of music as "Escapist, moving, transcendental, a shared experience (at a gig)" was linking the sense of escape and transcendence within the communal dimension itself.[16] The same respondent claims that loud music "has a physicality to it . . . not found elsewhere" and has favorite artists "Deep Purple, Led Zeppelin, Springsteen, Motorhead, Sisters of Mercy, Black Sabbath, Iron Maiden." The sense of togetherness at a communal gathering along with the physicality of the music may be sufficient for the transcendental element to be present. It is not clear that singing along is essential, though we acknowledge that participation normally occurs.

Participation is not, however, dependent on knowledge of lyrics. Important though singing along to known words can be, the sense of community/communion with others can be engendered by wordless participation. In the same way that soundscapes are important for the reception of, and participation in, Sigur Rós's music, so also wordless strategies for encouraging participation are adopted by bands. Three simple examples will suffice. In live performances Paul McCartney continues to make "Hey Jude" a key participative element within his concert experience. A master at promoting audience involvement, McCartney divides audiences up in friendly competition with each other until all sing together ("naaa, na-na, na-na-na-na, na-na-na-na, Hey Jude").[17] A more recent band, Elbow, found their song "Grounds for Divorce" evoking audience participation throughout (wo-oh-oh-oh-oh-oh-oh-oh-oh-oh-oh-oh). Perhaps one of the most prominent, deliberate contemporary attempts to turn arena-size gatherings into mass sing-alongs is Coldplay.[18] Lead singer Chris Martin actively encourages audience participation, especially for the song "Viva La Vida," which requires no knowledge of words, just a willingness to join in with "oh-oh-oh-oh-ohhhhhhhhh-o, oh-oh-oh-oh-ohhhhhhhhh-o." These are simple, almost banal examples. Yet they highlight the significance of the energy, communality, and sheer emotional power of music and togetherness. What matters most is the *sound* and the willingness and ability of those present to use their physical presence and the capacity of their human voice to contribute to the communal sound. The combination of a body of people and communally created sound enhances the sense of being transported, being "part of something bigger" (Eno), and being taken beyond oneself as an individual.

The Physicality of Transcendence

The *physicality of transcendence* must also be mentioned as a third way music can transport people out of themselves. The respondent (already referred to) whose heavy-metal interests were the context in which a "transcendental" and "shared experience" were enjoyed, explicitly highlighted the physicality of loud music. Another respondent was even more explicit about the ecstatic impact of heavy-metal music: "AC/DC gave me an orgasm without physical contact."[19] Whatever the truth of this claim, the listener wants us as researchers to understand the intensity of his experience of the music. This intensity, while deeply physical, is also bound up with a sense of losing control.

Getting "caught up in music" is another way to speak of the experience of being lost or absorbed in music. "I get completely caught up in the beat (I'm a dancer) or the lyrics and usually sing along," said a 21–30-year-old, white, female, US respondent in our survey. One male, over-60, white, UK respondent records his emotional experience of music as "absorption, fascination, contemplation." In contemporary popular music, study of the impact of the dance (club and rave) scene is an obvious way into this sense of being absorbed or lost. Behind the penultimate chapter of Gordon Lynch's *Understanding Theology and Popular Culture* lies some fresh empirical research into UK club culture.[20] There is surprisingly little direct reference to the physicality of the clubbing experience in the chapter. It could be that the agenda to assess the religious significance of club culture caused relatively little heed to this physical dimension, beyond where stimulants (alcohol and drug use) played a part in affecting the body.[21] For the clubbing experience, Lynch focuses more on the social and communal elements; the personal, developmental, and therapeutic dimensions; and the vital and joyful aspects. In offering our own definition, we shall refer to Lynch's discussion of whether these elements can be held to constitute experiences of transcendence.

The Power of Lyrics

Finally, as a fourth example of music's capacity to transport people out of themselves, we must not overlook the possibility that words themselves may provide the trigger. Though we are here examining popular music's role in taking people beyond themselves, we do not wish to suggest—despite our emphasis on sound, participation, and physicality—that words contribute nothing. Yet the approach we have adopted does remind us that when the poetry of lyrics contributes to transcendence—including in religious music (classical, ecclesiastical, or popular), where it can all too easily be assumed that it is primarily or solely the words that matter—it is as "musicalized" words.[22]

We have discovered that the way words function to take people beyond themselves often includes a sense of yearning. As one female respondent to our music survey indicated, "joy, contentment, yearning, aching" are all possible emotional responses to music.[23] Furthermore, it is no surprise that the articulation of such yearning often includes references to longing in love relationships or longing for love, as well as references to erotic desire (either implicit or explicit). When U2 sings the line, "Touch Me, Take me to that other place" (from "Beautiful Day"),[24] ambiguity is evident, though a horizon of the ecstatic, of joy, of hopefulness is clearly envisaged. Many love songs indicate that it is in the context of human relationships—in the search for human love, or through the complexities of developing partnerships—that encounter with some form of otherness is experienced. In the example of the gentle love song by Everything But the Girl, "I Didn't Know I Was Looking for Love," the search for love is denied, but then its impact upon the one who is found by love is spelled out ("A thousand stars came into my system; . . . if you left I would be two foot small").[25]

In the history of popular music, words have in another way proved significant in evoking experiences that may attract the label "transcendence": many bands have released so-called concept albums.[26] The way in which concept albums are designed to work was exemplified by Pink Floyd's March 2010 success in the UK courts against the record company EMI. The band secured a ruling that their albums could not be divided up into separate tracks for the purpose of assisting the sale of digital downloads. Some such albums tell a story (e.g., Genesis, "The Lamb Lies Down on Broadway"; Elton John, "Captain Fantastic and the Brown Dirt Cowboy"). Others have a theme. Their structure and purpose, however, is to be listened to *as a whole*. The lyrics may not always be profound, but are linked to a central motif. Although some such albums may be charged with undue pretension, the sheer intensity of a forty-minute listening experience, partly due to the lyrics, becomes a journey for the listener. This may be a journey inward or a form of escape out of oneself. But it certainly has the capacity to be an exercise in attentiveness.[27]

The experience of such intensive listening is well captured in Nick Hornby's 2009 novel, *Juliet, Naked*, where an early version of an album by musician Tucker Crowe is discovered. The novel then explores differing fan reactions to the discovery. One of the main characters, Duncan, first listens to the album this way:

> He went down to the sea-front. . . . The weather conditions were perfect for his needs. . . . He got himself a cup of takeaway instant coffee from the kebab shop by the pier and sat down on a bench overlooking the ocean. He was ready.
>
> Forty-one minutes later, he was scrabbling around in his pockets for something he could use as a handkerchief when a middle-aged woman came over and touched him on the arm.
>
> "Do you need someone to talk to?" she said gently.
>
> "Oh. Thank you. No, no, I'm fine."
>
> He touched his face—he'd been crying harder than he'd realized.
>
> "You sure? You don't look fine."
>
> "No, really. I've just . . . I've just had a very intense emotional experience." He held out one of his iPod headphones, as if that would explain it. "On here."
>
> "You're crying about music?"
>
> The woman looked at him as if he were some kind of pervert.
>
> "Well," said Duncan. "I'm not crying *about* it. I'm not sure that's the right preposition."
>
> She shook her head and walked off.[28]

The fictional album Duncan listened to was not a concept album. Our point, though, is to use Hornby's example of what a sustained period of focused listening has the capacity to do to an individual listener. Hornby captures the intensity and emotional impact beautifully.

It could, of course, be argued that in the age of the digital download, Pink Floyd's success is but a small act of defiance in the face of the inevitable commercial preference for bite-sized music. The band's legal triumph may appear quite a weak appeal to the value of intensive listening to whole albums when the notion of the album is itself dated. It may sound like nostalgia for U2 lead guitarist, Dave Evans ("The Edge"), to express sadness at the loss of the listeners' sense of how an album might have been constructed, with meaning in the order of the tracks.[29] Evans bemoans "the loss of depth" and the disappearance of the "ritual aspect" of listening that vinyl records were more likely to require. In his view, the depth comes from repeated listening, acknowledging that songs have a context within a whole album, a large listening experience.

We have sought, then, to show that when people report that music takes them to another place, this has specifically to do with sounds, participation, physicality, and words. Yet identifying these features does not fully explain music's working in the sense of reducing what is reported to these features. We are simply identifying features that surround the words used, to explore why music brings attention to that seeming human necessity to reach beyond what is experienced, even while enjoying the experiences of the moment (the music itself) and also what is referred to (e.g., love).[30] But what is to be made of these examples of what music does? Why are references to transcendence important? Are they important at all? Are such references made only by those already religious? Can a critical reading of such experiences gain anything from a religious studies perspective? To these questions we now turn.

Does Transcendence Matter?

We have raised the question of transcendence for two reasons: it is a word some listeners themselves use about their listening experience, and it is a word that features in scholarly attempts to define the kinds of human experience that are termed religious. At the outset, we should stress, we are not claiming that all listening to popular music merits the label "transcendent experience" (and is therefore really religious). And in communicating with anyone who believes that all claims for transcendence are reducible to chemical reactions in the body, we will not be able to convince such a person that what some music listeners call transcendence may be more than that. Our purpose is to probe the experiences so reported in light of what religion is and does. Our claim is straightforward: whatever transcendence may be, it is vital that we recognize the importance of the emotional, aesthetic, ethical, and cognitive work that occurs in the affective spaces inhabited by contemporary Western citizens when listening to and experiencing popular music, and acknowledge what is being termed transcendence within that space. Where the activities and experiences described do seem to require the use of that term, we suggest, then we need to recognize, too, that the sense of being taken beyond oneself is an essential element in developing a full appreciation of what it means to be human.

Charles Taylor, Frank Burch Brown, and John Carey offer three quite different readings of transcendence for us to work with. In Taylor's book *A Secular Age*, he sets off with a threefold understanding of transcendence, from the start identifying all three dimensions' close association with religion. The first dimension is the sense of "some good higher than, beyond human flourishing."[31] A second meaning is "belief in a higher power, the transcendent God." The third is the sense that "our lives extend beyond 'this life.'" Then Taylor extensively studies the impact of various secularizing dimensions on Western culture. At the end of his study, Taylor declares the contemporary importance of what he calls "immanent transcendence," the sense of "something beyond [merely human] flourishing," of "life beyond life," yet without the confidence that such a life can be affirmed, even while "a renewed affirmation of transcendence" seems both necessary and desirable.[32] Taylor observes that "the present fractured expressivist culture . . . seems very inhospitable to belief." What is more, "the level of understanding of . . . the great languages of transcendence is declining; in this respect massive unlearning is taking place. The individual pursuit of happiness as defined by consumer culture still absorbs much of our time and energy." And yet, Taylor reports, "the sense there is something more presses in."[33]

Popular music's role and use in contemporary Western culture is easily identifiable within Taylor's "individual pursuit of happiness." The evidence we have been offering also suggests, however, that popular music is part of that immanent transcendence, the sense that human flourishing is not enough. Expressive individualism—the way in which artists and performers express their innermost feelings and emotions (and potentially, beliefs, opinions, and ideas) *as* their art—is dominant, as Taylor notes. But we must be careful not to define the functions of media and the arts solely on the basis of such expression. When attention is paid to the complexity of what receivers (consumers, listeners, watchers) do with popular culture, then it is possible to argue that receptiveness to immanent transcendence (the expressivism of others) does not confine the listener to immanence. In their listening, listeners may either be grasping for a transcendence that, they sense, is fundamental to full humanity, or they may experience it without having had such intent. It is this, we suggest, that contemporary listeners are reporting in their responses to music, popular music included. The being taken out of oneself or even the desire to be taken out of oneself is itself a quest for otherness, a response to the limitations of self-containedness. Self-satisfaction will apparently not suffice.

"Immanent transcendence" is one of four forms of transcendence identified by the theologian Frank Burch Brown.[34] Brown is seeking to identify the different ways in which transcendence is mediated aesthetically. He presupposes that

God is mediated in the human realm. The issue is *how* this happens by artistic means. The first form, *negative transcendence*, functions in effect as a challenge to the success of God's self-mediation: "God appears only as the Absent One." Thus in artistic terms, because God is not there, yet still is believed in, it is as a yearning that God's presence is mediated and transcendence is represented. By *radical transcendence* Brown means God's otherness, "the infinitely distant one whom we cannot approach." Such otherness cannot, therefore, really be represented. Indeed, if anything we must be careful not to try, lest we end up worshiping the means through which we are seeking to channel such otherness. *Proximate* (or sacramental) *transcendence* accepts that earthly things can be used as means through which God's presence is mediated. This form is thus more positive about the value of tangible things. By *immanent transcendence* Brown means something slightly different from Taylor. As one form of four "varieties of aesthetic transcendence," this fourth form affirms the everyday. But God is so "immersed in the ordinary," it could be argued that God is not easily identifiable. Indeed, Brown himself refers to it as "a kind of transcendence," as if there may be some doubt that otherness is truly "other." The meeting point between Taylor's and Brown's definitions of immanent transcendence is thus the sense that while more may be yearned for beyond merely human flourishing, this can at best be imaginative. There may be no Other as such to relate to, no objective reality of God. Transcendence thus becomes a way in which we ascribe significance to what we feel or think.[35]

The question then arises as to who "we" are. This is where John Carey's approach to transcendence is helpful. In his discussion of Laski's work, Carey makes the following observation: "Claims to transcendence and universal knowledge are evidently a way of conferring significance on oneself and one's experiences, and are likelier to occur to those already in possession of social confidence and economic power."[36] This is difficult to dispute. What it does not tell us, of course, is whether such claims might ever be based on something more substantial than self-reference or a sense of social importance. The evidence we have gathered suggests that the reception and use of music is one key realm of Western culture where a sense of self-worth and appropriate self-importance are asserted. Where, however, some sense of going beyond the self (reports of escape, being taken to another place, transcendence) appears, we suggest that this is music's way of enabling people to discover that being human entails resisting self-absorption: entertaining some sense of otherness in one's life. The types of music enjoyed and ways in which music is used for such purposes will differ radically across age-groups, ethnicities, and social classes. Although this would require much closer empirical testing, we resist an assumption that particular kinds of music may automatically, or are always more likely, to evoke such a sense of transcendence.

This conclusion does not mean that a single form of (universal) transcendence can be discerned behind all music. The existence of a universal spirituality of music, or of a single notion of God, does not follow from this. But we are suggesting the limits of an understanding of immanent transcendence that would want to explain all experiences of music as, in some sense, an encounter with otherness as only psychologically or chemically induced. The tingle factor can indeed be variously accounted for. But in what at least some listeners are doing with music, and believe music does to them, they are saying more than "I am significant" (Carey's observation about transcendence). They are indicating that music is something through which they encounter otherness (proximate transcendence, in Burch Brown's terms).[37]

Of the ten people cited from our music survey at the start of this chapter, whose quotations we selected because of their content and without knowing their background, six are religious (all Christian), three have no religious affiliation, and one did not declare. It is not possible to conclude in any scientific way whether it is more or less likely that the already-religious may attach greater significance to the sense of otherness that music can produce. We do, though, need to acknowledge that religion at least provides a language for such experiences to be recognized and spoken about.[38] Whether content lies beyond the language is where the function of "the great languages of transcendence" and concern about the "massive unlearning" currently taking place, both identified by Taylor, come into play. Music of all kinds appears to keep the reminder alive that the great languages of transcendence will always be needed to enable people to make sense of the experiences that take them out of themselves.

Summary Comment: The Case of the Missing Dictionary Entry

What, then, is transcendence about? Does referring to the concept force the experiences of music reception described in an inappropriate direction? From his study of clubbers' experiences of "community and friendship, . . . intimacy, joy, and unity," Gordon Lynch reports that "it is particularly striking that these participants did not make use of any kind of 'transcendence' discourse to interpret these experiences."[39] The clubbers seemed to assume or conclude that their "oceanic states," though in many ways similar to religious or mystical experiences, were "intrapsychic events," within their experience only, with no link to anything beyond themselves. Lynch concludes that although clubbers' experience may be powerful and transformative, especially with respect to personal development and friendship networks, their experience still lacks a "deeper sense of transformation in which people in the club scene are challenged and helped to ask deeper questions about the meaning of their lives."[40]

There is much we have yet to investigate in the findings of our own music survey about the life structures and listening patterns of our 231 respondents. However, a striking difference between Lynch's conclusions and our own is that some music users clearly *do* use the language of transcendence, and related terms, to describe their experience. As admitted, we cannot conclude that all mean the same thing by "transcendence" or "being taken out of oneself." Furthermore, we are well aware that some of our respondents are actively religious, and hence, unlike Lynch's sample of clubbers, have access to a discourse of transcendence. But, we suggest, this highlights the crucial cultural importance of keeping the great languages of transcendence in active use. These languages are not just words. They are frameworks of meaning that do not simply label what is going on. They also interpret, shape, and extend the experiences being described. Music thus becomes more and achieves more when the ecstatic experiences that people report having as listeners are interpreted through such literary lenses.

There is no entry on "transcendence" in *The Oxford Companion to Philosophy*.[41] This is a striking though understandable omission. All matters transcendental may well be "beyond experience." But as this chapter suggests, that which is beyond experience (be it as a language or narrative of transcendence, or the Other that the language of transcendence tries to denote) proves vital to enabling us to understand the experiences we actually have as humans. The tingle factor puts us in touch with that which we cannot quite identify, but which is vitally important for human life, and which is very much the subject of theology.

pop music, ritual, and worship

If you've written any good tunes, you will be involved in funerals and deaths, you will be involved in weddings and births.

Richard Ashcroft, singer-songwriter[1]

Often a particular song reminds me of when I first heard it, and it brings back a rush of emotions that I associate with incidents at the time. More generally, music just relaxes me and helps me concentrate on whatever else I'm doing (I usually listen to music while doing something—driving, work, reading or whatever—and find it harder to do it without music.

Questionnaire respondent[2]

The quotation from Richard Ashcroft, solo artist and lead singer with The Verve, illustrates how popular music can be important for those key moments in life that might also be marked by some form of liturgical ceremony. Indeed, one of us attended the funeral of a teenager, where The Verve's *Bittersweet Symphony*, a favorite track of the deceased, provided both the basis for the minister's oration and the processional music when the coffin left the church. The second quotation from one of the respondents to our questionnaire highlights the connections between music and memory, extending the role of music in marking births, deaths, and marriages to its place within the wider world of everyday life. Both quotations therefore provide evidence of the role now played by popular music in dealing with life at major turning points and in its everyday form.

In this chapter we shall examine some of the major ways in which popular music functions as a form of ritual. Scholars in many disciplines have commented on popular music used as ritual.[3] We have not, however, come across an account of popular music's ritualistic functioning that does justice to the insights that knowledge of religion can bring—without either taking the purpose, reception, or use of music too easily *as* religion or explaining it away.[4]

Liturgies and the Handling of Life

In this chapter we first look at how the death of parents, alongside mixed and complex relations with Roman Catholicism, has significantly influenced the work of two musicians not (in any obvious sense) known as "religious artists": John Lydon and Madonna. Reaching well beyond religious studies, we also observe selected examples of ritualistic dimensions in popular music and how they are interpreted. From this material, we distill three areas for further discussion: religion and the public sphere; the nature of "self"; and the question of what constitutes "worship" or "devotion." Finally we shall explore the interconnectedness of pop music, ritual, and worship.

Seen It in Your Eyes: John Lydon and Bereavement

John Lydon was born to Irish Catholic immigrants in north London and became famous as Johnny Rotten, lead singer of the seminal punk band Sex Pistols. Following that band's split in 1978, he formed Public Image Limited (PiL), which initially took quite a different musical direction. After going through many lineup changes, PiL folded in the early 1990s. Later Lydon reformed both bands—Sex Pistols during 2006–9 and PiL from 2009 onward. According to a 2010 television interview with Andrew Graham-Dixon, Lydon feels that he is able to be "freer" and can be "into emotions in a much deeper way" with PiL than with Sex Pistols.[5] He continues, "I can cry my eyes out in half of these songs and usually end up doing exactly that because they're from the heart and soul." He explains that he deals with personal issues and personal pain in PiL whereas Sex Pistols is not the format for that.[6] Two examples are the songs "Religion" and "Death Disco," which were written in response to his mother's illness and death from cancer.

In the interview Lydon acknowledges that the Roman Catholic Church and school were constant parts of his upbringing but expresses deep disillusionment with the Catholic Church when he claims that priests wouldn't come to the hospital to give his mother the last rites unless money was involved.[7] This experience emerges lyrically in his bitter attack on the Roman Catholic Church in the song "Religion," where he lambasts what he sees as a sanctimonious priesthood that is interested only in extorting money from their flock, singing in his distinctive style: "This is religion and Jesus Christ / This is religion cheaply priced."

In the interview, he explains that he was asked by his mother to write a song about her impending death. This became "Death Disco," which he describes as "pain, agony and Swan Lake put together," and includes the despairing cry: "Never no more hope away, final in a fade / Watch her slowly die."

When Lydon's father died in 2008, he started playing "Death Disco" again, with its bleak response to an earlier death and the pain of bereavement returned. He reflects, "I really need to deal with these emotional agonies in a really proper, serious way, and Public Image is the only way I have of doing that. I've never understood death; I've never appreciated it or wanted it; I don't know where people go, but I miss them sadly."

Lydon remains a fierce critic of religion. In his *The Culture Show* interview, he remarks, "Religion has caused the most serious harm to the world as we know it. . . . I'd like to see it eliminated." Yet Lydon's experience shows that despite his hostility to organized religion, he has the same need as any human to give shape to emotion and deal with the deepest and darkest life experiences. Music has enabled him as a performer to give expression to his rage in the face of suffering and death. As he states in a July 2010 interview, he has found the fusion of music and words, rather than just words, to enable him to do this. He even qualifies the reference to "music" in his comments, accepting that he set words to "discordancy, noise, sounds," and this enabled him to "explain emotions much more accurately."[8]

For those who are not performers, the same process of release, or of handling difficult experiences and emotions, will not occur in the same way. We will, however, note how listeners too may be able to use music to serve similar functions.

There Was a Time: Madonna and Bereavement

Madonna is another performer whose personal experience and religious background inform both her songs and the choreography of her stage act. Also from a Roman Catholic background, Madonna was deeply affected by the loss of her mother, who died from breast cancer when Madonna was five years old. She has written and sung about this experience, most overtly in the track "Mother and Father" from her album *American Life* (2003). The song begins with a statement about her childhood in which faith is recalled with elements of naïveté rather than Lydon's cynicism: "There was a time I was happy in my life / There was a time I believed I'd live forever / There was a time I prayed to Jesus Christ / There was a time I had a mother, it was nice."

But this is replaced with the pain of death and parting as Madonna sings about the hurt she experienced through bereavement. She gives this a strongly autobiographical element as she lightly raps about how she spent all day crying over the loss of her mother. In a television interview from 2005, she says that for her

> religion is synonymous with not asking questions. And what I call religious thinking is robotic thinking. It's we do things because this is what our ancestors did; this is what my father did, . . . my grandfather, . . and as I was raised a Catholic and I had questions like [these]: Why did God create the world? And why is there so much sadness and why is there war? And why do good things happen to bad people and why do bad things happen to good people? My father could never answer those questions, and my religion never answered those questions, and when I studied Kabbalah for the first time, I felt those questions were being answered.[9]

It is difficult not to conclude that Madonna's embracing of Kabbalah mysticism in later life was a case of finding religious practice helpful at an appropriate life stage, and that she did not have, or take, the opportunity to ask what an adult form of her childhood Catholicism might have looked like. Even so, Madonna's video work and stage performances continue to provide evidence of her engagement with themes from the religious tradition of her youth. She cannot quite leave her Catholicism alone. Indeed, whatever criticisms she may have of the religious tradition and practices to which she was introduced when young, it is evident from her stage performances that it is not simply criticism that she wishes to offer.

Perhaps the clearest example of a positive and even missionary attempt to encourage those experiencing her music to see what Christianity might mean in the twenty-first century can be found in her 2006 Confessions tour. Onstage, Madonna performed her song "Live to Tell" while on a cross. Although raising accusations of blasphemy and questions of whether she is contributing to a feminist approach to understanding the crucifixion, it is difficult to conclude that Madonna is simply mocking Christian faith here. The performance juxtaposed the plight of African orphans with the cross in a striking way, making use of projected words adapted from the Gospel of Matthew (chap. 25) and reminding viewers/listeners of Jesus's commands to serve those who are in need. Just as U2 always seems to have a sermon slot (a point in their concerts when a clear ethical or spiritual message is communicated),[10] one could argue that here Madonna uses a striking—even shocking—piece of musical theater both to provoke thought, shake up people's commitment, and stimulate action.

Devils and Dust: Ritualized Behavior

Our intention in exploring the work of both of these musicians is less that of pointing out where and how religion appears explicitly in pop, than it is noticing where popular music operates in close alliance with ritual performance, both in the lives of those who produce it and those who receive it. Ritual performance is a typical aspect of popular music fandom, not just when it is linked to religion explicitly, and it occurs in more than a mundane way. All this is evident from Daniel Cavicchi's study of Bruce Springsteen fans.

Cavicchi finds that fans view the series of actions that constitute going to a concert as a ritual. "Fans see the role of audience member as very special and serious; they see the process of becoming a member of the audience as an elaborate ritual with many 'requirements.' Buying concert tickets or CDs involves lengthy road trips, camping on sidewalks, standing in long lines, and much strategy. . . . Fans feel that they must be involved in any Springsteen performance."[11] Even if developments in technology mean that the way in which one secures tickets for concerts has changed somewhat since 1998, a similar commitment and dedication to the cause is still required. The ritual is, then, not just the musical event itself. As an aspect of what it means to be a fan, what happens *around* the event (before and after) proves just as meaningful. Hence, for fans, a concert "is not a single theatrical event but rather a ritual in which they regularly participate over time. . . . [It] is not about fun but rather about results."[12] Hopefully it will be enjoyable entertainment! But for the committed fan, a Springsteen concert is to be viewed more "as a ritual rather than as entertainment" and "is not a break from, but a continuing reaffirmation of, their everyday lives."[13] To quote Cavicchi again, "Fans' descriptions of their listening indicate that the significance of the music is not limited to the musical encounter but resonates long thereafter. . . . [It is] an ongoing process of deepening the connection between their hearing and their lives . . . [and] is not simply about making sense of music; it is about making sense of the world in which music is created and shared."[14]

On this basis, it is not surprising to find Springsteen fans themselves declare:

- Seeing Bruce in concert is like a religious experience.
- It's a spiritual experience.
- One leaves a Bruce Springsteen concert with the feeling that one has just been to a religious revival, and there is a reaffirmation of Faith and Hope and Joy![15]

Cavicchi himself is reluctant to conclude that Springsteen fandom *is* religion.[16] Even though a reading of Springsteen fandom invites such an interpretation because of the ways in which fans speak about the intensity of their experiences, Cavicchi finds it more appropriate to conclude that "both fandom and religion are addressing similar concerns and engaging people in similar ways."[17] Yet it is vital that the ritualistic function of music use by fans ("a complex kind of listening")[18] is recognized at the heart of such practice.

Ritualized use of music, then, surfaces for writers/composers and for performers in the context of use (at significant life stages and in the course of everyday life by fans). But what remains is the question of whether such ritualized use indicates religious use or not, and if religious, whether it is a new form of religion, a replacement for traditional religion (as Rupert Till argues). In this book we do not seek to offer a conclusive answer to this more sociological or cultural question. We shall, however, in part 3, need to take account of this de facto development in offering a theological response to what is happening. At this point, however, we must at least explore the relevant issues that the many dimensions of the ritual use of popular music raise for our inquiry.

Ritual in a Secular Age

In the songs, interviews, and fan responses just considered, we can begin to identify significant social changes that have taken place in Western culture and altered the place and role of music, faith, and liturgy in the lives of individuals and communities. Some have called this development a process of secularization, and there has been much debate about the nature of those changes and the value of that word. We will not deeply consider the debates on the secularizing process, but refer readers to the work of Peter Berger, Steve Bruce, David Martin, and Charles Taylor for detailed discussion. However, we need to locate our analysis in the continuing conversation about the changing place of faith in the world. This must include (1) an understanding of how the category of religion emerged within a secular public sphere; (2) a consideration of how a contemporary understanding of self has developed; and (3) an appreciation of the nature of Christian worship within the broader context of human ritual. So it is to these issues that we now turn.

Religion and the Public Sphere

In his description of how the secularization of the public sphere within Western culture has come about, Charles Taylor sets out a key question: "Why was it virtually impossible not to believe in God in, say 1500 in our Western society, while in 2000 many of us find this not only easy, but even inescapable?"[19] In seeking an answer Taylor argues that in the past, three key factors played a role in preserving faith: the natural world testified obviously to divine purpose and action; God was deeply implicated in society since a kingdom could only be conceived as grounded in sacred order; and people lived in a premodern, "enchanted" world of spirits, demons, and moral forces. During the intervening five hundred years, our social and intellectual framework, including these three elements, changed significantly, leading to the present secular age. For example, the place of divine purpose in the natural has become an area of intellectual dispute.[20] Furthermore, the role of God in social order has been overturned by anticlericalism and revolution.[21] All of these changes have had far-reaching impact on how faith is perceived in the contemporary world.

Thus with the songs and interviews in which Lydon and Madonna reflect on the deaths of their mothers, we can sense how for them the natural world does not obviously testify to divine purpose nor does the social order support a belief in God. Both artists struggle to make sense of their experiences and also question the church, which fails to provide answers that they find credible. Perhaps the only one of the three elements identified by Taylor that still has some effect is a lingering or lost sense of enchantment. Lydon yearns for some explanation ("I've never understood death; I've never appreciated it or wanted it; I don't know where people go, but I miss them sadly"), while Madonna has clearly found the kind of answers she was looking for in the teachings of Kabbalah mysticism. The link between memory and enchantment was made by one of our respondents (a white female, age 21–30 years) who wrote about how "many, many, many of my memories of music are tied up with friends and good times and dancing and festivals."

Daniel Cavicchi commented on his interviewees: "[They] spoke with enthusiasm and clarity, recounting experiences that were rich in emotion, memory, and complexity, sharing with me whole realms of meaning about which no one in the modern university seemed to care."[22] Our contention here is that it is vital—in academy, faith communities, and society—for us to recognize what is happening to the ways in which people shape and cope with their life experiences. We further examined the emotional dimensions of music use (the tingle factor) in chapter 6. Most relevant for our discussion here are changes to the enchanted world.

We agree with writers such as Grace Davie, Danielle Hervieu-Léger, and Taylor that rather than disappearing completely or fading into indifference, religion changes, mutates, or evolves into different social forms.[23] If this is the case, we must be able to find new forms of religious expression that are developing in the contemporary world. We are not arguing for a direct equivalence between a mutation of religious ritual and the contemporary use of music within Western culture. We are not saying that religion has been replaced by music. Nor are we saying that religion remains unchanged by such social mutations.[24] More precisely we maintain that the developing and diverse use of music is taking place against a backdrop of changing faith practice that may well be affecting *both* practices.[25]

As social practices, religion and music are linked in a number of ways, and this can be illustrated historically. Christianity made a decisive contribution to pre-Reformation European life by providing a ritualized marking of time.[26] This form of liturgical enchantment is gradually receding, but we can argue that, given the important role of time in music, the contemporary place of music in Western culture is one of the ways in which the human desire for enchanted time is being fulfilled.[27] It is striking to find this notion of marking time echoed in Cavicchi's work, providing evidence of the human need for ritual recognition of time periods, whether or not these are labeled as religious practice or identified as having any connection with religion.[28]

Another significant social phenomenon to emerge from the mutation of religion is the reordering of the public sphere in terms of affinity groups, which is itself a reemergence of the tribal nature of humanity. French social theorist Michel Maffesoli has linked social developments in the Reformation and Renaissance periods with the tribal nature of contemporary society, while drawing attention to artistic and religious manifestations of social "effervescence."[29] Thus he contends that for everyday forms of Christianity "before becoming dogmatized in faith, popular religiosity—pilgrimages, the cult of saints and other various forms of superstition—was above all an expression of sociality."[30] Given Maffesoli's case that tribalism is an essential part of Christianity, we can question the extent to which it makes sense to describe it as becoming "dogmatized." We contend that Christianity has always been a fluid, diverse, and tribal phenomenon, so, in that respect, religion shares characteristics with music. Thus Maffesoli points us toward an important social link between worship and music: adherents to Christian worship exhibit behavioral traits similar to behavior of music fans. In addition to the evidence provided by Cavicchi with respect to followers of Bruce Springsteen, we can see a clear social link between worship and music in the calls for heavy metal to be recognized as a religion for census purposes[31] and in Sarah Thornton's observation: "Taking part in club cultures builds . . . affinities, socializing participants into a knowledge of (*and frequently a belief in*) the likes and dislikes, meanings and values of the culture."[32] This idea has been developed most recently by Rupert Till, who has argued that popular music has developed traits similar to cults or new religious movements for various reasons, including this one: "They are usually focused around one individual or group of figures who are treated as being special or more important than anyone else and are often worshipped as though they were divine." In addition, he believes that the music scene can involve high levels of participation, obsessive behavior, brainwashing techniques, and "shadowy figures" who work behind the scenes to increase the profiles of pop icons.[33] Despite certain similarities between pop fandom and cultic practices, we still prefer to see this form of activity through the lens of tribal affiliation rather than that of new religious movements, and we shall return to this when considering the nature of religious ritual.

Nevertheless, the role of personal and communal faith, including worship, has changed significantly over the past five hundred years and continues to do so. Within that broader cultural narrative, the role of music has also evolved. Another important factor in the story has been the developing notions of self. Who is this self that believes or does not believe? Who is this self that worships or does not worship? Who is this self that appreciates one form of music rather than another or in some cases has no interest in music at all? We now turn to an understanding of the reflexive self.

The Reflexive Self

The roots of a generalized understanding of "self" as reflexive being[34] have variously been traced back to the 18th-century industrial revolution, the 17th-century scientific revolution, the Protestant Reformation in the 15th and 16th centuries, and even further back to Augustine in the 5th century. As Taylor argues:

> It is hardly an exaggeration to say that it was Augustine who introduced the inwardness of radical reflexivity and bequeathed it to the Western tradition of thought. The step was a fateful one, because we have certainly made a big thing of the first-person standpoint. The modern epistemological tradition from Descartes, and all that has flowed from modern culture, has made this standpoint fundamental—to the point of aberration, one might think.[35]

Nevertheless the notion of the "reflexive self"—the recognition that humans are aware of, and can reflect upon, their own existence—has been and remains a vital facet of Western culture.

The reflexive path from Augustine to the present is long and complex, yet within the context of this book, it is worth bearing in mind Alasdair MacIntyre's identification of the role of music in this journey. In particular, he contends that in Northern Europe the blurring of the line between "religious" and "aesthetic" within music played a key role in creating the secular space for the Enlightenment.[36] Although this process of creating the reflexive self can be seen as extending through history, it also has an impact at a personal and immediate level. One of the respondents to our music survey observed: "Music for me is food for my soul. . . . Without music my life would be less rich. . . . Music is a medium which I use to change my inner world but also brings me a sense of getting in touch with my innermost thoughts and feelings."[37] Not only does the role of music continue to be important within a contemporary philosophical, sociological, and theological understanding of reflexivity; music also plays an equally important role in the everyday practice of our using it to reflect upon our lives and their meaning.

Another influential thinker who has looked at this strand of human activity is Anthony Giddens. He believes "self-identity today is a reflexive achievement" and that a "reflexively ordered narrative of self-identity provides the means of giving coherence to the finite lifespan, given changing external circumstances."[38] This shares common ground with what DeNora calls our search for "ontological security," and she argues that music plays a crucial role in this process: "In the course of daily life, many of us resort to music, often in highly reflexive ways. Building and deploying musical montages is part of a repertory of strategies for coping and for generating pleasure, creating occasion, and affirming self- and group identity."[39] This focus on self has not only become a significant factor in the *secular* realm. It has also had a major impact on those who identify themselves as *religious*, as their attention turns less to traditions of belief and more toward a concern about who they truly are. At its most negative, as one observer has noted, this tendency leads to replacing spirituality with narcissism.[40]

Against this background, most people in Western culture seek contemporary self-identity in the marketplace of consumer capitalism. Another factor in play here, bringing together religion, music, and identity, is the importance of naming. In his discussion of how protection of a brand name is fundamental to the aesthetics of commodity, Kieran Flanagan observes that the significance of "naming" can be found as far back as the biblical book of Genesis.[41] But this is not a remote or archaic issue. In 2010 the *Wall Street Journal* carried a story titled "From Abba to ZZ Top, All the Good Band Names Are Taken"; it reported that because of the accessibility of the internet, any band is able to announce their presence and make a claim for the identity of their group. One musician expressed his frustration at finding a name for his new band: "Think of a great band name and Google it, and you'll find a French-Canadian jam band with a MySpace page."[42] Whether this turns out to be a genuine problem in the long term is probably not important. The story highlights how the lack of a named self-identity is perceived as a serious issue for late modernity within the context of a commodified world of reflexive consumers of music and culture.

The role of music and brands in constructing identity for the reflexive self works at many levels. For example, the phenomenon of "sonic branding" highlights a further consideration. North and Hargreaves define such branding as "the attempt to use very short periods of music and other auditory cues to convey brand values and prime brand recognition whenever customers come into contact with their company."[43] A good example is the musical cue we receive whenever we turn on our computers. This is the aural equivalent of a brand name or trademark. However, the impact of music on identity can be both positive and negative. Some research has suggested that "64% of 14 to 25-year-olds cited music as their greatest influence when selecting between different brands." By contrast other studies show that "fans can particularly resent 'their' music being appropriated for commercial ends."[44]

The role of brands in the creation of self-identity is clearly significant and has strong links with the tribal nature of human behavior. Even in this short discussion it is clear that for the worlds of music and faith, concepts of self, self-identity, and group identity play a vital role. How ritual functions as the means by which enjoyment of, or participation in, musical activity (playing or listening) contributes to the establishment or development of the self or personal identity (individual or group) surely raises the question of worship. For wherever religious or religion-like activities are discernible in other social practices (such as music), then the intensity and purpose of the practices merit scrutiny. "Devotion" denotes at least a high level of intensity. Music lovers and fans are readily called "devoted." It is necessary to ask: What is the nature of

"Jacob's Ladder" by Pete Seeger
and by Bruce Springsteen & The Sessions Band

Folk singer Pete Seeger and rock star Bruce Springsteen are not obvious musical brothers-in-arms. Both are American and troubadours of popular culture, but their differences outweigh their similarities. Seeger was born in 1919 into a family that was affluent, Protestant, and musical. He was under no pressure to learn an instrument, but he took up the ukulele before learning to play the banjo. Springsteen was born forty years later in 1949 into a family that was relatively poor, Catholic, and not particularly musical. He was inspired to take up music at age seven after seeing Elvis Presley on *The Ed Sullivan Show*. At thirteen, his mother bought him his first guitar for $18.

Seeger was blacklisted during the McCarthy Era, then in the 1960s emerged as a prominent singer of protest music in support of disarmament, civil rights, and the environment. Springsteen spent seven years searching for a breakthrough before being signed to Columbia records, with the help of the same person who signed Bob Dylan to that label. Success was still elusive. It was only with his third album *Born to Run* in 1975 that he hit the big time and from then on continued to achieve enormous popular and commercial success. Not only were their backgrounds poles apart, their musical genres were different. It has rightly been said that Springsteen was "no folkie."[45] Over time, however, he has been willing to explore and learn from different musical traditions.

Both artists have recorded versions of the traditional spiritual "Jacob's Ladder"; examples of their live versions can be found on YouTube.[46] Seeger's relatively gentle version was recorded in the secular setting of Wolf Trap, Washington, DC, in 1993 yet still has ritualized aspects of "call and response" which generates the kind of shared, collective reaction found in many forms of worship. By contrast Springsteen's much more energetic performance is closer to the types of ritual found in black gospel churches, and some comments made in response to the YouTube video point to the religious nature of his performance. Viewer Joelt6502 comments on the version recorded at St. Paul's Cathedral: "As close to a religious experience one could get outside a church! Amen!, brother Bruce!"[47] Another version, recorded in a decommissioned church in London, comes even closer to recognizable Christian ritual when Springsteen introduces the song with a short homily, saying that Jacob kept getting things wrong and that by God's grace he was given further chances until he got things right–which is an interesting combination of grace and works (or a Protestant and Catholic take on the song).[48]

that devotion? How do insights about worship contribute to what music and its reception are achieving in society today?

Defining Worship and Devotion

In her classic work on the subject, Evelyn Underhill begins by defining worship as "the response of the creature to the Eternal." She extends this theological understanding of the phenomenon beyond the merely human sphere, arguing that "we may think of the whole life of the Universe, seen and unseen, conscious and unconscious, as an act of worship glorifying its Origin, Sustainer, and End."[49] Whether or not people of all religious traditions would accept this working definition, derived from a Christian writer, as wholly adequate, it points to a basic sense that whatever humans are doing when they worship, they are "responding" first and foremost. "Devotion" therefore denotes a consistent, disciplined practice of worshiping. Though both worship and devotion may be undertaken in both public and private, and be social or individual, "public worship" and "private devotion" are commonly used phrases, thus denoting different settings and styles in which regular, disciplined "response . . . to the Eternal" may occur.

Given the material we have been considering throughout this second part, it is inevitable that many of the ways in which music is regarded and used invites consideration through the lens of worship. It may be claimed that worship of the Creator has become redirected toward worship of the creature (such as, seeing pop stars as idols or worshiping the body). It could be argued that the expressiveness or creativity evident in music, and enjoyed in responses of dancing and singing, celebrates no more than human creativity. And yet the continuing, ritualized use of music (as we have observed in this chapter) suggests that all may not be so simple or so easily explained away. What, then, does the use of music look like when seen through the lens of worship?

We begin by admitting that worship, prayer, and devotion can be areas of social conflict as individuals and groups dispute issues that extend far beyond the apparent source of disagreement. To cite a historical example, in England the sixteenth-century Reformation dispute over whether prayers should be said in Latin or English continued in later centuries with equally heated debates about whether prayers should be read from the Prayer Book in a formalized way or whether they should be impromptu and spontaneous. As one writer has observed, "What to the establishment represented a successful mechanism for edifying large numbers of people was to the non-conformists a spiritually deadening imposition upon minister and congregation alike."[50] At issue immediately, then, is the question of how the Eternal should be addressed, and by whom. The issue remains live in churches across the world (what language to use, whether to sing accompanied by instruments, what styles of music to use). In contemporary music beyond faith communities, the question can be sharply posed: can *any* music *really* have the potential to be seen as a response to the Eternal?

Lori Branch has explored how the continuing conflict over spontaneity versus conformity became much more than a simple binary relationship with respect to the practice of praying. She argues that the debate played a significant part not only in the rise of secularism but also in the emergence of modern capitalism and a new economic system. In essence she contends that many of the means for structuring social life and personal identity were removed in the aftermath of the Reformation. She claims that numerous expressions of religious and cultural spontaneity following from the late seventeenth-century Restoration in England were part of a profound process of cultural sense-making and establishing meaning for individuals. The formation of individual identity was a key element in the process that Graham Ward has termed the globalization and privatization of religion.[51] Branch argues this reached an apotheosis in the poetry of William Wordsworth: "The question which Wordsworth's poems should raise, and which is more relevant at the start of the twenty-first century even than the nineteenth, is the extent to which spiritual practice in the formation of persons and identities might be the basis not necessarily of escapism (though it may be that) but of a constructive politics and of a powerful yet vulnerable, nonviolent resistance to coercive societal and economic forces."[52] In other words, how people are being shaped and how they themselves contribute to their process of being shaped through what they do or consume (and listen to, watch, sing or play, for example)—all this is complex. But the individual is to be formed freely rather than coerced. Only in this way would such a response to the Eternal be fully authentic.

But this also means that although worship can be "the response of the creature to the Eternal," it is much else besides. In both popular and literate forms, worship, devotion, and prayer are part of complex social patterns and practices of identity formation. As we begin to examine this elaborate web, we can see that something similar is true of music as well. DeNora speaks of music as a vital constituent part of an individual and collective "life-web" that is formative of reflexive and social meaning through what she calls ritual "procedures" and "gestures."[53] However, DeNora does not define what she means by ritual in these contexts. As we seek to understand how such life-webs take shape, what functions they serve, and what conceptual frameworks they operate within, we could benefit from examining these life-webs through the lens of religious practice. Therefore we turn next to the connections between music, ritual, and worship.

Pop Music, Ritual, and Worship: Some Critical Reflections

Ritual and Individual Identity

Burning Man is an annual celebration of the arts that takes place in the Black Rock Desert of northern Nevada. The centerpiece of this festival is a towering wooden figure called the Burning Man, which is incinerated as the climax of the event. Lee Gilmore has written a participative, ethnographic study that reflects on her own involvement in Burning Man since 1996 and explores some of the ritualized behavior associated with the festival, through the ideas of Victor Turner, Catherine Bell, James Carey, Ronald Grimes, Graham St. John, and others.[54]

From her observations and interviews with those attending ("Burners"), Gilmore mentions the highly ambiguous role that religious ritual plays in this event. On the one hand, people bring the religious language and imagery from their everyday lives and use it to inform, shape, and illustrate their temporary life in the desert: "Participants' engagements with and narrative about ritual at Burning Man demonstrate how thoroughly religious ideas and symbols permeate our culture and are recursively mapped onto individuals and communities while at the same time rendering the semantic flexibility and instability of those concepts transparent. This can be seen in Burning Man's most prominent rituals."[55] On the other hand, it is steadfastly maintained that the event has no religious stance, and many of those questioned admit to either no faith or to a faith that is not linked to any particular religion or denomination: "Burners . . . by and large locate themselves within those elements of society that resist and reject normative religious structures. Yet for many of these individuals there remains a desire for a spiritually informed life, a connection to a larger, or ultimate reality, meaning, or purpose, as well as a sharpened, expanded, and reflexive sense of self."[56]

From the work of Gilmore and others, it is clear that although ritual, music, and worship are certainly not coterminous, they do overlap in significant ways. This can be demonstrated by noticing how three writers who have individually approached one of these topics while working from quite different perspectives nevertheless share some common ground in their results. We shall briefly examine Tom Driver's work on ritual, Tia DeNora's observations on music, and Graham Hughes's inquiry into the nature of Christian worship.[57] By its very nature this can be only a sketch of each scholar's ideas; yet by looking at their analyses, we begin to see how these expressions of human experience are linked.

In his work on ritual, Driver observes, "One obvious aspect of ritual is that it not only brings people together in physical assembly but also tends to unite them emotionally."[58] He illustrates this with reference to Colin Turnbull's account of experiencing ritual music performed at times of crisis by the Mbuti hunter/gatherers in Zaire:

> In an instant it all came together: there was no longer any lack of congruence, and it seemed as though the song was being sung by a single singer, the dance danced by a single dancer. Then I made the mistake of opening my eyes and saw that while all the others had their eyes open too, their gaze was vacant. . . . [I was] the only individual consciousness; all other bodies were empty. Something has been added to the importance of sound, another mode of perception that, while it in no way negated the aural or visual modes of observation, none the less went far beyond them.[59]

From this participant observation, Driver highlights three key elements of ritual behavior: communal gathering, performative cooperation, and mystical participation. He argues that in this ritualized setting the members of the group, "although interacting with each other only in the singing and not with eyes, spoken words, or physical touch, were yet as much united as it is possible for human beings to be."[60] Driver comments that ritual is essentially social in nature and that modern society offers few opportunities for this level of mutual participation.[61] Let us see how the ideas of DeNora and Hughes relate to Driver's insights.

In her discussion of how music is used in everyday life, DeNora also recognizes the importance of ritual: "Particular configurations of meaning (value, authenticity, affect) can be stabilized through ritual procedures and practices over time." She quotes national anthems such as "La Marseillaise" and "The Star-Spangled Banner" as examples of this process.[62] DeNora extends this analysis into exploring how music acts as a device for social ordering across a whole range of relations, from small gatherings and one-to-one relationships through to retail space and work areas. Therefore music and ritual both function as means of shaping communal life: "Music has organizational properties. It may serve as a resource for daily life and it may be understood to have social 'powers' in relation to human social being."[63]

Music also plays a key role in the process of self-identity. DeNora describes music as "semiotic particles" that individual human actors or agents use in the process of shaping feelings and identities: "Music is a material that actors use to elaborate, to fill out and fill in, to themselves and to others, modes of aesthetic agency and, with it, subjective stances and identities."[64] There is a tension between individual and group experience similar to that noted by Driver in his discussion of ritual, since music functions as a means of self-identity *and* as a means of negotiating social relationships. Furthermore, it also shares common ground with the mystical participation of ritual. In her conclusion DeNora touches on how music can be seen as a "drug," with the ability to effect psychological changes in moods and attitudes.[65]

Ritual and Communal Identity

Graham Hughes also observes a dual role for liturgy in individual and communal identity. He acknowledges Emmanuel Lévinas's assertion that Western thought evinces "the return to the self" together with the significant place that Lévinas gives to "the face," "otherness," and a presence not my own.[66] Hughes argues that in worship we are experiencing two kinds of "otherness": the first is in the communal experience of liturgy, and the second is in imagining "how things are in the presence of God."[67] In developing his understanding of the communal dimension of Christian worship, he argues that liturgy uses metaphors and signs to produce a field of meaning not unlike DeNora's life-web.

For DeNora, ritual and music have organizational properties for human society; the same is true for worship in Hughes's discussion. He draws on the work of Paul Ricoeur and Orthodox Christian thinkers in contending that worship is the primary expression of the church's theology, in which narrative "emplotment" (forming a narrative from historical events) plays a key role. The process of sign production, sign reception, and meaning-making that Hughes describes is essentially a communal experience: "It is a collaborative process in which the responsibilities (for meaning) are evenly shared between the producers and the recipients of signs."[68] This leads him into the area marked out by Driver's discussion about mystical participation and DeNora's observation about the ability of music to effect psychological change. For Hughes, worship is a boundary experience that brings us to the edge of the known or the edge of chaos. This is characterized by three things: an intensification of ordinariness, religious potential, and a sharpening of alterity.[69] All three of these characteristics can be illustrated by the music of worship, which consists of notes and words found in everyday contexts yet in liturgy are patterned for a specifically religious gathering; in this context they can give a glimpse of the "bright mystery" by which our lives are surrounded.[70]

The insights provided by Driver, DeNora, and Hughes suggest that music, ritual, and worship share a great deal of common ground in that they (1) help to shape self-identity, (2) assist in the organization of communal life, and (3) allow humans to experience alternate states of being. These features exist in creative tension with one another and with other elements of human experience. For example, individual self-identity and expressions of communal life have an impact on each other; alternate states of being interact with our everyday lives. In his work on wonder, Robert C. Fuller observes: "Music, like abstract visual art, also affects the human nervous system without relying on human words or gestures. . . . Music communicates meanings that in some way refer to concepts, memories, or emotional states that exist independently of music itself."[71] An important element of these independent factors is the process of narrative emplotment: what sense-making stories are being told by those who are listening to music, engaging in ritual, and performing worship?[72] To follow Michel de Certeau, what is it that we as consumers are making of these experiences when we are consuming them?[73]

Concluding Reflections

We began this chapter by exploring two personal reflections on bereavement in the contemporary world and how they had influenced two songs by quite different artists: John Lydon and Madonna. We then noticed ways in which concertgoing and listening to music are evidently functioning as ritual for users of music. We argued that the attitudes and practices in evidence highlight significant changes to the role of religion in Western society and begin to provide evidence of where the (necessary) function of ritual has shifted. From this we explored further issues around the relationship between music and worship—in a broad sense of that word. Thus we have examined how (1) the category of religion has emerged within a secular public sphere, (2) a contemporary understanding of self has developed, and (3) worship is more than a "response of the creature to the Eternal" but has involved social, political, and economic factors as well. Thus we have argued that public expressions of faith and religion have been in a state of flux, particularly during the last five hundred years of Western culture. Against this background, perceptions of self (going back at least as far as Augustine) have also been changing and developing; during this same period Christian worship has been part of a process of negotiated identity for individuals, communities, and churches.[74] This wider social context provides the framework for examining how ritual, music, and worship share a good deal of common ground: they help consumers and communities develop a sense of their own identities and bring individuals and groups to an edge of wonder.

Once again this discussion can be charted on our Spectrum for mapping affective space (see chap. 2). Gilmore's study of ritual and spirituality at Burning Man provides a good example of how this works. If we place the festival participants at the center of the Spectrum, we can see them appropriating language and symbols from religious institutions. Despite the fact that to a large extent the content and symbols remain under the control of a magisterium, the participants are appropriating them for their own eclectic and personalized rituals. There is clear tension between the individual freedom people have to do this and the claims religious symbols arguably might make on them. Yet they *can* choose. Individual freedom is real. However, a couple of caveats should be added. First, Gilmore observes that there remains a disconnect between those creating these hybridized rituals and those accessing them. Although temples are created at Burning Man for spontaneous celebrations, they nevertheless demonstrate "the extent to which Burners will happily embrace an explicit ritual intention and even an explicit meaning, *so long as the purpose rests lightly upon itself and leaves lots of room for personal interpretations and expressions.*"[75] Second, even at this point on the Spectrum, there are important tribal distinctions to be made. There appear to be those at Burning Man who seek to make a distinction between its true adherents and those who belong to the disparagingly termed "Ibiza set."[76] It is precisely the same dynamic as Cavicchi found in a music setting, such as the tension between (true) Springsteen fans and "ordinary audience members." It becomes clear, then, that the notion of affective space works best (or perhaps only works at all) when the participant has a conscious level of commitment to the specific practice.

Without wishing to press the tribal distinction too far, we can see that ritualized actions remain part of human behavior for (1) those who are adherents to a faith tradition, (2) those who are spiritually inclined but not members of a religion in any formal way, and (3) those who have no faith commitment at all and yet might accept or attribute some form of religious implication to, or interpretation of, their own conduct. Rupert Till discusses how, as an observer of electronic dance music culture in the UK, he perceived many of the traits found there to have religious or shamanist parallels. Yet when he asked clubbers if there was a religious element to clubbing, they replied in the negative.[77] Like Gilmore at Burning Man in the USA, Till found that the negative connotations of institutions that have clearly defined magisteria meant that participants operated with a very narrow definition of religion, which often depended on the negative experience of religious institutions they had encountered. In due course we shall argue (in part 3) that moving beyond such restricted understandings of religion and ritual allows for a much more fruitful understanding of the encounter between faith, worship, and music. In spite of all religions' faults and specific religions' faults, there is no escaping the need for human life to be shaped by and for individuals and communities. Thus there is some explaining to be done about how and why religious beliefs and practices persist, and how and why humans constantly seem to need them in their societies. The shaping work needed is indeed human work. Yet it may inevitably have to include tapping into already-existing rhythms of nature and past human cultures. Whether such available rhythms and cultures (including religions), and the ways they are used, are true in any objective sense, or can be known to be true—all this may not be knowable. But that we must act *as if* our life-shaping rituals are true seems beyond dispute. It is why religions and religion-like practices become so important and also so potentially dangerous.

what's on your ipod?

Classics, Canons, and the Question of What Matters

If, even once, a person has experienced a text, a gesture, an image, an event, a person with the force of the recognition: "This is important! This does make and will demand a difference!" then one has experienced a candidate for classic status.

David Tracy, author[1]

If you stick to the canon, you are less likely to waste your time.

John Carey, author[2]

His songs are my bible.
A Bruce Springsteen fan[3]

Collecting Tracks, Defining Selves

You need only take a walk in a local park, pay attention to people's habits on buses or trains, or be aware of discussions about how people use their MP3 players to realize that technological advances are having a huge impact on how people listen to music and use it.[4] The MP3 player's appearance is, however, but the latest in a long line of developments that have increased people's capacity to listen to the music they want, whenever they want. From the invention of the phonograph in 1877, to the appearance of the gramophone and the ensuing struggle between the cylinder and the disc for the most accessible way to play recorded music, to the emergence of cheap mass-produced disc records in the middle of the twentieth century—the move toward listener autonomy has grown.[5]

The question of *what* a person might be listening to, though, introduces issues of market forces and patterns of consumption along with the recognition of increased listener autonomy. The growth of recorded music through computer downloads has been accompanied by the development of radio. Always interconnected with market-related issues in the sale and purchase of music, radio itself has been part of the technological shift as radios have become more portable. Unlike MP3 players, however, radio has a more limited playlist. Listeners exercise choice of music by deciding which station to tune in (be it easy listening, rock, pop, country, Christian, or whatever the main local station is playing). Radio listening makes it clearer that you are susceptible to market forces in what is made available to you. Your MP3 playlist has at least been constructed by you, yet here too you will surely (even if unwittingly) have been influenced by someone else's skillful marketing.

Yet music lovers *do* have a playlist. Whether or not it is on an MP3, takes the form of a CD collection, or is loaded onto our laptops, it is our favorite music. Our playlist is the music we want to come back to time and again. It is the music that, in our personal views, merits repeated listening. This may be because it is popular: everyone's listening to it just now, yet later we might delete it. It may be because it carries particular emotional resonance: it reminds us of someone, or a place, or a time in our lives, or when we heard it live. In the previous chapter we noticed just how important memory is for the narratives we create about our own lives, and the importance music can have in the remembering and in the construction of those narratives. Particular music may be on our playlist because the sound or the words move us. But our playlist is an important stock of material with which we interact, engaging in a practice that is meaningful to us: our playlist manages our mood, gives us pleasure, or passes the time while we run, walk, jog, or drive.

Yet we must ask why a piece of music *remains* in someone's collection. We might get rid of some pieces after a while, even after paying to download them. We may be bored by them and decide that they do not merit *that many* repeated listenings. No one else may be listening to the tracks anymore, and we do not want to appear to be out of touch. But the reasons selected music remains significant for us open up a range of important issues and questions. Along with the fact that we might just like it, we keep on listening to a particular track or piece of music because it is part of our story. Because there is emotional resonance, or because it moves us, it has become part of our life story. The image of "soundtrack" may be overused, but it is still accurate: the playlists we create are the soundtracks of our own personal lives.[6] The construction of a playlist thus contributes to, and is an expression of, the identities we have found or made for ourselves. Whatever rituals we participate in, and whatever form our fandom might take, our own personal playlists have been shaped by some means and relate to the stories we tell of ourselves.

Here are some examples from our own music survey. One female respondent said that music is "a soundtrack to life to reflect or oppose your reality. An audible expression of mental state."[7] A male respondent commented: "Music acts as a soundtrack to life. Certain songs have special meanings associated with certain times or moments in my life."[8] Another male respondent spoke of the cultural identity to which listening to music contributes.[9] Others spoke of the way in which music is "woven into my life" or of the way in which "my life is grounded in music."[10]

It is easy to overestimate the extent to which we can shape our identities, for we are very much a product of what we are given through our upbringing, and through the cultures we have been part of without our choosing. Yet we also maintain some say in who we become. Whether the self can be quite as freely constructed as individualist readings of the Magisteria-Ibiza Spectrum (chap. 2) suggest—those who deem that we really can occupy the right-hand end of the Spectrum, with little input from the left—and as questioned in chapter 7, understandings of the self have certainly become more fluid. Moving beyond the fixed self of modernity, according to which there is an essence of the self to be *discovered*, much postmodern Western culture implies that a self can indeed be *constructed*. For those to whom music is at all significant, then, music is part of the self-shaping process and a means of discovering and expressing who we believe ourselves to be. In a clear sense, we *are* our playlists.

Compiling Playlists, Encountering Classics

How, though, have we constructed our playlists? In large measure, a playlist is chosen, though also, in part, suggested and sold to us. Particular music may have come into our collections and remain there, yet not simply because of market forces. It may be there because it has achieved classic status. By "classic" we do not mean classical. Much classical music is classic, though not all. Not even all works by Bach and Mozart may be considered classics. After all, they had weekly worship commitments to meet (Bach), money to raise and commissions to fill (Mozart). They had off days. Not all classics are equally classical. By "classic" we mean "has proved itself over time as worthy of repeated listening, because it keeps on being moving, informative, inspiring." If it were a literary text, then we would say it "keeps on generating new meaning." In other words, the range of interesting interpretations a text is capable of producing seems inexhaustible, even while it is not tenable to make a text mean simply what you want it to mean. A text places constraints on the possible range of meanings even if no single meaning may exhaust its potential. When speaking of music, the parallel is not perfect: what are "meanings" in music?[11] It is not always as easy as it is with written texts to point to multiple interpretations. Yet music of all sorts surely speaks to, and finds a response from, many different people, even if its hearers may not always be able to articulate what it is doing to and for them. And if particular pieces keep on moving, inspiring, stimulating, and proving meaningful for us, then they may well deserve to be called classics.

Let us consider some examples. The Beatles song "Yesterday" is probably the most recorded song in modern music history. Its origins are documented and much reported.[12] As a tune, it appeared in Paul McCartney's head some time in 1965. He woke up one morning and simply went to play it. Concerned that he might have heard it elsewhere, he spent some time checking with others on whether he was mistaken in thinking it was a new tune, but he could find no one who knew it. The words came later. As a successful fusion of music and words, however, the results have been clear ever since: it is moving, enjoyable, and useful. As Steve Turner comments: "All the listener needs to know is that it's about someone wanting to turn the clock back, to retreat to a time before a tragic event. The application is universal."[13] Listeners cannot justifiably attach just *any* meaning to the song. But the song can undoubtedly function as a means through which they can articulate or deal with a sense of regret. "Let It Be," the final song to be released as a single during The Beatles' life as a band, also has a specific point of origin.[14] Written at a low point in Paul McCartney's own life, as the breakup of the band was imminent, it articulated his cry for help. Using the ambiguity created by reference to his being visited by his (long-deceased) "mother Mary" and by the hymnlike musical form, he has made it possible for any listener to use the song when needing comfort at a time of isolation or despair. The beauty of both songs and the flexibility of their function make them classics.

"Classic," though, is admittedly an overused word. Thus DJs may sometimes call a recently released piece of music "a classic." Strictly speaking, this is a misuse of the term. It should not be possible to call a newly released track a classic because it has not had *time* to prove itself.[15] A classic needs time, and it needs a proven audience—a group of people who agree that a piece of music merits revisiting again and again. But how does this work? How does a piece of music attain the status of a classic? Is it simply a case of lots of fans agreeing, over time, that a song is great? Is it about music *critics'* agreeing that a piece of music is well structured, well written, well sung, or marks a new departure in the world of music? In truth, the latter is more likely to determine whether a piece of music is *called* a classic. But as Detweiler and Taylor observe in *A Matrix of Meanings*, the power of technology and the expansion of a more democratic voice in popular culture mean that it is no longer the experts alone who determine what counts.[16]

We are making no claims that our own CD collections or MP3 playlists are composed only of classics. Yet even so, we suggest, the notion of what is classic music and what is not comes into play if we are to address adequately the question of how music is currently functioning in the contemporary West. We were talking to someone who expressed interest in this book, is a regular attender of music festivals, and spoke of her own enthusiasm for both live and recorded music. As she described what is on her iPod, she began talking of her favorites and also speaking of what "should" be there and what she knew she "should have" listened to by now. She had picked up a sense that there is a "canon" of music—even a canon of "popular music"—to which people are expected to listen. In other words, whether we know it or not, we are influenced not just by commercial concerns. We do not *just* listen to music that marketing departments want to sell us. We listen to music also because it has established its worth, usefulness, or fame in some way, however we have had that worth communicated to us. We listen to it because someone else has deemed it important.[17]

There is a sense, then, in which our MP3 playlist or CD collection is our own personal canon of music. This soundtrack of our own life is also our own authoritative list of pieces of music that mean the most to us, have shaped us, keep us happy, inspire us, make us think, remind us of our beliefs and values, turn us on, make us move, move us. We can call it a canon, though there is a more precise understanding of the concept of "canon" that we also need to consider in order to see how talk of a "personal canon" is understandable but not wholly appropriate.

From Classics to Canons

One meaning of "canon" is "list."[18] It can also mean "measuring rod." The term is used in religion, literature, and music to denote an authoritative collection of texts or works that demand attention and function as a norm against which other texts can be measured. In the case of religion, a canon of material usually functions in the form of a set of scriptures (key writings) that become influential upon followers of a specific tradition because of the authority that canonical texts carry.[19] In Judaism and Christianity, for example, the Hebrew Bible and the Christian Bible (Old and New Testaments, in Protestant and Roman Catholic forms) are canons of Scripture that function in this way. In English literature there have been lively discussions for decades about what constitutes the literary canon: texts that any self-respecting educated person in the West should read. Harold Bloom presents perhaps the boldest case for such a list, though he has his critics too. His list is long, and he clearly likes Shakespeare![20]

Bloom's selection of material is focused primarily on aesthetic criteria: what makes for good literature? He explicitly opposes any attempt to commend texts on political or moral grounds.[21] Whatever is made of his selection and the debate surrounding his choices, the *process* of recognizing a proven set of resources that are worth returning to, that are then fenced off and commended to ensuing generations, is clearly something that human communities do. We need to know what is worth spending time on—even amid our enjoyment and as we make use of our leisure time. But what does this have to do with MP3 playlists and CD collections? Do we not listen to music for sheer pleasure? If we try to bring into consideration of our music-listening habits these rather weighty reflections on the value of literature and of religious texts, do we not overburden our listening? From all the chapters in part 2, though, it should be clear by now that even while we may indeed listen for pleasure, much else is reflected in our listening habits.

Considering canons in relation to music is important for three reasons. First, there are various suggestions for what musical canons themselves contain. Appendix 3 to Roy Shuker's *Understanding Popular Music Culture* contains an "album canon."[22] The list of thirty albums is adapted from a sociological and aesthetic study of the most influential popular music albums.[23] The study from which Shuker adapted his list recognizes that musical criteria are never the only factors at work. Yet music takes its rightful place alongside literature and religion here. It provides auditory material that commands our attention, and our discussions about what is worth listening to are a crucial feature of our culture.

Second, we must recognize that even in the case of literary canons, more than merely literary factors are at work. In making allowances for sociocultural and class factors in any suggested list, canons exist in part to give people guidance on how to live. In effect, the existence of literary canons—despite what Bloom suggests—does imply, "Read these texts, study them and play off against them, and you'll be a better person for it." Carey notes this, if somewhat obliquely: "Literature does not make you a better person, though it may help you to criticize what you are. But it enlarges your mind, and it gives you thoughts, words and rhythms that will last you for life."[24] Similarly we can say: "Listening to popular music may not make you a better person. But it will stretch your sense experiences, bring you into the company of others who think similarly or differently, tease your emotions, confront you with much of what life is about (often at the extreme ends of human experience), and give you something to think about." There is, therefore, a moral dimension to any process of canon building. This may sit uneasily with the notion of reading for pleasure (and thus, in turn, with listening to music for pleasure), but the moral aspect is there.

Third, canons relate to communities. This is prominent in the case of religious texts, which function canonically, as scripture, for specific communities (historical, local, and global). At their most extreme, religions seek to form communities that are detached from the rest of life, living according to a canon of texts that most of society ignores. Even in post-Christian times, however, Bibles and other scriptures are not wholly neglected, and in practice it is hard to ensure that scriptures are read in isolation, other texts disregarded, and communities formed that enable such detached reading to occur. We suggest that musical canons also relate to communities, even if less tangibly than in religious communities. In the case of popular music, canons relate to fan bases. Whether those fan bases are virtual (all listeners out there, fan clubs, or online fan communities) or real (gathered communities of fans at concerts or festivals), there is a body of people who enjoy, are stimulated by, and expect to benefit from their engagement with their chosen artist's body of work.

We are suggesting, then, that it is worth pursuing the number of ways in which canons of musical material function. While people do have their own personal music collections, which are highly individual, these inevitably interconnect at some point with more publicly accepted lists of what is deemed worth listening to. These lists exist not simply according to musical criteria, but they also carry other freight—things to do with ethics, politics, class, religion, philosophy. What is more, how these lists exist and are used relates to the communities to which a listener belongs (be this groups of friends or fans). In the case of fans, the devotion with which one may follow a particular performer or band may lead to intense engagement with a particular set of "texts" (i.e., piece of music). The regular engagement with such material, and the pleasure in revisiting and reinterpreting such texts through persistent enjoyment of them, makes one a committed community member.

Music fans thus are like religious believers insofar as they are devoted to their favorite band or performer, they constantly engage with their favorite music, and they may even idolize the performers. Such a point has often been made.[25] But we are saying something more and something slightly different. Whether or not we call such music-listening behavior religious, the actual function of the practice of listening attaches significance to the music and to the practice for the listener on a number of levels. Interpreting such practice in the light of attention to canons and communities is informative even if the religion-likeness of the practice is denied.[26]

Classics, Canons, and Communities of Listeners

How, then, do canons work for those who use them? Different parts of a canon have different functions. The canon of English literature suggested by Bloom, for example, contains tragedy and comedy. Different types of literature teach and provoke discussion about different issues and prove useful at different times. The Christian canon of Scripture contains historical narratives, hymns (psalms), books of pithy statements and erotic poetry (Wisdom literature such as Proverbs, Ecclesiastes, the Song of Songs), collections of prophetic speeches, life stories (Gospels), and letters. Such diverse texts cannot all do the same work. People need and use them at different times, to address different challenges and contexts. Music is no different. People draw on a canon of music—be it personal or critically agreed upon—for a variety of purposes, in diverse circumstances. At one moment it may be to manage mood ("I need soft music to calm me down," "I'm playing loud music because I'm enraged").[27] On another day one may want to be encouraged to laugh, to receive reinforcement for a view one holds (Dylan's "You Masters of War"), to seek a peak experience of some kind ("There's a lady who's sure, all that glitters is gold"),[28] or to enjoy physically the experience of singing along to The Beatles' song ("Na Na Na Na-na-na-Na, Na-na-na-Na, Hey Jude").

Such an approach to a musical canon is challenged by reference to other fields in which canons function. Such an individual approach to a canon implies that one is always in control of the music one chooses, and that there is always conscious intent in listening to a particular piece of music. Yet such intention may not always be clear.[29] Furthermore, just putting something on—and even more so, having an MP3 permanently set on shuffle mode—serves as a potent reminder that often we simply listen. Being addressed by one's music collection, though, has strong similarities to being confronted by the contents of a literary or musical canon. Admittedly, in a personal collection all the music has been chosen to begin with. Even so, as we have seen, some music will be there "because it should be there." So even in the most personal of collections, there can still be elements of surprise and challenge. The music may "speak" in the form of a song frequently listened to yet now offering something fresh, or through a song hidden on an album we chose to download and now presented by the MP3 player. How canons work is well demonstrated by such happenstances.[30]

Again, an example will make this clear. Bob Dylan is known as much for his sheer longevity as for his music. As we write, he is still on the Never Ending Tour in his early seventies. But it is not simply his age or the length of time his music has been around that have kept him famous and musically well respected. Nor indeed is it his voice or ability as an instrumentalist, both of which have received criticism. It is not merely that he has written many memorable songs, songs that have been covered and recorded by many other artists across five decades. His contribution to modern music, and his rightful place in any popular music canon, is because he has written a great many songs that have proved evocative, provocative, and inspirational in many ways to a great many people. Beyond any technical deficiencies in the performance of his own songs, he has created a body of work that as a whole resonates with, informs, and stimulates a great many listeners, even those who may not call themselves fans.[31]

Hence many popular-music fans may load up a great many albums, or have a shelf of Dylan CDs in their collection, for the sake of owning a few particular songs ("Blowing in the Wind," "Mr. Tambourine Man," "Forever Young"). Yet when listening to them, others rear up and challenge them. "Maggie's Farm" addresses the issue of exploitation at work, a theme that reappears on much more recent work by Dylan ("Workingman's Blues #2," on *Modern Times*). "Not Dark Yet" is one of a number of tracks released by Dylan since the 1990s and articulates his awareness of his own mortality and the approach of death. "Like a Rolling Stone" carries an impact and draws a listener into self-expressiveness despite Dylan's drawl, even when the lyrics may be unclear. Its sneery protest and the way it digs the listener in the gut both operate beyond lyrics.

To have a range of Dylan albums in a collection, in other words, does more than feed a fan's interest or simply entertain. It confronts a listener with a range of topics to reflect on, stories to hear, issues to debate, and emotions to feel. The novelist Nick Hornby's humorous account of how he built up his own collection is worth quoting:

> I'm not a big Dylan fan. I've got *Blonde on Blonde* and *Highway 61 Revisited*, obviously. And *Bringing It All Back Home* and *Blood on the Tracks*. Anyone who likes music owns those four. And I'm interested enough to have bought *The Bootleg Series Volumes 1–3*, and that live album we now know wasn't recorded at the Royal Albert Hall. The reviews of *Time Out of Mind* and *Love and Theft* convinced me to shell out for these two, as well, although I can't say I listen to them very often. I once asked for *Biograph* as a birthday present, so with that and *The Bootleg Series* I've got two Dylan boxed sets. I also, now [that] I look, seem to own copies of *World Gone Wrong*, *The Basement Tapes* and *Good as I Been to You*, although this, I suspect, is due more to my respect for Greil Marcus, who has written so persuasively and brilliantly about Dylan's folk and blues roots, than to my Dylanphilia. And I have somehow picked up along the way *Street Legal*, *Desire* and *John Wesley Harding*. Oh, and I bought *Oh Mercy* because it contains the lovely "Most of the Time," which is on the *High Fidelity* soundtrack. There are, therefore, around twenty separate Bob Dylan CDs on my shelf; in fact I own more recordings by Dylan than by any other artist.[32]

Hornby's narration of the way he built his Dylan collection offers evidence of the way in which a music fan feels he "ought" to have certain things in his collection. We are suggesting that once such a collection is gathered, it functions for a listener in many different ways, yet contributes to a person's development by its range of songs that support, challenge, and move, even while entertaining. The notion of a person's collection containing only "things I like" is therefore misleading. When it is recognized that the proven impact of pieces of music is what makes them classics and canonical, then for listeners they can function politically and ethically, as well as musically and aesthetically.

The popular music canon thus challenges listeners on the basis that a long and dispersed community of listeners (including informed critics within it) has determined "you should listen to this." In practice, of course, we rarely listen to a piece of music in order to be taught to think or to be preached at. But the art of the musician may be to provoke all those things even while a listener wants to listen for pleasure. So when we talk of "respecting the canon"—be that of music, literature, or religion—we open ourselves to the influence of others' wisdom. In musical terms this may prove to be demanding. Often Dylan is not comfortable listening (even for fans). But the existence of a canon of popular music, however disputed and open-ended it will always remain, provides listeners with a standard, authoritative playlist with which to experiment and by which to be challenged. The accepted wisdom of a community of listeners past and present suggests that such music is ethically, emotionally, philosophically, musically, and spiritually rewarding.

Four Hallmarks of Devotion

Fans can be intense. The reason for fan devotion to an artist is because they have formed an affective alliance with a band or singer.[33] This means that listeners are connected with an artist in such a way that they expect to gain something from the practice of listening or experiencing a performance. They invest emotional energy and devote time to the practice of listening because of their attachment. It is not our purpose here to critique this practice. At times it may be an unhealthy form of attachment,[34] so we do not suggest that it is always positive. For our immediate purposes we simply recognize that any emotional bond formed can be a feature of the intensity with which fans listen to music. We note *intensity* as the first of what we are calling "four hallmarks of devotion." The potential of "devotion" as a term linking music listening with religious practice results from the level of involvement and commitment that fans often demonstrate.[35]

A second hallmark of devotion is the *meditative* element that can occur in the practice of listening. Clearly, this does not occur equally with all types of music. Heavy metal is not the most obviously meditative form. That said, technological developments in the practice of listening to music—especially the Walkman and the MP3 player—have increased the extent to which music listening can be an intensely private practice, stimulating inner work.[36] People can be lost in their music.[37] One possible definition of meditation is "thinking about things, whether the emphasis is on intellectual rigor, acuteness of perception, or devotional fervour."[38] We must free ourselves from understanding meditation within a narrow frame of reference, such as requiring set body postures and always being accompanied by gentle music.[39] Many forms of music can foster meditative listening.

Third, in this chapter we have noticed the importance of a repetitive element in the listening process. When allied to the proven significance of classic (even canonical) material, *repeated listening* is formative. At its most basic, repeated listening is a form of mood management. But when linked with fandom, it can function ritualistically. A person returns to bands and tracks that have proved their worth in order to recapture a particular meaning or to reinforce a sensibility or opinion.

A fourth hallmark of devotion is the *authority* that one ascribes to the object of one's devotion. It may seem surprising for us to introduce this theme, yet

"Dance in the Dark" by Lady Gaga

In an apparently surreal moment one accountancy website asks readers to imagine that the Archbishop of Canterbury and Lady Gaga find themselves seated next to one another at a dinner party. What common ground can they possibly have to talk about? The answer is that they are both figureheads of markets perceived to be in terminal decline but are actually growing in terms of revenue. While fewer people are buying gig tickets these days, each person is paying several times what they were a few years ago for that ticket—well over inflation. Likewise, the archbishop's flock is diminishing, but each member is putting more coins in the collection plate each Sunday.[40] While this financial similarity between religion and pop is both suprising and interesting, it is not the deeper affective alliance that the makers and consumers of popular music are seeking.

A good example of a more devotional connection can be found in Lady Gaga's track "Dance in the Dark" from *The Fame Monster* album (2009). At one level the song is about a woman's concern for her body and her self-esteem[41] and in that respect it is seeking an affirmative alliance with many women (and perhaps not a few men?) who have such anxieties. The lyrics reference a litany of females who died tragically: Marilyn Monroe, Judy Garland, Sylvia Plath, JonBenet Ramsey, Princess Diana. Given that Lady Gaga's birth name is Stefani Germanotta and that she comes from an Italian-American, Roman Catholic background—not unlike that other US female, pop icon Madonna—it is possible to see this list being modeled on a roll call of saints and martyrs. In an ambiguous line she sings of finding Jesus or Kubrick in the music—a reference to American movie director Stanley Kubrick, who spent much of his life in England living as an outsider, a recluse with an unorthodox view of God. Lady Gaga's contrast between Kubrick and Jesus is significant. She suggests an affirmative alliance between herself and her fans with Jesus and Stanley Kubrick as outsiders in their cultures who wrestled with some of life's key questions and issues, just as some of her songs also engage such themes.

it is undoubtedly present in the way music functions for listeners. Canons are authoritative lists. If one pays heed to the accepted musical canons in any sense, then an authoritative voice ("this is worth listening to") is being respected. The notion of having a personal canon merely indicates that favorite tracks are being treated as especially valuable. We will say more about the role of authority in listening to popular music since so much popular music (especially forms of rock music) are antiauthority, or at least antiauthoritarian. For the moment we simply identify that value judgments are made within the practice of listening. People may know what they like and store favorite music on their iPods. But more is at stake in the way choices are made about what music is listened to (and why) and therefore in the functions that listening carries. Furthermore, here at the end of part 2 of this book, after looking at many different dimensions of the practice of listening to popular music, we focus on the way in which the individual choices made about music (as expressing personal freedom) meet with the way in which authoritative voices nevertheless contribute to our act of choosing. There is no better way of illustrating how sections A and B of the Maigisteria-Ibiza Spectrum (chap. 2) stand in tension yet also in close relationship with sections C and D.

There must surely be a point at which this parallel (which is more than a mere parallel) between music, literature, and religion—according to which a canon functions authoritatively—breaks down. Music and musicians, while they might engender a passionate following, are not in themselves religions. What is more, there is no single worldview or philosophy that can be distilled from music per se. As a phenomenon, music is so incredibly diverse. How can a Latin American rumba, an Indian bhangra, a Rolling Stones song, a Beethoven sonata, a Schoenberg opera, a sung psalm, a bluegrass instrumental, and a track by the Carpenters be reduced to a single philosophical foundation or background? And that is without even considering the influence of the social contexts within which such different pieces of music might be heard.

They cannot, of course, be reduced in this way, even if appeal is made to spirituality as a universal human phenomenon, claiming that all humans have a spiritual dimension. Even if music is a channel through which such a spiritual dimension is discovered and developed, the cultural specificity of both music and its reception needs to be addressed. We shall address this question directly in part 3 as we consider how Western popular music and Christianity may or may not interact fruitfully.

part 3

pop music
and theology

the discipline
of listening

How (and Why) What We're Doing
with Music Matters Ultimately

There is an intense inwardness about true religion, and in this it overlaps with
the current fashion for spirituality.

Richard Harries[1]

In part 1, we sketched the context in which this work is offered to the field
of theology/religion and popular culture, and we summarized a theoretical
framework (the Magisteria-Ibiza Spectrum) within which the consumption of
popular music may be understood. We also explored different ways in which
arts and culture have been handled recently within Christian theology, even if
not always directly with regard to popular music. In part 2, we drew together
a range of findings about how popular music works and what it is doing to and
for people. We used studies drawn from many different academic disciplines
in addition to drawing upon the data of our own survey of music fans. Unlike
many studies in popular culture (in music, media, or cultural studies), we
kept religious studies alive as one of the disciplinary lenses through which the
phenomenon of music use can be examined. Our concern was not simply to
offer a religious or theological reading of what we encountered. Insofar as it is
possible, we sought to respond to how music is actually being listened to and

to note the functions that music has. We wanted to "let the music speak for itself," while knowing that such a phrase can imply neutrality on the listener's part or in academic study of listening patterns, neutrality that is simply not tenable. In other words, we are fully aware that music fans, religious believers, and academics all have interests, and that as authors we are in all three groups.[2] Throughout our investigation we also identified points at which religious matters surfaced anyway (such as in the alliance between the selling of music and religious practice, or in the lives of musicians reacting to their religious pasts at significant times of their lives).

Our purpose now is to return to the specific disciplinary and committed interests of the world of theology/religion and popular culture within which this work is situated. Given the material presented in part 2, what shall we make of contemporary use of popular music in relation to the ways in which people make meaning? What part (if any) do religions, and Christianity particularly, play in understanding such meaning-making? And if the answers are that there is no real link, and religions contribute little, then where does this leave religions and theology in the West today, given the seeming ubiquity of popular culture and popular music?

We divide this concluding part of the book into three chapters and one brief postscript. In this chapter we look at the significance of the *practices* of listening. In chapters 10 and 11 we look at the *content* of what is listened to and ask how this can be processed in the life experience and thinking of the listener. Finally, in the postscript, we assess what this means for a range of educational contexts.

In a theological project such as this, we must first establish that such "listening to listening" is worth doing at all. We must, in other words, show that what we do in the next two chapters amounts to more, say, than just picking up (preprogrammed) insights from chapter 3 in the light of chapters 4 through 8. We need to show how the approach we set out in chapters 1 and 2 can be balanced by a *theological* method that will take serious account of the findings presented in part 2. Rather than just taking chapters 4 through 8 as illustrations of theological views already held, how are we to know that "listening to popular music" can or even should have something substantive to offer theology today? And if it is to contribute something, how does it do that?

A "Theology of Engagement" for Popular Music

In chapter 3, we drew on the work of David Brown, Tom Beaudoin, and James K. A. Smith in seeking to orient ourselves theologically within the terrain we are exploring. In chapter 11, we shall return to the substantive issues they have raised. While introducing their work, we admitted that we needed the help of others when seeking a methodology for reading popular culture (and thus popular music). In this chapter we pick up the issue of theological method.

In his 2003 work *A Theology of Engagement*, Ian S. Markham has mapped out a framework within which our current undertaking is best understood as a *theological* method.[3] Markham's is an important and yet undervalued study, taking the unfashionable risk of questioning conservative and liberal alike, and positioning his approach at odds with the much-debated Radically Orthodox approach to theology.[4] Although we think that he limits the range of necessary dialogues required by his approach, we wholeheartedly applaud his undertaking and make practical use of it here.

Markham's basic thesis is that good theology—Christian or otherwise—must recognize the way in which it constantly interacts with, and receives material from, sources beyond its own tradition. He works from within the Christian tradition, and hence his interest is especially to demonstrate to Christian theologians how a "theology of engagement" works (and has always worked throughout Christian history). As a way of doing theology, however, his approach need not be seen as a Christian methodology alone. The attention Markham pays to religious traditions other than Christianity, and to the interactions between religions, highlights the degree to which his work must not be seen as simply a Christian project.

The theology of engagement that Markham expounds comprises three dimensions: assimilation, resistance, and overhearing. By "assimilation," Markham means

> the *constructive use* of a category or, more often, a set of categories, *from a non-Christian source*. . . . ["Resistance" is] when a theologian decides that *a certain approach*, albeit tempting for various cultural reasons, should be rejected as *incompatible* with the heart of the Christian revelation. . . . [Finally,] overhearing comes into play when a theologian finds *significant illumination* from the arguments and positions of theologians within another religious tradition.[5]

These are valuable perceptions with respect to how theology actually works, whatever theoretical models may exist that try to play down the influence of sources outside of a tradition in shaping a religious tradition. We do, though, notice significant limitations about the usefulness of these three dimensions for our project.

First, Markham's primary concern is with philosophy and ethics. This means that his analysis of examples of engagement past and present, even though very practical at times (e.g., with respect to human rights),[6] remains highly conceptual and restricted in its range. Second, there is no place in his study for explicit engagement with the arts or popular culture. This is especially puzzling given that his method would inform the discussions that have gone on for some time about the arts/culture and theology/religion. Third, despite the "open orthodoxy" of the theology of engagement espoused, and the recognition that theology must continually "relocate" itself to do its work, Markham still feels the need to support a church-centeredness in his approach. We shall return to the third point in due course. But for the moment, we can rectify the limited reach of Markham's project as evidenced in our first two observations by looking at each of the three dimensions—assimilation, resistance, and overhearing—with respect to popular music.

Assimilation

"Assimilation" need not mean a fully worked-out set of categories with which theology must engage in order to be deeply influenced. In the case of popular music, two examples can be cited. One idea that comes from much popular music is the continuous insistence on the importance of embodiment, as reflected in dancing and an emphasis on sexuality; this may be seen as a mere reminder of incarnation. It could equally be taken as a challenge (a greater challenge than theologians are often willing to acknowledge) to how Christian theology does justice to what the embodiment of God means, and how that embodiment affects human thinking and behavior.[7] Some might argue that Christianity has exhibited a fear of sexuality that is reflected in its current uneven and often shoddy handling of the complexities of human relationships. However, the relationship of the body to faith has always been hugely complex, and we can see this in the Hebrew Scriptures,[8] the New Testament,[9] medieval Christianity,[10] and contemporary theology.[11] As Bryan Turner has observed: "The body has many meanings within human practice, and can be conceptualized within a variety of dimensions and frameworks. . . . There appears to be an intimate connection between the exterior order of the socio-political world and the equilibrium of the human body, so that instabilities within the body are thought to reflect instabilities within the wider social system."[12] The variety of embodied religious and social frameworks that Turner identifies is also reflected in the extent to which Western citizens turn to a wide range of resources in arts and popular culture, including music, in order to do their feeling and thinking about such important topics.[13]

A second challenge of assimilation from the world of music is that of the wordlessness of an experience of transcendence or a deity. In a striking passage from Tia DeNora's *Music in Everyday Life*, she recognizes the way in which music "provides . . . a 'ground of being.'"[14] The theological resonance of this term with the way in which twentieth-century German-American Lutheran theologian Paul Tillich chose to speak of God (as "Ground of Being") is clear.[15] Tillich used the term in order to be unconstrained by any particular linguistic usage in trying to grasp something of God as experienced reality, as opposed to word or concept. In the case of music—even popular music[16]—we observe the way particular music, or the listener's response to music, evokes in a person a sense of connectedness to the divine source of all existence. What is being assimilated here may again be construed as a reminder of reality over linguistic constructions, of the fact that no thinker or tradition really knows how to speak of God wholly adequately. But even if so, the power of the reminder is needed lest too much be claimed for what is or can be known about God. God may no more be a sound or a feeling than a verb.[17] But it is vital, in order to maintain the primacy of attention to God as reality in all theological thought and practice, that ways are found to maintain an emphasis on divine being and action, which is superior to human language and construction about God.

Resistance

This is not, however, to say that anything and everything that people believe or think about God is acceptable, or that any and every form of artistic or cultural life might be conducive to the development of theological ideas and beliefs. This is where "resistance" must be seen as a crucial aspect of a theology of engagement. We can use one of the previous examples in a different way here. In the process of (potentially positively) enabling listeners to begin to appreciate their bodies and explore their sexuality, popular music can also sell people woefully short when it comes to understanding human love and fulfilling relationships. It can actively distort the development of positive, healthy feeling and thinking. As musician Frank Zappa, not known first and foremost as a theologian, has rightly said: "Romantic love songs are a sham that perpetuate a lie on unsuspecting young kids. . . . I think one of the causes of bad mental health in the United States is that people have been raised on 'love lyrics.'"[18] Zappa's comment is not ultimately supported in Levitin's discussion, given the latter's positive affirmation of love songs. But the quip remains telling and important: a vital aspect of human life can be easily cheapened as it is handled in popular culture. If popular songs are used at all in assisting theology in its task of exploring the meaning of love (human and/or divine), then the need for critique is essential. The point was brought home to us starkly when one of the respondents to our music survey listed as his favorite song of all time Lil Wayne's "Every Girl," a rap song with explicitly sexual lyrics.[19] The problem is less the explicit lyrics than the sentiments expressed (e.g., "I wish I could f—k every girl in the world"). It is an isolated example, but the thought of a regular diet of such lyrics would not, we suggest, easily be offset by whatever impact the music might have in terms of affirming body consciousness or the development of positive, mutually supportive relationships. If Christian opposition to such music at local churches and through national campaigns is sometimes too strident, too hasty, and unreflective, it is nevertheless understandable.

Here is a further, quite different example of where resistance might be necessary: the potential for the practice of music consumption to be so highly individualistic an exercise that any sense of the social dimension of what it means to be human is underplayed. Rather than being qualified by the social aspect of fandom, the experience of concertgoing, or even a sense of "being part of something bigger" through the phenomenon of listening to music on the radio, listening might be so intensely private for a person that the wider world disappears from view. Here, then, it is less an issue of lyrics per se (though the impact of private listening might be extended still further by particular choices of songs about individual freedom) and more about practice.

In a theology of engagement, it may appear strange to suggest that the significance of such privatized listening might be resisted. After all, is this not the same, in formal terms, as private religious devotion? Could it not be like the mystic who enjoys a direct relation to the divine without the mediation of religious institutions? And are the arts not about personal development, self-expression, self-discovery, and testing what constitutes appropriate and inappropriate forms of assertiveness? This is all true. But at the same time it must be recalled that religion is always both a public and a private phenomenon: even mystics do not have experiences outside of a tradition. In unpacking what goes on in the affective space where music is listened to attentively, then, we need to, based on theological grounds, resist a tendency to let the practice of listening be interpreted solely on the basis of what occurs on the right side of the Magisteria-Ibiza Spectrum. Theology, like all forms of wisdom, needs a tradition to work within, and that means drawing on what happens on the left side of the Spectrum.[20]

Overhearing

There is, however, a third dimension to Markham's theology of engagement that is less stark than the positive appropriation of material implied by assimilation or the rejection of ideas and beliefs as acknowledged in resistance. It is the practice of "overhearing." In many ways, all of part 2 is an exercise in "overhearing." We have been listening to what is going on in the world of popular music, hoping and expecting that through our eavesdropping we might be challenged to think in fresh ways about the Christian traditions we stand within, to be encouraged to have new thoughts and to notice what needs special emphasis now, even what might need to be dropped (either temporarily or for good) from Christian self-understanding and articulation. It is through such overhearing that assimilation or resistance is possible. Overhearing, then, is being open simply to what is there. In the case of popular music, unlike Markham, we are not listening just to philosophers and theologians. Our discipline of listening means that we listen to music by people of many faiths and no faith, sometimes by people indifferent or hostile to faith. But nevertheless music is there, shaping the world of Western citizens, people of faith and no faith, and filling the airwaves and the echoing spaces of shopping malls across the Western world. It is necessary to ask what our overhearing produces: do we find significant illumination in response to what we hear?

These are, then, the three aspects of a theology of engagement. Out of our experience of overhearing we shall (in this and the next chapter) assess what can be assimilated and what must be resisted as we look at what Christian theology learns from contemporary popular music and how it critiques such music. As we do this, we observe also (along with Markham) that the same theme or topic may be assimilated and resisted in different ways.[21] This has actually already occurred above in the examples given. We noticed that attention to embodiedness, sexuality, and the development of relationships in popular music can be considered in positive and negative ways.

The Theologian's Location

Where, though, is a theologian located in undertaking such overhearing? At this point we return to the third limitation we identified in Markham's approach. Markham observes:

> Rowan Williams writes, "I assume that the theologian is always beginning in the middle of things." By this he meant in the middle of a pre-existing community— i.e., the church—participating in the unconscious theological life as expressed in hymns and liturgy and facilitating clarification. Although this is undoubtedly true and important to remember, [that] theology always belongs to the church, I am suggesting [that] the theologian needs to be both in the middle and on the edge.[22]

> The theologian must be in the middle of the believing community. We are servants of the church. We should not delude ourselves: it is the church that is interested in theology, and we depend upon the church for our vocation. However, we must also be at the edge of that community, forcing that community to listen to the truth of God as it is in non-Christian traditions.[23]

We dispute none of what Markham says about the importance of the church for anyone undertaking Christian theology. Our dispute is about where the theologian must stand in order to overhear non-Christian resources. We are arguing that overhearing extends beyond philosophers, theologians, and ethicists. We are also arguing that because God may be discernible within the work and responses of those who are not even trying to be religious or theological, close listening and careful attention are needed, including from the perspective of those who participate in the world of popular music (as producers, performers, and listeners). To do this, theologians need not be just at the edge of the church, but in the middle of popular culture. We have no desire to be melodramatic or romantic about this; though the apostle Paul encouraged Christians to be "all things to all people" (1 Cor. 9:22), he did not mean using drugs illegally in order to get inside the drug culture associated with some forms of popular music.[24] Being in the middle of popular culture as well as in the church does not mean that the theologian can be or needs to be everywhere. But we are suggesting that the listening must be intense and genuine: it must take account of what performers and listeners want to say and do, and not just what we happen to (want to) hear. We sought to show the results of this intense listening in part 2, and throughout our study we want to take full account of producers/composers, performers, and listeners. As Markham himself says, "A theology of engagement is a perpetually relocating theology."[25] We agree. But theologians need to be more in the middle of public, popular culture in order to be better church theologians than Markham's approach appears to allow. It is this, we suggest, that constitutes an incarnational imperative.

In his introduction to the 2007 essay collection *Everyday Theology*, Kevin Vanhoozer remarks: "Four doctrines in particular have a special bearing on a theology of culture and, more specifically, on the issue of whether God reveals himself in and through popular culture: the incarnation, general revelation, common grace, and the *imago Dei*. Running through all four as a common theme is pneumatology."[26] Markham's theology of engagement is, we suggest, a practical unfolding of the theology for overhearing popular culture, with which we have been working. It is a deeply incarnational method. But it is conducted in search of the divine Spirit at work in the producers and receivers of all forms of popular culture, including music. It is now time to turn to the task of discerning further—to adapt Vanhoozer's framework—how God incarnate might be revealed and the image of God be evident in traces of common grace in popular music. We turn first to practice, and to the discipline of listening to what we have been overhearing, summarizing our findings about what music actually achieves.

Summarizing Seven Functions of Music

We must admit that music is not important to everyone. Strange though it is to music fans, there are people in the world who do not choose to listen to music, who just don't get it and are irritated by the extent to which music pervades daily life. Within music itself, fans of one type of music are puzzled by how fans of a different type can find music so meaningful. Rock fans may not understand classical music. Classical music fans may have little time for rap. But even if music as a phenomenon is not reducible in easy ways so that it is possible to say, "Music always does this or that," part 2 of this book has suggested how it can function in many key ways as an important life-enhancing practice. Even if music is only one form of cultural practice (and popular music a more limited form still), then it constitutes an example of what occurs in the affective space that, as we have suggested from the outset, all humans inhabit in some form as they make sense of life.

How, though, are those key ways to be understood? From our findings in part 2, we must first distill the main functions of popular music. There are seven in all.[27] First, music *orders and organizes time*. In the case of the popular music studied, it does this in many different ways. It is used by people at key points in a day (beginning or end, when making journeys to/from daily places of work or study). It thus marks the time on a daily, weekly, or other periodic basis. Fans who attend music concerts regularly may have their month (or year) marked out by attendance at concerts. Music also organizes time by accompanying people as they do other things (running, driving, cooking, cleaning, or doing other domestic chores). It not only makes tasks that may not immediately be pleasurable more bearable, even enjoyable; it also assists the pacing of such tasks.

Second, music *brings people together*. In part 2, we saw many ways in which music achieves this. It literally gathers people—for concerts or festivals. But music also connects people emotionally in the similar responses that fans may have to particular music or a specific artist. We saw an extension of these responses in how music creates virtual communities of many kinds (fan clubs, fan sites) that reflect this emotional connectedness.

Third, music *exercises the body*. The physicality of the experience of music listening was especially prominent in chapter 5. Dance and the physical aspects of singing benefit the body. The chemical stimulus of music's feel-good factor also contributes to the body's well-being.[28] Music's emotional function must be seen as directly related to the body's health.

Fourth, music *expresses values*. Such expression is clearly defined in the context of a public event (e.g., when a national anthem is used), at a religious service (e.g., words embodying a belief system, or instrumental music having a specific liturgical function at an appropriate point within the ritual), or for political purposes (e.g., at a protest, or at a party rally). The expression of values may be less clear in personal or more informal use of music. Yet it is not merely the lyrics of popular music that carry the values of those who use them. The *practice* of music use is itself wrapped up in the value systems that people espouse, through the alliances they make and the values systems they choose to inhabit or construct. For example, listeners may associate with particular artists because of their political stance, without necessarily finding the music the most enjoyable in their collection. An example of this is the protest that occurred in the UK at Christmas 2009 to encourage people to download Rage against the Machine's "Killing in the Name" to prevent X Factor winner, Joe McElderry, from having a Christmas No.1 hit. The way in which music expresses values may thus be much more about what occurs in the interplay between listener/consumer and artist/song than what is contained in either alone.

Fifth, music *enables participation*. At a number of points in part 2, we noticed the contagious element in music: music includes people, draws people in, even encourages them to do things they may at other times consider embarrassing or inappropriate. Karaoke is an extreme, popular form of such involvement. The "empty track" (no vocals) leaves the words to be filled in by the live singer, thus requiring participation. Similar and more structured participation occurs at sing-along showings of films (e.g., *The Sound of Music*, *Mamma Mia!*). Singing along happens, though, in plenty of other less embarrassing forms: at large-scale concerts (though rarely at classical choral events), at national celebrations, at political and sporting occasions, and at religious services. Here the focus is clearly on "a certain kind of solidarity and shared experience."[29]

Sixth, music provides a way of *channeling emotion*. In chapters 5 through 7, we noticed this in different ways. As Clarke, Dibben, and Pitts observe: "Music has long been recognized as a powerful means to elicit emotional responses, and as a channel for the sometimes unfocused and unarticulated emotions that people may feel in the face of shocking or bewildering situations."[30] This insight relates directly to the ritual aspect of popular music's use when we explored, in chapter 7, the powerful capacity of music to assist when shocking or bewildering situations must be dealt with. But as we have also acknowledged, this same capacity has a more everyday function in enabling listeners to respond to emotions being felt or to evoke desired emotions. "Mood management" is the term commonly applied to such a use of music. It may be too weak a term, given the range of emotions to which music can relate or that music can evoke. It may also too easily imply total control on the part of the listener, as if a person can always manage one's mood. In this regard we recognize that shocking or bewildering situations do arise that cannot be easily managed. The notion of channeling emotion is thus significant, especially when the use of music in formal settings is considered. Music can be a means of acknowledging which emotions are simply there and which cannot be changed, handled, or removed.

Finally, as a form of summary of the other six functions, music can be seen to *shape life* for those who are committed listeners. Insofar as it organizes time, has social functions (brings people together and encourages participation), contributes to bodily well-being, expresses values, and helps people address emotion, music is shaping their lives as a whole. When people allow music to do all of these things, and even actively use music in order to help them in these different ways, then the practice of listening has clearly become more than just listening. Yet what we are calling music's life-shaping function is not itself static. Throughout life, music may not be used in exactly the same way or with the same selections. When we acknowledge that music can have a life-shaping function through the many ways in which it works, then we also recognize that the ways in which it is used may change at different life stages. In the same way that musical fashions, fads, and enthusiasms may change, so also the extent to which people participate in music, or use it to express emotion or values, may occur in different degrees at different points in life. There is a world of difference between the emotional uses of music by a teenager, and the correlation between values and music that a middle-aged listener may be choosing to express and explore. Nevertheless, a life-shaping element is present in the practice of music use. We are certainly not claiming that all six functions of music already cited must all be present, even if in greater or lesser degrees, for this seventh, life-shaping function of music to be evident. We simply observe that because music has so many functions, many of which are usually very active for frequent music users, the scale and nature of music's significance command attention.

It could, however, be claimed that we are still operating only in the realms of sociology or psychology of music in making these observations. In using Clarke, Dibben, and Pitts's work as our starting point, we indicate that we have not yet begun to process the material of part 2 from a religious or theological perspective. Nothing we have yet said requires any kind of *religious* reading. Though we have cited religious ritual as possible examples of music's function, the truth or falsity of such social practices has not been at issue. Furthermore, no metaphysical assumptions are required to affirm what has been said so far. In the next section, then, we shall need to build on this formal sketch of what music achieves with more focused considerations of why and how it is worth reflecting critically on music's functions from a theological perspective. From here onward we shall seek to show, first in the practice of use and then with respect to music's content, why a theological reading of popular music consumption is necessary for healthy discussion of music's function in Western society.

Listening as Spiritual Practice

It would be a huge leap to move from the evidence and reflections gathered together in part 2 and the seven functions of music to a conclusion along the lines of declaring that listening to popular music is a form of religious devotion of today. We are not going to make the leap. It would be too simple and too forced. That said, there is too much evidence of music listening happening to deny its importance as a social, ethical, and political practice. Whether it be deemed definitively a philosophical or religious/theological practice too will depend on further factors and more extensive debate than can be entered into here. Music listening always will be in part religious for those who already are religious. It may be more philosophical and religious than people who are not religious recognize. But our purpose is not to win that argument conclusively. By looking at music listening through a religious/theological lens, we have the more modest goal of highlighting what we can understand about contemporary practice and what observations need to be made about its significance.

We argue that it is legitimate and necessary to conclude that listening to popular music can be viewed as a spiritual practice. By "spiritual practice" we mean a practice in and through which people actively work on their development of an inner life. People may do this with different levels of awareness. But as we shall show, the greater the conscious awareness of what people are doing with music, as fans, the more religion-like the practice becomes, and the more density the practice of listening takes on. We shall develop our case by examining three aspects of practice: intensification, fandom, and respect for the other/self-transcendence.

Intensification

For many years now, in the context of our dialogue with each other as friends and coauthors, we have referred to the concept of a "journey of intensification" with respect to music we have been listening to. By this we signaled to each other our being engaged in a sustained encounter with a particular musician's work. We might have been to a concert without much prior knowledge of a particular artist and then chosen to sample tracks from their back catalog. We might have prepared for a gig in a similar way. Or we might simply have had an artist recommended to us or stumbled across the musician on our own, someone we may or may not have liked but who seemed interesting.[31] In conducting our research about the way popular music is used, we have been able to identify this intensification as simply a normal aspect of fandom. Though for each of us the seriousness with which we have practiced our listening might well have been informed by our experience of being versed in religious devotion (i.e., we know what it means to engage in a sustained, focused practice), such listening is not in itself immediately religious in any other sense than the categories of "binding," "regular," or "committed." But it is a normal expression of sheer enthusiasm.

It is, however, striking that such intensity denotes a depth of engagement and an expectation that time devoted to the activity will be worthwhile. It is quality rather than quantity of listening that counts. As Cavicchi says of Springsteen fans, "Even though fans may not spend an inordinate amount of time listening to Springsteen, when they do listen, they tend to concentrate intensely on the music rather than use it as background."[32] Yet intense listening and serious engagement in music could indeed prove to be close to, if not identical with, what Graham Hughes refers to as "an intensification of ordinariness" with respect to the practice of worship,[33] as reflected in the title of David Brown's volume *God and Grace of Body: Sacrament in Ordinary*.[34] In noticing something that is an everyday practice for a music fan, yet which leads somewhere as it takes a person to a place of depth, we are seeing more fully what occurs in the affective space that a music fan inhabits. A fan is able to make a journey of intensification with great regularity, through familiarity with a particular artist or artists, through a discipline of listening, through simply knowing what to do and how to let oneself go into a song, whether singing along or just listening. What is produced is likely to be greater self-understanding. It can also produce deeper reflection on the world around and on how to live, as a consequence of attention to one's own situatedness in the world.

Fandom

The journey of intensification is, however, but one aspect of what it means to be a fan. We identified aspects of ritualized listening (in chap. 7) and hallmarks of devotion (in chap. 8). These are features of fandom. We also noticed that there seems to be a difference between what it means to be a fan and what it means to be an ordinary listener or audience member. A criterion therefore emerges for establishing whether a person is likely to get much from their listening. Are they a fan or not? Are they going to put some effort into repeated listening, to listening to the canon, to learning more about a performer? Becoming a fan admittedly sounds like going through an initiation rite or becoming an insider after being an outsider. It is no surprise to find anthropological and sociological categories (as used also with respect to religion) to describe what occurs. But the similarity is important and deserves being pressed. Rewarding listening means hard work, demands effort, and will not always be successful. Fandom is not about instant gratification. It is different from participation in the cult of celebrity yet may overlap with it at times. In the same way that religious devotion can be mundane and unfulfilling, so fandom is about loyalty and about the recognition that sometimes, in the middle of a sustained and mostly enjoyable practice, true highlights, profound insights, and a regular ongoing process of personal development will come about. To use terminology from performance studies, a fan's use of music will move a listener's engagement with it well beyond mere entertainment. In the midst of enjoyment, there will also be efficacy.[35] Listening will do something to and for a person, even if not on every occasion (to expect such would be unrealistic anyway). To use our own framework of interpretation, a music fan knows that in one's own conscious inhabiting of affective space in the listening experience, the fan has the chance, through sustained, focused, informed listening, to be enriched personally, both in their inner life and in thinking about how to act. When such fandom proves to be consistently efficacious, then it is not surprising that it shapes a person in a religion-like way.

Transcendence (Once More)

The third way in which music listening proves to be a spiritual practice is in how it contributes to a person's transcendence of mere self-interest. We saw this as a dimension of music's transcendent effect (chap. 6). Here we are not making any claim for music's intrinsic transcendent quality. Some music may indeed be argued to have something in it to enable a person to be pushed beyond themselves or to be provoked—if only in their imaginations—to move beyond their own limited world and experience.[36] But our claim here is that whatever the quality or type of music being enjoyed, it is in the intensity of a fan's music consumption that the possibility of self-transcendence is possible.

When allied with the communal awareness that comes with listening—either in the context of live performance, through explicit contact with other fans, or even through a sense that one is connected with others—self-transcendence can also entail respect for the Other. Again, there need be no requirement that a divine Other is being referred to here. A music fan might be quite explicit in holding to atheism, even while acknowledging an experience and a self-awareness that may be termed "transcendent." But the significance of regularly being taken out of oneself, so that a person is attending to who is around them, should not be underestimated. In this sense the practice of music listening can become a regular exercise in attentiveness.

A Note of Caution

A note of caution should, however, also be sounded. Being "taken out of oneself" could seem a similar experience to being "lost in music." Both are the kinds of statements that music lovers use. In the one case, however, the loss of the ego could promote attentiveness to others. In the other case, the loss of the self could be more of an absorption of all things around it, even while looking like an absorption *into* music. In exactly the same way that religious fervor while striving for the loss of self can become narcissism, so also a fan's music listening may appear to be a journey of intensification, while being no more than self-indulgence. Genuine fandom will always be more than self-indulgence when undertaken with appropriate intensity and in the interest of enjoyment, yet with a view to being challenged and encouraged into personal development.

For these reasons and because of these three aspects of music-listening practice, we suggest that engaged, sustained listening may be regarded as a spiritual practice. No matter how the term "spirituality" is used (something we shall examine in the next section), it is difficult to dispute that some form of inner life is being acknowledged and cultivated by engaged, sustained listening, whether or not the listener is explicitly religious. We suggest that it is important to acknowledge this so that we also recognize the crucial significance of such practice alongside or in place of religious practice in contemporary Western culture. Such spiritual practice is filling the affective spaces that contemporary Western citizens inhabit.

Spiritual Practices and the Making of Meaning

Spiritual practices are not contentless. In chapter 10, we shall take a more detailed look at questions about the content of listening, examining how Christianity manages the content of its theology and how this might relate to the substance of popular music. For the moment we must simply state that although dedicated listening, as opposed to indifferent and casual listening, may be deemed a spiritual practice, it could only constitute a "spirituality" in a weak sense. "Spirituality" is currently a common term in Western culture. Often used as a positive counterpart to the more contentious concept "religion," people who use it of themselves (as either "having" a spirituality or "being" a spiritual person) are usually indicating that they have an inner life, that they work at their inner well-being, and that they are trying to be a good and kind person. The distinction often sharply drawn now between "religion" (institutional, oppressive) and "spirituality" (communal or individual, liberating), however, also indicates that to be seen as positive, a "spiritual" person needs to distance oneself from organized religion. Being "spiritual but not religious" may sound good. Yet the claim also raises questions about which traditions a person might be drawing on, consciously or unconsciously, in order to have a spirituality at all. Ideas and beliefs do not come from nowhere. It is no accident that in the history and study of religion, spirituality has required an adjective so that something more specific can be said about the spirituality being referred to; hence we hear of Jewish spirituality, Christian spirituality, Hindu spirituality, and more recently, Green spirituality and Celtic spirituality. While people may not consciously participate in forms of spirituality specifically because the forms function authoritatively for them, by virtue of using them they do enter a world in which elements of authority come into play. As the Magisteria-Ibiza Spectrum showed (chap. 2), communal frameworks influence the choices we make even when we are acting and choosing as individuals.

Acknowledging adjectives does not mean that spiritualities can simply be stitched together in the practice of an individual. "Pick 'n' mix" approaches (a bit of Buddhism here, a bit of Judaism there) might be attractive but may not always work easily in practice. This is an issue we identified in our discussion of the Burning Man festival in chapter 7, and it now reappears sharply here. It has also become a topic of media discussion in its own right. In an article posted on the CNN website in June 2010, John Blake asks, "Are There Dangers in Being 'Spiritual but Not Religious'?"[37] In representing a number of perspectives, Blake is evenhanded, though the article clearly recognizes how difficult pick 'n' mix spirituality might be to achieve. Blake cites Jennifer Walters, dean of religious life at Smith College in Massachusetts, who comments: "Hymn-singing, forms of prayer and worship, teachings about social justice and forgiveness—all these things are valuable elements of religious wisdom. . . . Piecing it together by yourself can be done, but with great difficulty."

To identify engaged listening to popular music as a potential spiritual practice thus does not yet tell us very much. It shows that there are different kinds of listening. It shows that popular music can be taken seriously. It shows that we are not dealing with the content of popular music understood simply in terms of its lyrics. This all supports where theology/religion and popular culture have moved to: respecting what goes on between the receiver and the text (broadly understood). But to admit that "spirituality" is insufficient as a term to denote what actually goes on *beyond practice* reminds us that there is work to be done about the *content* of the practice. In the same way that spirituality does not tell us enough about which values, beliefs, or ideas a spiritual person considers important, so also identifying engaged listening as a potentially significant spiritual practice does not yet tell us whether popular music has any particular core values or emphases, or whether a particular emerging spirituality depends solely and wholly on which individual artists or types of music one is listening to. Or again, are the music and its lyrics largely irrelevant? Is it simply what one brings (such as a worldview, a philosophy, a theology, a religious outlook) that determines everything? Can I actually make use of *any* music for my own purposes? Is listening so individual a practice that even if I cannot legitimately make any song mean what I want it to mean, I can listen to what I want, listen to music for fun, and enjoy most musical types, yet simply select what I think is helpful for the worldview I already have? To use Markham's terms, is spiritual development all about assimilating and resisting while overhearing, all in a highly individualized way? If so, this may mean that popular music and its use merely highlight that meaning-making in the contemporary West really is now so highly individualized that the notion of any firm, coherent connection with theology is gone. Orthodoxy is simply hard to sustain anymore. Thus if any claim is to be made that engaged listening to popular music, as a potential spiritual practice, assists contemporary Western citizens to make meaning, then what precisely is the meaning of this meaning that people might make? We turn to this question directly in the next chapter.

three steps to heaven?

On Negotiating Meaning between Popular Music and Christian Theology

Sting, Jay-Z, Brad Paisley, Bon Jovi, The Killers, Michael Jackson, Queen, The White Stripes, Dolly Parton, The Clash, Stevie Wonder, Eminem, Genesis, Joni Mitchell, Elvis Presley, Adele, Switchfoot, Elton John, Alison Krauss, Editors, Fugees, The Eagles, The Undertones, Arcade Fire, George Michael, Bill Haley and the Comets, The Beatles, U2, Billy Bragg, Eric Bibb, Carole King, Reba McEntire, Doc Watson, The Proclaimers, The Eurythmics, MGMT, Randy Newman, Kings of Leon, Gillian Welch, Spiritualized, Rolling Stones, Lady Gaga, Roxy Music, Moby, REM, Deep Purple, Radiohead, Madonna, Bob Dylan, Black Eyed Peas, Imelda May, the Blind Boys of Alabama, Paul Simon, Public Image Limited, Dr. Dre . . .

The list could be varied much more and yet could easily be the result of using the shuffle facility on one person's MP3 player. More unlikely, though feasibly, it could be a radio station's playlist for a few hours.[1] But it would be a profound mistake to assume that any such playlist constituted a single, coherent worldview. For one thing, songs are not always intended to pass on any worldview at all. They may be story songs, relatively detached from those who sing them. They may be fun songs, with no particular purpose but to entertain. It is true that all songs and all music come out of a particular value system and framework of thought. But the musical piece may not pass this on or commend it in any obvious way at all, and may never intend to do so.

And then there's the sheer diversity (in politics, philosophy, religion, ethical outlook) of all those performers. It would be nonsense to suggest that, after all, "popular music" means this or that, or does this or that, to those who listen to it. We can only ask: "Whose popular music? Which listener are we talking about anyway?" As Rupert Till has rightly said of popular music cults and culture, "They lack a coherent, consistent system, the purpose, direction, history, maturity and coordination that mainstream religions offer."[2] The potential for plurality of form, content, and influence of popular music more generally is even greater than this. There is no single philosophy (or theology) of popular music. Popular music is much more a type of music with multiple forms that people enjoy and use for a range of purposes. Why, then, might we possibly want to bring our study of this type of music alongside a systematic understanding of the theology of a single religious tradition (Christianity)? What could be the benefit of such a critical juxtaposition when it is evident that in so many respects the two worlds are far apart?

Our two questions "Whose popular music?" and "Which listener are we talking about anyway?" echo Alasdair MacIntyre's observations about competing notions of justice within traditions of rationality, particularly these: (1) the Aristotelian *polis*; (2) the Augustinian tradition of religious orders within secular communities; leading to (3) the tradition of universities; from which emerged (4) the tradition of liberalism.[3] MacIntyre contends that liberalism began "as a repudiation of tradition in the name of abstract, universal principles of reason, [then] turned itself into a politically embodied power, whose inability to bring its debates on the nature and context of those universal principles to a conclusion has had the unintended effect of transforming liberalism into a tradition."[4] The key aspect of this observation for our purposes is the dynamic established here between "tradition" and "repudiation," which clearly shares common ground with our Magisteria-Ibiza Spectrum, with affective space being shaped by different types of tradition or authority on one side of the Spectrum, balanced by various forms of self-expression or nonhierarchical experience on the other. In chapter 4, we argued that various manifestations of Christianity and popular music exhibit similar creative movement through tensions between stability/innovation and tradition/imagination. It is arguable that along with the traditions of Christianity and other religious communities, popular music is also developing traditions that have narrative coherence and group identity.

Yet by now it should be clear that there are a number of reasons we must look at the two worlds together. For one thing, both the use of popular music and participation in Christianity are influential contemporary practices. A great many people are engaged in both simultaneously, and for some there is a considerable overlap. Second, without needing to argue that use of popular music by committed fans *is* religion, we have seen enough evidence that such music is certainly something *like* religion (at least for some) in the intensity with which people follow it. So in examining how popular music is used, we are looking at a case study of popular culture as a religion-like practice and perhaps even as a direct replacement for religion. Third, people do have assumptions and make choices regarding how to live. Whether people make much conscious critical examination of their values, they will hold, discuss, and sometimes vehemently maintain political and ethical viewpoints in the face of challenges. Christianity is a religious tradition with a wide-ranging and complex theological structure within which orthodoxy makes sense, and yet there are many theologies within Christianity. It is an example of a religious tradition that both creates communities and informs the way people live. Its theology functions as a conceptual framework—a structure of beliefs and ideas—within which people make sense of life. It would be useful to see if what Christianity addresses is comparable to what people might get from committed interaction with popular music. In other words, if people are committed fans (whether or not they are religious), what themes and issues might they inevitably come to face, think through, or find emphasized through their listening? There may well be no system to popular music, but there are certainly narrative communities and emerging traditions within popular culture. But does popular music square up with the "six songs" that Daniel Levitin identified as summing up the whole of music?[5]

To explore these questions we shall follow four steps, three in this chapter, and one in the next. First, we will summarize the findings of a published analysis of popular culture by the Christian theologian Kelton Cobb. We shall present what Cobb thinks are the main theological themes discernible in and through popular culture. In overhearing Cobb's discussion of popular culture, we shall also map his conclusions onto the framework presented by systematic theology. Which of systematic theology's themes, in other words, does Cobb believe are most prominent in popular culture? What can we identify as lacking?

Having set up the framework from systematic theology, we shall then take our second step and ask, on the basis of the representative studies offered in part 2, how does our analysis of popular music fit in with the framework that systematic theology presents? In essence we are asking: If someone chooses to consume a diet of popular music, what kind of emphases do they end up with in life? What things will they be preoccupied about? What kind of person might they become? Within the themes of theology particularly, what is emphasized, what is missing, and how does our analysis of popular music compare with Cobb's review of popular culture more generally?

As a third step, we shall then revisit Levitin's six songs and look back across our findings to see if his reading of what music (in general) achieves applies to popular music. We shall map all of this diagrammatically against some of the different themes that make up Christian theology. A comparative chart of the different emphases will help us throughout to see more clearly what dominates and what is missing. In chapter 11 we shall then take our fourth step and draw out some theological conclusions from the comparative undertaking. What is to be said now about some of theology's key themes? And which themes need rethinking anyway (and why)? In taking this fourth step, we shall be asking, finally: What does the world of popular music offer Christian theology? What does Christian theology have to say to popular music?

We accept that our approach can be trivialized in certain ways. We need only think of poor-quality popular music with trite lyrics and a formulaic beat and conclude that a diet of popular music can be unhealthy.[6] We also accept that our approach begs many questions, both with respect to *what* people listen to and *how* they listen. Here we build on the previous chapter's distinction between fans and ordinary listeners or ordinary audience members. Thus at the outset of this chapter, we assume that amid all the enjoyment of music, our undertaking is serious because we are dealing with people who take music seriously. The listeners we have especially in mind are those who are willing to recognize that their listening is doing something to and for them, whether or not they have any explicit intention of thinking theologically or doing anything resembling philosophy. And even for those who are less serious in their listening, much else may be going on. We are not presenting an argument that declares—for serious or nonserious listeners—that we and we alone know what is really going on as they listen. Our attempt is more modest: we are locating the act of listening within the interpretative framework that Christian theology provides. If this is deemed fruitful, then a different understanding of the act of listening itself results. At that point theology as a living discipline and listening as a disciplined, theological practice can come into view.

A Working Theology of Popular Culture

We turn first to Kelton Cobb's theological summary of the achievements of popular culture. In *The Blackwell Guide to Theology and Popular Culture*, Cobb makes a brave attempt to survey the preoccupations of popular culture and distill evident key emphases of a theological nature. His undertaking is distinct from our own. Cobb's goal is "to discover what sorts of things popular culture, drawing entirely upon its own resources, has to say on these theological topics."[7] In other words, Cobb does not attend much to practices. He is mostly concerned with content and is looking for the explicitly theological. Nevertheless his interpretative effort provides a helpful yardstick to measure our own findings. We accept the limitations of our respective undertakings. No individual—indeed no team of interpreters, however large—can do a fully adequate reading of popular culture as a whole. There is only so much television, so many films, so much music that one can watch and listen to. And every reading is both perspectival and, in academic terms, affected by a disciplinary slant. But you must start somewhere. Cobb ends up writing five chapters: "Images of God," "Human Nature," "Sin," "Salvation," and "Life Everlasting." We look briefly at each in turn.

God

In a chapter that draws on film (*Fight Club*, *The Big Kahuna*, *Dogma*, *Wings of Desire*), music (Tori Amos, Joan Osborne), and especially literature (Nikos Kazantzakis, Douglas Coupland, and extended studies of 1990s novels by Franco Ferrucci, James Morrow, and Laurence Cossé), Cobb sees popular culture as reporting on God's dynamism, yet also God's elusiveness.[8] Evident too is a deep distrust of "hypocritical piety," alongside a search for ultimate benevolence, even if needing to be sought outside of mainstream religious traditions and practice, and recognizing that such desires and convictions are expressed while staring into "the abyss."[9] In the second half of his "Images of God" chapter, Cobb seems to lose sight of the substantive element required in such theological searching; yet he still feels able to conclude that popular culture has a "doctrine of God." Even if it has a "strange profile," it reflects "a great willingness to entertain the possibility of divine transcendence in its various modes."[10]

Humanity

In his chapter on human nature, Cobb makes considerable use of television, observing in particular how police series, or cop shows, invite viewers to reflect on how society handles human vice. He also highlights a wide range of music and literature that celebrates the "triumph of the ordinary," the "common" person, finding that a clear thread runs through "the anthropology of popular culture": "the common sense and simple virtue of plain-speaking people whose grasp of reality has been shaped by the most mundane pressures of life are more real and praiseworthy than those of the pampered, privileged classes."[11] The notion that such wisdom of the ordinary is easily won, conveyed, and received is surely too simple, as Cobb himself acknowledges. But in making the tenable claim that the doctrines of original sin, the priesthood of all believers, and the conviction that God shows no favoritism suffuse this approach to where wisdom is to be found, Cobb shows how deeply Christian theological convictions have been shaping Western popular culture.[12]

Inevitably, in exploring the task of identity construction, which must occur for a person, the role played by memory, and the many features that distinguish humanity from robots, Cobb must make frequent reference to how humans handle their emotions. His use of social psychologist Daniel Gilbert's work is instructive, reminding us of "the endless restlessness of our affections," and the degree to which we should be cautious about trusting the level of emotional satisfaction we might receive from what we expect to make us happy.[13] In an age when entertainment "ceases being a way to relax during our leisure time and becomes itself a way of life," we are invited to be circumspect. The would-be demotic enjoyment promoted by popular music could thus be interpreted as part of popular wisdom.[14] Or, building on Cobb here, we are perhaps reminded once more that without entertainment becoming efficacious, then the wisdom of "plain-speaking people," which may be present in and through popular music and its reception, may not have a chance of being heard. In other words, if it is clear that it certainly is not lyrics alone that make popular music "work," then it is crucial to highlight the way in which popular music helps people construct an understanding of what it means to be human. What makes music efficacious, rather than being merely entertainment, is its evocation of memory, its functioning within personal narratives, and its formation of communities. Cobb's conclusion that popular culture presents the human being as a "pleasure-seeking *bricoleur* [trying anything]" is balanced by the recognition, present in popular culture too, that a "flesh-and-blood person cannot live on simulacra alone."[15] The distinction of being a fan rather than an ordinary listener—seeking efficacy rather than mere entertainment—is thus reflected in the quest for the authentically human.

Sin

Cobb's chapter on sin begins with loud appreciation for country-western music.[16] Cobb observes the way in which its lyrics log "the transgressions human beings perpetrate against one another." Then he lists other examples of how popular culture reports on human waywardness. Cobb also recognizes that such records are often reflections on fallenness because paradise myths—as scholars of religion and anthropologists have long reported—are found across cultures. Whatever may be the storied extent of the tales we tell ("Are these narratives true?" we ask ourselves),[17] our stories are ways of describing and handling our condition, in both its positive and negative aspects. In Cobb's discussion of sin, music and films presenting a gothic theme feature prominently. The gothic accentuates the struggle of goodness to prevail in the way it enables us to "correlate current social pathologies to past transgressions." Yet in Cobb's view the gothic functions as one among many witnesses to the lingering tension in popular culture's handling of the human condition, contrasting the paradise myth and the shortcomings all too evident in human conduct.[18]

Salvation

Salvation is at hand, even in popular culture. In the chapter devoted to this topic Cobb offers his most extensive engagement with popular music. This is where Cobb comes closest to identifying the significance of the *practice* of listening, along with the content of the music.[19] Cobb states starkly (and in our view wholly accurately): "We fill our lives with music as a kind of soundtrack to train and amplify our emotional awareness about the contents of our lives, or what we wish were the contents of our lives."[20] That such a statement should appear in Cobb's chapter on "Salvation" and in a section headed "Soteriology in Song" is profoundly instructive. Cobb suggests that the ritual elements, the motif of protest, the engagement with the theme of love, and the frequently present mystical element all come together to connect with the theme of salvation. When allied with the theme of confession and forgiveness, which Cobb draws out more fully with respect to films, we are encouraged to recognize that "we turn to popular culture to prod, entice and feel ourselves into believing that our sinful ways can be redeemed, that obstacles to our happiness can be overcome and that we can enjoy more fulfilling lives."[21]

We shall reflect shortly on how this squares up with our own conclusions. For now we simply notice that Cobb's discussion focuses on the experience of salvation for the one "saved." While not simply a study of individual experience—a social (ecclesial) motif does appear—there is little need for Cobb to explore the means of salvation other than through the efforts that humans themselves expend. Salvation is not to be equated with a therapeutic process, though Cobb needs to show that salvation means more, even if containing much from therapeutic culture that is worthy of respect.[22] Strikingly absent, from a Christian theological perspective, is much engagement with savior figures. Even allowing for the fact that the search for Christ figures across popular culture is overplayed, one might have expected more than Cobb offers as a potential product of the self-reliance motif that pervades the chapter. This surely is not Cobb's fault. He is seeking to reflect what he finds. And we support the caution he demonstrates in not equating salvation too quickly or too closely with happiness or self-fulfillment. Yet it will be important to see if and how popular culture has a chance of enabling salvation—understood as being rescued—to be discerned when transcendence, such as can be found through music, can too easily be self-induced, deforming "self-transcendence into self-absorption," and not in any sense being a gift.[23]

Eternity

Cobb's final substantive chapter on a theology of popular culture is devoted to "Life Everlasting." Along with examples from the visual arts, Cobb is able to find extensive examples of popular culture's preoccupation with death and with life after death in films and on television.[24] Especially notable in this chapter is the way the diverse ethnic and cultural backgrounds inform thinking about life beyond death despite the fact that people might participate in the same religious tradition. As a meeting point of multiple influences, popular culture displays the uncertainty—and lack of knowledge—that all humans of necessity wrestle with in the field of eschatology. That said, Cobb makes the point well that while all seek to transcend what we do know, in fashioning visions about what we believe for the future, "cultural artists" and "religious communities and their theologians" alike can lose their way. Yet we must continue to shape those visions, for what we believe about what lies beyond shapes what we believe and act upon here and now.

Summary

Cobb has offered us a 160-page systematic theology of popular culture. It might be disputed whether all the artistic and cultural resources he draws on are truly popular. And, as stated at the start of this section, he acknowledges himself that there is an impressionistic dimension to any such undertaking. But his five focal points are helpful by both what they present and what they ignore. This can be summarized diagrammatically as follows:

Figure 10.1. Cobb's reading of a theology from popular culture
(related to loci of Christian theology)

Revelation	God/Trinity	Christ	Spirit	Salvation/Redemption	Human being	Church	Sacraments	Last things/Eschatology
	God "on the move"			(Sin) Human shortcomings evident	Triumph of the ordinary	(A social dimension of salvation)	(A ritual element in salvation)	The role of the dead among the living ("communion of saints")
	Elusive			(Salvation) Human effort to save the self	Construction of the self	(A present dimension of "life beyond")		
				(Contains a ritual, social dimension)	Search for authenticity			
				Linked to transcendence				

Kelton Cobb, *The Blackwell Guide to Theology and Popular Culture*

On Systematizing Dominant Themes from the Use of Popular Music: A Working Summary

We turn next to a substantive summary of what we have discovered in our own work on popular music. In contrast to Cobb, we have focused less on content and more on the practice of listening, though without ignoring content altogether. How might the practice of listening to popular music be mapped theologically, given what we presented in part 2? Accepting that popular music is not a single phenomenon to be summarized in any easy way, it must still be possible to address the issue of what popular music might be doing to and for people. In teasing out the content of what we were working with throughout part 2, we shall at times come close to theology explicitly; at other times we shall seem far away. But it is necessary to undertake the overhearing, if we are to stand any chance of judging what a theology might need to assimilate or what it must resist. Four key themes emerge from our analytical reflection on the material we presented in part 2: transcendence, embodiment, connectedness, and ritual.

We consider each of these briefly in turn; then at the end of our exposition, we will add them to the chart alongside Cobb's conclusions.

Transcendence

Transcendence relates to a number of theology's themes: revelation, doctrine of God, Christ/incarnation, Spirit, salvation, eschatology. It relates to *revelation* in being a gift from outside of present experience. No matter how much a sense of transcendence may be related to (or seem explicable in terms of) physical, psychological, or sociological processes, the sense of Otherness experienced leads the person who reports the transcendent feeling to speak of being addressed, caught unawares, and encountered in such a way as not to be in control.[25] Therefore experiences of transcendence immediately raise questions about the nature of the reality by which one is reportedly addressed or encountered. Within whatever framework of meaning a music listener may then locate an experience of transcendence, theological and religious frameworks are close at hand. To speak of an experience of transcendence as revelatory, then, can legitimately be interpreted as an experience of God (a deity/divine reality) in whatever form "God" is understood.

A *doctrine of God* is another theological theme that relates to transcendence. There is, however, no specific religious content to such a doctrine of God without further reflection and thus closer location of such an experience within a particular cognitive worldview. The practice of interpreting a human experience by locating it within some form of worldview or framework (or to accept that the experience is actually already located as such—a claim that always merits examining)[26] is, then, the process of finding or making meaning. It is this process of reflection that contains within it the potential to enhance life experience. Whether it is a necessary process is a moot point. Plenty of people argue that life is to be enjoyed, not reflected on. True. The further question is whether life would be enjoyed more by being reflected on, and whether the result of such reflection would constitute a fuller human life. To speak of "God" at this point—when the existence or presence of God cannot be proved— sharply poses the question of what functions religious traditions (and all philosophical and ethical traditions) play in being available to people as life is being interpreted.

A third dimension of transcendence within Christian theological reflection is christological. Within a specifically Christian reading of human experience, transcendence must relate to Christ by virtue of the attention given to the human body. It is a simple point, and we shall say more on this shortly, but a sense of being "taken beyond oneself," or made aware in and as a body of what is beyond oneself, requires us to *be* bodies. Contrary to appearances and common assumption, Christianity's intense engagement with the body of Christ is not a preoccupation with the first-century Palestinian figure, Jesus of Nazareth. It is about the enfleshment of God and the fact that matter matters to God.[27] It is also a corporate phenomenon. To cite Graham Ward's interpretation of the apostle Paul: "The body of Christ is both a collection of people and a coordination of operations."[28] A christological interpretation of transcendence, then, refuses to be bound by the experience of the embodied individual. Being taken out of oneself throws one toward the concrete Other—the other person to whom I relate, as friend or as person in need. In and through such relatedness to a human other is also how a person may encounter God.

Transcendence is experienced in and as a body, but it also reminds us that we are not *just* bodies. *Spirit*—a fourth dimension of transcendence within Christian theology—relates to soul, to inner life, to dynamism, to creativity. In being correlated with transcendence, attention to (Holy) Spirit emphasizes that being (divine or human) is not reduced to the material. The fact that it is easier and more acceptable in the contemporary West to speak of spirituality rather than religion indicates a current attentiveness to the nonmaterial, though this tendency overlooks the framework of practices within which such attentiveness is maintained. Spirituality needs its institutions and traditions too. Furthermore, with Ward, we are reluctant to speak of inward and outward aspects of what it means to be human, but we too "can think of no better way of putting this."[29] Transcendence is to be understood in relation to both bodies and that which takes us deep within or beyond our bodies. Transcendence identifies something that happens to us in, and as, bodies *and* spirits. The dimension of Otherness contained within the reference to transcendence means that this is not simply inner or individual human experience.

A fifth dimension of transcendence is seen as an indication of *salvation*. Perhaps the experience of transcendence is in itself redemptive and liberating, whatever form it takes. With respect to the reception of music, when a listener links experience with a reference to transcendence, musical ecstasy is perhaps being referred to. Though some listeners do use terms such as "thrilling" for the nature of their listening experiences, it is more appropriate to demand less of all such musical experiences and use the term "well-being." While this term better correlates with salvation, we must accept that the link is tenuous. Salvation in theological terms, while it includes an inner sense of well-being (the ultimate "feel-good factor," one might say), is claiming much more about what happens to a person who feels "liberated" or "redeemed." We will return to this (in chap. 11) as we explore the similarities and differences of the contemporary search for happiness and well-being on one hand, and beliefs about liberation, salvation, or redemption on the other.

Finally, transcendence is linked to *eschatology*. No matter how the relationship between bodies and spirits is understood, and whatever form beyond physical death one believes a person might take (if any), any claim for transcendence includes within it an implied understanding of existence. This understanding will then be reflected in how one views the so-called four last things (death, judgment, heaven, hell) and related themes.[30] We cannot explore all of this here.

Yet we must recognize the link: a worldview/faith that is especially influenced (dominated, even) by eschatological concerns, will also inevitably be affected by these other themes of theological transcendence. Eschatology is arguably the most difficult of theological themes to address; therefore, if overemphasized, it is the most likely route to distortion of other themes.

Transcendence is, then, a crucial theme raised by the exhilaration and the sustained sense of Otherness that listening to music can create. As such it can readily be mapped onto the topics through which a theological framework interprets human experience (see fig. 10.2 below). There are, however, three other themes to be addressed. We turn next to embodiedness.

Embodiment

As we saw in chapter 5, so much of the production, reception, and use of popular music relates to a focus on the body. As Heaney states: "In music, one listens with one's whole body, and the body (mind included) is affected by it."[31] Religions have different ways of handling the theme of the body and are often assumed to subjugate the body in favor of the spirit. Heaney describes this: "The philosophical and theological background of Western thought has left us with an 'uncomfortable' relationship with our bodies, which may be one of the reasons why we are uneasy with strong rhythms in a faith context. Our dualistic mind frame, which favors abstract intellect over bodily sensations and lacks the tools to integrate and unify both, can feel threatened by the powerful bodily awareness provoked by certain rhythms."[32] There is something in this charge: a certain amount of world renunciation is present to a greater or lesser degree across most religious traditions, and approaches to the body are inevitably influenced by this.

In practice, though, religious attitudes to the body are much more complex. Dietary customs are about care of the body; attention to the inner life need not deny the body but keep it healthy. In Christian theological terms, strains of world renunciation and the negation of the body are undoubtedly present. Yet the extent to which Christians have gone, and do go, to renounce the worldly and the bodily can appear to be a puzzling and stark denial of the Christian commitment to the incarnation of God in Christ. However, it is worth bearing in mind that the body (including Christ's body) has always been a locus for theological conflicts within the church and wider society.[33] Even if the strong Christology (and thus an accentuated theology of embodiment) that should result from the commitment to incarnation does not endorse all that goes on in the name of popular music (something we shall explore further in the next chapter)—dance, physicality, and the embodied pleasure of music are all wholly consistent with an incarnational Christology. To understand music "in Christ" means to celebrate its bodily aspects.

It is no coincidence that the "body of Christ" (as developed conceptually and practically in Christian tradition) should be correlated with embodied and corporate experience. Nor is it surprising that the concept of body became one of the key images by which Christians understand and express what it means to be a church.

Connectedness

These aspects of theological reflection and practice flow into the third theme we draw out from our study of popular music and its reception: connectedness. In part 2 we saw many different ways in which music listeners reported a sense of connectedness: with one another in a specific place (e.g., at a concert), with others not present (e.g., in a fan community, or with those who share similar tastes), with the music itself or the performers in a kind of spiritual union, with a cause (e.g., political), with ultimate values. None of this is necessarily religious, nor need it be interpreted as such. But what we are identifying here is a social-psychological element of the practice of music listening that informs, and can be informed by, theological reflection. Our work shows that the body-spirit experience that music at its most intense can create is not to be accounted for or wholly encapsulated in terms of what happens to the individual listener. The experience requires us to respect a social dimension. Indeed, we are arguing that it requires us to respect a spiritual aspect of the social dimension. Though a conceptual leap from "connectedness in music," in a general sense, to "body of Christ," in a specifically Christian form, cannot be made in any simple way, the legitimacy of the connection is difficult to dispute.

To express this in bold and clear theological terms: any form of human connectedness that fosters human well-being and flourishing is to be interpreted, in Christian perspective, as the work of God in Christ, effected by the Spirit. It is a manifestation of redeemed humanity, taking concrete form in the body of Christ as an anticipation of ultimate (eschatologically) redeemed humanity. In this way it can be argued that human experiences revealing glimpses of that sense of (transcendent) connectedness are anticipations of that eschatological unity, whatever form they take (e.g., music) and regardless of whether they take social shape in explicitly ecclesial form (as church). God, Christ, Spirit, salvation, church, and eschatology connect together conceptually to make sense of what a listener experiences.

Is this, then, a version of the "communion of saints"? Undoubtedly, even if in a weak and undeveloped form. It must not, though, be implied in any lazy sense that Christianity is ahead of things and popular-music fans are simply catching up. Here we anticipate what we shall be addressing in the next chapter: What might popular music have to teach theology via its creation of exhilaration, intensity, and forms for sensed connectedness? To express matters starkly: Do Christian notions of the communion of saints or anticipations of the coming eschatological reign of God expect Christian disciples to feel as connected with one another and with the ultimate destiny of humankind as those leaving the arena might feel after a Springsteen, U2, Dixie Chicks, or Mumford and Sons concert?

Ritual

The final theme for us to consider is ritual. In chapters 5 and 7 of this study, we variously noticed how habits of listening indicate not only how, when, and where people choose to listen; they also show how listeners are shaped by their practice, form communities of listeners, handle life stages and crises, and express and explore who they are as people. Theologically speaking, such ritualistic functions of listening link with the theological topics of humans and church. Crucially, ritual and sacraments also need to be brought close together. In this way we have come full circle from chapter 3, in which we explained how three recent thinkers have stressed sacramentality as a key way of understanding how popular culture and the arts function theologically.

First, though, we must recognize how ritual relates to the theological theme of *human being* (theological anthropology). The serious listening that a music fan undertakes—beyond the casual listening of the ordinary audience member or occasional listener—is clearly constitutive of such a person's identity construction.[34] As we suggested in chapter 9, listening is a kind of spiritual discipline. This means that serious listeners are conscious of the way they are being shaped, and they choose to be influenced by the music to which they devote their time. Given the patterns of consumption we examined in chapter 4, however, we must also notice the link between the assumed freedom to purchase and the extent to which listeners believe they may have control over their identities. The question arises regarding the extent of freedom that people truly possess to be what and who they want to be. Constraints imposed by genes, upbringing, social context, income levels, climate, geography, and politics—all come into play in shaping the kind of people we are. Without pressing a deterministic case, many theologies strongly argue for a high level of givenness in human identity, as a reflection of the gift of existence.

That said, the notion of human freedom is not solely a modern phenomenon. While post-Enlightenment modernity has undoubtedly accentuated the extent to which human freedom is to be acknowledged and prized, philosophies and theologies of freedom have been around for a long time. In Christian terms, God's freedom, as reflected in God's free decision to create the world with its own freedom to be, is reflected in the freedom of the created order (human and nonhuman), which contains within itself the freedom to be or not to be. In the case of human creatures, this includes the freedom to make conscious choices, including the freedom to reject God entirely.

Choice of music, the freedom to listen and not to listen, to be shaped and to resist—these all feature as part of the shaping of the self. As people consume their music of choice—while also being bombarded with much music they do not choose (be it national anthems, looped tapes, shopping mall musak, hymns at school or college [at least in the UK], marching bands at sports events or on military occasions)—in many different ways, they assert, resist, conform. By inhabiting the affective space in which they undertake their sustained listening, they come to be the people they are.

The second aspect under which the theme of ritual can be explored theologically is that of *church*. Though church is seemingly distant from the practice of listening to popular music, four dimensions of church as understood in Christian thought merit mention. Church is, first, a concept that relates to a *tradition*. It is, second, a (large) collection of people *across time and place*. Third, church is an *institution*, with aspects of its structure appearing internationally, nationally, regionally, and locally. In its most concrete form, fourth, church means a *gathering* of people—not always wholly like-minded—in a locality.

The Christian *tradition* that the church carries may not be quite as diverse as the history of popular music, yet it indeed is very diverse. We have already made the point that popular music is not to be systematized. We therefore are not claiming that listening to popular music is akin to participating in church in this first sense. There is no orthodoxy—however broad and generous—in popular music, in the sense of a single worldview emanating from popular music, a view to which all listeners subscribe.[35] There are, however, orthodoxies created in the context of fan discussions about artists' and bands' music. Interpretations of music are debated and policed. It may be easy to remind listeners that there can be no single right way to understand a song; yet in exactly the same way as academic and religious discussions show, there may be some wrong ones. And in certain cases, it may be morally and politically important to clarify what those wrong interpretations are.

Listeners to popular music constitute a large, motley group of people *across time and place*. They subdivide into lots of interest groups (styles and levels of commitment). As we saw above, at times they may be something like a communion of saints, even if their theology is not explicit or well formed. Through the connectedness between people brought about by music, there is a sense in which the consistent engagement with music, in a ritual-like way, contributes to the social shaping of a listener.

There is, of course, no requirement that any act of listening to music is inevitably deemed a social experience. Listening to music on an MP3 player, putting on loud music in solitude in the comfort of one's own home/apartment/room, and building up one's own personal canon—all these are expressions of the extent to which listening is an individual pursuit. There need be no real or evident sense of the third or fourth forms of church (*institutional* and *local*). All we are noticing here is that attention to the theological topic of church requires that we examine what social contexts a person operates within in order to be shaped and to contribute to construction of oneself. Sociologically speaking, this will be their "church"—a key (perhaps the primary) social group in and through which they discover or form their identity and develop personally and spiritually. For music fans, some form of music community, real or virtual, will play this role. For Christians who listen to popular music, Christian church and fan community will almost certainly interweave, regardless of whether or not the fan community to which a Christian relates exists for a "religious" performer.

The final way in which the theme of ritual relates to a topic in Christian theology is through *gathering* and giving attention to *sacraments*. Sacraments are more than signs and symbols. They do symbolize, but they also convey something of that to which they refer. Hence the sacrament of baptism uses the symbol of water. But while the water symbolizes purification, as a sacrament the practice of baptism is held to effect cleansing. It is God who cleanses and purifies, not the water that is symbolically used. The point is that notions of sacrament go beyond the merely symbolic. Similarly, bread and wine are just that: bread and wine. But when understood sacramentally, the many dimensions of what occurs in a service of Holy Communion/Eucharist/Lord's Supper ensure that the use of bread and wine goes beyond the symbolic. It is not necessary to reenter or resolve the Medieval, Reformation, and Post-Reformation debates about what, if anything, happens to the bread and wine to be able to see that claims for sacramental efficacy can be maintained without detailed conclusions about changes occurring in the elements. Holy Communion/Eucharist/Lord's Supper is a whole act of worship, an extended practice, which has ongoing significance in the rest of the participants' lives. The action of God in the lives of participants is thus being understood much more fully than merely at the point of receiving symbolic food.

To explore the ritualistic aspects of listening to popular music with reference to sacraments means developing a number of the points just made. Three are immediately apparent. First, we observed how it is not sufficient to see a concert or gig alone as a religion-like ritual. Committed fans are clear that a threshold is crossed from eavesdropping listener to serious fan-community member, from outsider to insider. There is an issue of membership here, a clear sense of a group to which one belongs. Second, this means that however ritualistic an act of listening may be in itself (be that live performance or focused listening to recorded music), it is part of a much wider engagement with and use of a performer's work. The ritualistic engagement has an impact on the rest of life. Third, there is no escaping the communal dimension of this engagement. As Jennifer Porter says of fan communities, "They are, or at least can be, a place that embodies a person's and/or a community's expression of the essence of all meaning: what it means to be human, to be in community, to be in space and time, to be moral and immoral, to be finite or eternal, to simply be."[36] We add to this that the ritualistic, religion-like participation in a fan community actually conveys the sense of connectedness (community) and of locatedness (space and time). The sacramental quality of listening, in other words, comes from what is conveyed to, in, through, and beyond the body. One is being shaped as a

Figure 10.2. A diagram of Cobb's and our understandings
of popular culture and music (related to loci of Christian theology)

	Revelation	God/Trinity	Christ	Spirit	Salvation/ Redemption	Human being	Church	Sacraments	Last things/ Eschatology
Cobb		God "on the move" Elusive			(Sin) Human shortcomings evident (Salvation) Human effort to save the self (Contains a ritual, social dimension) Linked to transcendence	Triumph of the ordinary Construction of the self Search for authenticity	(A social dimension of salvation) (A present dimension of "life beyond")	(A ritual element in salvation)	The role of the dead among the living ("communion of saints")
Part Two	Givenness of transcendence/ Otherness	Does one God mean one universal theology/ spirituality? Does the plurality of theologies/spiritualities therefore challenge monotheism? (ch. 6) Transcendence as/and Otherness (ch. 6)	Bodies matter profoundly/ Flesh matters (ch. 5) The physicality of transcendence (ch. 6)	Transcendence as spiritual (yet do we ever escape the body? (ch. 6)	Musical ecstasy as salvation? (ch. 6) [Celebrities as savior figures?]	We choose who we are (what we buy shapes us, but can we control our consumption? ch. 4) Rituals express/ shape identities (chs. 5 and 7) We have "personal canons" (yet authoritative voices shape our choices) (ch. 8)	How much choice do we have about who we belong to? (ch. 5) We connect with others (chs. 5 and 6) Fan community (chs. 7 and 8)	(Ritual is vital for human beings) (chs. 5 and 7) Rituals actually convey something (e.g., self-understanding) and evoke gratitude (ch. 7) Rituals accompany life-stages (ch. 5)	Transcendence as "beyond the body"—does this mean "beyond death" too? (ch. 6)

person by the practice, partly out of choice (by choosing to belong) but partly as gift (one receives more than one has chosen).[37]

Once more we are not claiming a necessary intentionality on the part of the participant for this to occur. We are just trying to enhance understanding of what is already occurring in a person's shaping. More can happen, and be seen to happen, by being interpreted sacramentally. But much is already happening by virtue of what is being done.[38]

We will say more about the significance of this analysis of what contemporary listening to popular music can achieve with reference to sacraments. Here we simply state that we have come full circle from the theological content of chapter 3, returning to an emphasis on the sacramental as a way to appreciate what occurs in the arts and popular culture. Have we, though, lost sight of the important journey apparently made by the history of theological critique of popular culture ("from sin to sacramentality" in chap. 3)? Have we ended up being too positive about the body and its needs? Is our strategy one in which we become blind to the demands of holiness and end up being simply too optimistic about humanity? Before we address such questions directly, we must complete the third step of our summary inquiry by asking how our study of popular music and its use fits into Daniel Levitin's map of the world of music.

"Six Songs" and Popular Music Culture

In the previous section we mapped the findings of part 2 of our study onto a framework provided by the themes of systematic theology. We sought to show, via the ways in which popular music works for keen listeners, how selected themes in theology inevitably come into play in the task of understanding what is happening in the life experience of the listener. In the process we began to compare our findings with those of Kelton Cobb's distillation of the theological themes prominent in popular culture. Our purpose is not to suggest that a theological agenda is either implicit or explicit in popular music, as if this is what all popular music is really about. It is an exercise in cultural interpretation, using the lens of theological and religious studies, an approach informed also by other disciplines involved in the task of interpreting popular music.[39] Our intention remains the analysis of the function and significance of popular music, whatever the multiple purposes of its producers and users may be. Before we offer (in chap. 11) brief programmatic explorations of the theological themes we are beginning to identify as especially significant, we must undertake one final piece of mapping. Having introduced the work of Levitin in chapter 2, we must now return to his reading of the functions of music per se in society. How do Levitin's "Six Songs" relate to the themes that theology addresses? And what does the practice of listening to popular music look like in light of this? In this way we extend our mapping exercise beyond theological and religious concerns alone. We can then more suitably identify the themes that come from the practice of listening, and more clearly identify the agenda that popular music sets theologically today. We shall now locate within our grid the six songs identified by Levitin. (Since we have already expounded and discussed the detail of Levitin's argument in chapter 2, we do not need to repeat it here.)

We recall that Levitin identifies six particular types of song that persist in human development: friendship, joy, comfort, knowledge, religion, and love. If this is so, then one should expect popular music's main interest to reflect this combination of themes. If theology (as a conceptual world) is meant to relate to the whole of life, then one can justifiably expect that the six songs may be plotted across the framework of systematic theology. We shall see if this works by undertaking a theological mapping of Levitin's songs.

In theological terms, the theme of *friendship* as developed by Levitin relates most clearly to the theological concept of church. Here the primary focus is placed on the quality of human relationship. Here "church" is not to be narrowly understood in clearly defined institutional terms, though the importance of respect for church as having a concrete form should not be underplayed. Church is here to be understood first and foremost as a living community: a primary community to which one belongs and in relation to which one's values are worked out. It is not, however, an idealized community. "Church" is thus a concept that also denotes the struggle, the difficulty, of what it means to establish and maintain good human relationships, yet also the necessity of finding a context, a forum, a network with which to do this. It is striking that singing of all kinds occurs "in church," both to create community and to maintain and celebrate it.

In making the theological link between Levitin's identification of friendship songs and the concept of "church," we are still some distance from any sense that the friendship groups created by music are a "sign and instrument of God's intention and plan for the world."[40] But the theological challenge we take up shortly is the extent to which attention to people's primary meaning-making communities causes a reassessment of what it means to be church.

Joy and *love* can both be correlated with the quest to identify and fashion what it means to be truly human. If "the glory of God is a human being fully alive"[41] then in theological perspective the quest for the joyful, loving human being is at the heart of human culture. This is not an insight exclusive to theologically interested people. Yet so much in Levitin's discussion of songs of love invites theological interpretation. Love is clearly the most significant of the six types of song.[42] It is clear too that attention to human love requires us to be taken out of ourselves: "Love is about feeling that there is something bigger than just ourselves and our own worries and existence."[43] In its larger sense, love is "the sweeping, selfless commitment to another person, group, or idea." As such it is "the most important cornerstone of a civilized society."[44] It requires "an almost irrational trust and faith in another person."[45] We reach a point, then, of apparent convergence of interest between the reception of music and participation in religion. Here the search for the fully human means refusing to accept any self-absorption on the part of an individual and emphasizing the importance of being turned to others/an Other. To acknowledge this will take us beyond reason alone. A "musical anthropology"—an understanding of humans accessed through the enjoyment of, and reflection upon, music and its reception—brings us, in short, to a theological place that is strangely familiar.

Songs of *comfort* may seem quite different from any kind of interest in salvation. Though there may be a notion of a happy ending (rescue, liberation), salvation can be understood only when sin is taken into account. Human frailty, weakness, and sometimes downright evil are therefore in view here. That said, there is an undoubted alliance between comfort and redemption. "Solace" may be the common ground here, or the quest for contentedness or well-being. People listen to music of all kinds to help get them through. We have each spoken to many people who refer to music as helping them "cope with life."[46] Yet we should not read "comfort" as some kind of weak or vague escapism, anymore than we should detach salvation from the concrete realities of current lived experience. While further exploration is needed in Christian and other religious narratives and traditions about how God "saves," we should recall that what we are dealing with here is how humans, with external support, face who they are honestly and address all that life presents to them.

We may need to accept here that music may not be the easiest form of art or culture through which people can explore and experience salvation. Perhaps films and literature—stories of redemption—work more readily. Even acknowledging with Cobb that some forms of music, lyrically speaking, may do similar work (e.g., country), our claim (that music listening as a *practice* may imply that the listener is seeking salvation through ecstatic experience) perhaps suggests its limitations here. Effective approaches to salvation need narrative.

That said, the way people frequently use music to narrate their life stories—thereby constructing a meaningful narrative out of sometimes jumbled and disjointed life experiences—shows how the use of music can be brought to bear salvifically, beyond the context of individual pieces of music. The notion of music as soundtrack is again important here. Identity discovery/creation depends on some notion of a linear, sense-making narrative that responses to music can help create, thus providing comfort at key points in life.[47]

Knowledge songs, says Levitin, "are perhaps the crowning triumph of art, science, culture, and mind, encoding important life lessons in an artistic form that is ideally adapted to the structure and function of the human brain."[48] In terms of theological tradition, that is clear. The songs referred to here would include not only hymns but also liturgies, ways in which truths about life are preserved and passed on. Even those who might question the truth of religious songs can acknowledge their function. As Levitin himself says, "Superstitions, while inaccurate, nevertheless represent an attempt to encode knowledge."[49] Knowledge songs, then, provide all sorts of cognitive material for us to use.

In the case of Christian theology, Christians live primarily within narratives about God. The point at which knowledge songs are to be located is at the key point of the systematic theological map. Though knowledge of God comes through all of the subthemes of theology (e.g., Christ, Spirit, church), this understanding feeds into a working knowledge of God in the form of a tradition, a collection of stories by which participants in Christianity are shaped. In theological terms, personal narratives (life stories, narrated soundtracks) are mapped onto an overarching story (metanarrative) of God. When understood and used in a living way, God (as reality and story) does not stifle individual experience, even while shaping it. A person who is open to God *wants* experience to be shaped theologically. This is done dialogically with God (i.e., prayerfully). Prayer and acknowledgment of God's presence can then be recognized as practices that contribute to a flourishing human life. In musical terms, it is necessary to show how music and its reception encourages attention to such ultimate meaning, inviting the listener to respect a point of reference that grounds what it means to be human.[50]

In Levitin's account, songs of *religion* are primarily related to ritual. It is inevitable that in trying to map these songs onto the schema of Christian systematic theology, they link with sacraments, for here is where Christianity's ritual element is most pronounced. At this point in his account, Levitin recognizes the necessity of ritual for human community and survival. It is too simple to argue from this that theology is therefore also necessary. But it is most helpful to acknowledge that what is deemed to be anthropologically essential can also be viewed in theological perspective. We have indeed come full circle: from the contemporary interest in correlating use of culture—including popular culture—with sacramentality (in chap. 3), to Levitin's recognition of the vital character of ritual in human life. Yet the arguments for the theological significance of reference to sacramentality take us well beyond Levitin on "songs of religion." We shall address this shortly. For the moment we need simply to diagram results of all that we have drawn together in this chapter. They are presented in figure 10.3 below.

Questions from the Comparison: Where Next?

In light of the three stages of our mapping exercise, sharp questions now arise. In comparing Cobb's conclusions with our summary of part 2 and with the framework that Levitin supplies, where are we? We could take our inquiry in many directions. In simply noticing possible directions, we are largely suggesting work for us or others to take up. There is space in our most explicitly

Figure 10.3. A diagram of Cobb's, Levitin's, and our understandings of music and popular culture (related to loci of Christian theology)

	Revelation	God/Trinity	Christ	Spirit	Salvation/ Redemption	Human being	Church	Sacraments	Last things/ Eschatology
Cobb		God "on the move" Elusive			(Sin) Human shortcomings evident (Salvation) Human effort to save the self (Contains a ritual, social dimension) Linked to transcendence	Triumph of the ordinary Construction of the self Search for authenticity	(A social dimension of salvation) (A present dimension of "life beyond")	(A ritual element in salvation)	The role of the dead among the living ("communion of saints")
Part Two	Givenness of transcendence/ Otherness	Does one God mean one universal theology/spirituality? Does the plurality of theologies/spiritualities therefore challenge monotheism? (ch. 6) Transcendence as/ and Otherness (ch. 6)	Bodies matter profoundly/ Flesh matters (ch. 5) The physicality of transcendence (ch. 6)	Transcendence as spiritual (yet do we ever escape the body?) (ch. 6)	Musical ecstasy as salvation? (ch. 6) [Celebrities as savior figures?]	We choose who we are (what we buy shapes us, but can we control our consumption? ch. 4) Rituals express/shape identities (chs. 5 and 7) We have "personal canons" (yet authoritative voices shape our choices) (ch. 8)	How much choice do we have about who we belong to? (ch. 5) We connect with others (chs. 5 and 6) Fan community (chs. 7 and 8)	(Ritual is vital for human beings) (chs. 5 and 7) Rituals actually convey something (e.g., self-understanding) and evoke gratitude (ch. 7) Rituals accompany life-stages (ch. 5)	Transcendence as "beyond the body"—does this mean "beyond death" too? (ch. 6)
Levitin		Knowledge (Love)	(Love)		Comfort	Joy Love	Friendship (Joy) (Religion) (Love)	Religion	(Comfort)

theological chapter (next) to follow only one of these avenues in any detail. But the many potential pathways are worth identifying.

First, it would be possible to reflect on the gaps evident across the chart. Why are Christ and Spirit so absent in Cobb's reading, and Spirit-related issues lacking in Levitin's? Even when the subtext of an attention to Christ (the incarnate God's commitment to the materiality of the created order) is respected, why does Christ remain so hidden? Or if this is a mapping mistake, what is to be made of areas in which the doctrine of incarnation is implicit and needs to be made explicit? This approach would be tantamount to assessing the theological limitations of popular culture.

Second, one could focus on the areas of concentration, where activity on the chart is most dense. We would need to develop reflections especially on the human being and on salvation (Cobb and part 2) and on church and sacraments (part 2 and Levitin). The former area of concentration is not surprising; the element of human interest or real-life-relatedness in popular culture is compelling. The latter may seem more surprising, though it is merely the human interest element now set in a social key. This approach would highlight specific ways in which popular culture accentuates themes in theology, at possible cost to other themes.

Third, we could identify the agenda set by the topics that our analysis of popular music disclosed, then let that agenda play the lead role. By that we mean that although we have mapped our findings onto the framework of systematic theology, it is not *as* a series of doctrines that popular music works. Even though we shall want to clarify how contemporary theological reflection and formulation is informed by the way in which popular music functions and is used, the step from our analysis to the mapping exercise we have undertaken may still be too great.

We have decided to focus on three theological themes. This approach arises from the third possible way forward, though it links interestingly with the first two possible approaches. By reflecting on the four dominant themes we identified in our study of popular music—transcendence, embodiedness, connectedness, and ritual—we concluded that explorations of contemporary understandings of incarnation, church, and sacraments would be an appropriate conclusion to our study. Embodiedness invites a theological exploration of incarnation (and vice versa). Connectedness requires that attention be given to church and its surrogates. Ritual cannot be detached from sacraments, even while not being exhausted as a topic by being addressed through a sacramental lens. Given the emphasis on the sacraments in the theologians considered in chapter 3, it is also an appropriate place to end up. Transcendence figured extensively in the way we mapped the experience of listening to music (in relation to revelation, God, Christ, Spirit, eschatology). However, at this stage in our investigation, we considered that transcendence would prove too vast a topic to cover, and in chapter 6, we anticipated some of the relevant material and the direction such a discussion might take. Our purpose now is, rather, to offer three short dialogical, theological explorations at the point of encounter between the popular-music-listening experience and the task of contemporary theological construction. In exploring incarnation, we address a theme that was prominent (embodiedness) yet does not surface readily in the form that Christian theology might wish (Christ). Hence we try to explore a gap in what popular culture does or does not deliver—a dimension of the first approach suggested. In looking at church and sacraments, we explore dominant themes in popular music use (connectedness and ritual)—an aspect of the second possible approach sketched above. In giving full rein to the forms in which the themes are invited, however, we are seeking to permit a much greater playfulness and critical interaction in the dialogue being overheard between popular music and theology than might have been possible with a straightforward thematic theological starting point. In his stimulating volume *Poetic Theology: God and the Poetics of Everyday Life*, William A. Dyrness declares that "the implications of a poetic theology are still largely to be worked out."[51] We agree, though we hope that this initial attempt to reflect creatively on theological themes that arise directly from a particular practice of everyday life goes some way toward addressing what Dyrness rightly says is necessary. Theologians must not speak just to one another, nor must the church look only within to discern what God is doing. This is the theological assumption that drives Dyrness's project as well as our own.

embodied social rituals

Revisiting Theology through Popular Music

In the previous two chapters we showed how listening to music functions as a practice that, whether or not located within a specific form of religiosity, can be seen to operate in a religion-like way (chap. 9). Rather than make any claim that music fandom *is* a religion, however, our purpose was simply to suggest that attention be paid to the elements of listening that reveal it to be a spiritual discipline for many users. Whether or not music listeners explicitly recognize this element in their own practice, this aspect of the study of contemporary music use enables the pro-spirituality/antireligion outlook to be acknowledged. It enables us to establish a positive base upon which to pose a set of questions about the explicit practice of religion and the subject-matter of theology.

In chapter 10, we turned from form and practice to content. We offered an interpretation of the material presented in part 2, locating this within a more general theology of popular culture (Cobb) and within an anthropological reading of the function of music in society (Levitin). By mapping all three onto a framework of systematic theology, we were able to notice emphases and gaps in the way sustained and serious listening to popular music relates to the content of theology. We are now in a position to take matters a stage further. In keeping with a concern in the dialogue between theology/religion and popular

163

culture not simply to log material that illustrates what theology already knows, we must now venture some suggestions of what the experience of listening may contribute to theology in the present. We offer three worked explorations—case studies—of theological themes where we can see music-listening practices constructively affecting the contemporary construal of these themes. The three themes to be explored are incarnation, church, and sacraments. At the very least the explorations press for sharp, contemporary articulation of these three themes. We suggest, however, that the explorations go further in showing major weaknesses in how these themes are often currently addressed.

Embodiedness/Incarnation: The Divine Value of Materiality

Incarnation and an Incarnational Principle

Christianity is caught between its clear commitment to the incarnation and its espousal of an incarnational principle. It rightly seeks to maintain both, though the balancing act necessary to do this is not always easy. "The incarnation," as Oliver Crisp observes, "is the central and defining event of Christian theology. The doctrine that the Second Person of the Trinity assumes human nature, becoming a human being in order to bring about the salvation of fallen human beings, lies at the heart of the traditional teaching of the church."[1] A number of observations can be made about this summary. First, the primary reference is to an *event* rather than a doctrine. This is worth highlighting in order to maintain the emphasis on an action of God in history, rather than on the interpretation that surrounds it. Second, when interpreted doctrinally, this event is instantly linked to other doctrinal themes, specifically, Trinity and salvation. From the outset, then, the incarnation is not to be viewed in isolation, even when contextualized in relation to a fixed point in history. Third, it is important to keep in mind Adrian Hastings's observation of what he calls the "necessary incomprehensibility of the Incarnation" since human understanding depends on "classes of things and comparisons, on what we can measure experimentally. None of this is available for the Incarnation. . . . Here is something by definition unique."[2]

The historical specificity of the incarnation (God did something in the past, in the person of Jesus Christ, that occurred at a fixed point) can, however, lead us to downplay the impact of the incarnation throughout history, and its connection to other doctrinal themes. In doing this we would be giving short shrift to the incarnational principle that needs to function in order to say something about the God who was and is incarnate in Christ. If incarnation (en-flesh-ment, coming into flesh) says something about God, it says that the creator God is profoundly committed to the created order, wishes to redeem it fully (rescue it from any wrong turnings), and engages with the created order in all its frailty, fragility, vulnerability, and wickedness to enable this redemption to be possible.

This means, as is often said, that matter (all matter) matters to God, not only the good or beautiful bits.[3]

From Crisp's essay on incarnation, however, it is possible to gain the impression that the (doctrine of) incarnation has the purpose solely of speaking of Christ with respect to clarifying the natures of Christ back then (in the first century). Crisp summarily dismisses challenges to classical Chalcedonian Christology and makes no attempt to explore what the doctrine of incarnation means beyond the clarification of natures within the person of Christ.[4] Thus Crisp does not consider the notion of an incarnational principle that flows from what *is* explored, which is saying something important about how God acts and can be encountered now, in light of interpretation of the incarnation event (of Christ).

Crisp is being true to the preoccupations of much of early Christian tradition here and is no doubt working within the limitations of the edited volume for which he wrote. So he can perhaps be excused for his emphasis to some extent. That said, there is something rather alarming about a contemporary Christian theological textbook that makes no effort to articulate the full significance of "the central and defining event of Christian theology."[5]

Our contention is that the way in which popular music works, and the reflections that inevitably flow from observations about its working, require fresh attentiveness to the meanings of incarnation. Christian commitment to incarnation inevitably implies a positive view of the body. Christian concern about overattention to the body or idolization of the body may often seem to be more dominant across the church scene, however.[6] Youth workers and parents across the world express anxiety about the early and oversexualization of the body. These concerns are real and understandable. But our theological task here is to explore what *positive* view of the body can continue to be maintained even in the face of the apparent idolization of embodiment. It is imperative that the positive Christian stance toward the body is not lost beneath concerns about a descent to hedonism. The body is a source of delight and pleasure, and enjoyment of popular music cries out for this appropriate respect to be given.

Christian Ambiguity about the Body

As we examine the function of popular music in this respect, however, we must freely admit the theological tension that is present all through Christian thought and practice. We have wrestled with it as cowriters. One of us is more steeped in the liberal Catholic Anglican/Episcopalian tradition, the other in Free Church Protestantism. We have noticed that this has produced a more and a less favorable stance toward the body, respectively. Rather than allowing this difference in our standpoints to hinder our exploration, we offer it as evidence of Christianity's ambiguity about the body, despite its commitment to an incarnate God. We each acknowledge ambiguity at Christianity's heart about the body. In the realms of both theory and practice, Christianity both affirms the body (God's incarnation in Christ supports this) and denies it (the flesh is suspect, the body must be subjugated, and the passions must be kept in firm check). But Christian thought and practice can be read in different ways. On the one hand, we recognize that the body has played an immensely complex role within Christian history and theology, and that Christianity in both East and West has at times taken a positive as well as negative attitude to the body and the material world. Neither view can be shown to have proved finally dominant; yet the body itself has become a site of conflict for numerous theological, ethical, and political issues over time.[7] On the other hand, it could be argued that despite this ambiguity, Christianity has too often seemed to favor a negative approach to the body—to the point where a near-gnostic attitude has been too close to the surface throughout its history. In the modern period, especially post–World War II, the reaction against Christianity's negativity about the body has been keenly felt. Even if it could be argued that this negative view (within Christianity) was very much shaped by Christianity's opponents, there is no escaping the fact that the opponents were at least latching on to a potential, and in some cases actual, Christian tendency.[8] Throughout the 1960s, popular culture, including popular music, challenged the negative attitudes toward the body and was part of a general movement to present "unorthodox religious ideas" or "criticism of the church."[9]

What is, then, the challenge issued to Christian thought and practice by the huge attention paid to the body in the practice of popular music—simply by the way music works? What is to be done theologically with that emphasis? As admitted, there is much that can be cited as questionable or negative about contemporary obsession with the body. It is no coincidence that thriving modern popular music, associated with freedom from tradition and institutions and with promotion of individual self-expression, has often implicitly and explicitly encouraged unbridled sexual self-expression and experimentation and abetted drug use, whether with alcohol or with hard (addictive) or soft (less harmful) drugs. Moral questions instantly arise when we explore these associations. Here is not the place to begin the important critical discussions about the role the churches have sought to play and must undoubtedly play in dealing with moral issues. We must simply recognize that although forms of extreme behavior may appear to be easily labeled as morally dubious, the Christian stance can equally easily indicate a refusal to address questions about the body's needs, pleasures, and potential.

Theological factors prove crucial in such deliberations. Music listeners may explicitly pose philosophical questions about their existence, questions that theologians want to hear: Is this my only life? Am I subject to the chemical processes of my body even when I think I have free choice? Do I survive physical death in any form? Whether or not music listeners raise such questions, the music survey we conducted shows that the body is viewed as a vehicle for transcendence. Music itself, alone, may take people to the edge of human experience, in and as a body. But the quest for, or interest in, experiences of transcendence discloses a desire to go as far as one can *as a body* in search of something that takes us beyond the everyday. There is a sense in which the extremes of experience, which practices that often accompany music listening—sex, drugs, and alcohol—may provide are but recognition of the desire to go to the edge of embodied experience, even while recognizing that it is only in and as bodies that such experiences can be enjoyed at all. If excess is puzzling and deeply damaging at times, it is also an acknowledgment of the body's importance and its capacity to enable ecstasy and fulfillment to occur.

A Christian moral judgment about damage done to the body is easy to make, on the grounds of disrespect for the body as divine gift; nevertheless, to fail to enjoy the capacity of the body could be regarded as equally sinful. Not to use the body physically, and not to glorify God by enjoying the body's receptiveness through whatever senses a human has access to is to fail to respect the body's God-given grace. Popular music's celebration of embodiment, when seen in positive terms, is thus an accentuation of the gift of embodiment in keeping with the Christian affirmation of God incarnate. Though it is understandable in historical, contextual terms why post–World War II churches struggled to come to terms with the rise of popular music, it is now theologically baffling how opposition could continue in any unqualified sense.[10] However, while churches might still display caution and express opposition to certain lyrics and to the harmful excesses of behavior that are connected with popular music, the growth of Christian rock and popular music, inside and outside of worship, demonstrates at least an acceptance of the form of such music and celebrates the pleasure of the body.

But if the basis of such a judgment is an incarnational principle (matter matters to God, and God is active in and through bodies), what has all this to do with Christ? And what might such theological reflection then have to offer, if anything, to a Friday-night clubber? We offer an answer to the second question at the end of the chapter. In response to the first, here is precisely where Oliver Crisp's approach to the doctrine of incarnation, and others like it, is found wanting. It certainly is necessary to outline the purpose behind early Christian explorations of the human and divine natures of Christ. Furthermore, it is vital to emphasize the close relationship between Christology and soteriology. Only God could and can save, and only by God's taking full part in the created order (and not remaining detached from it) could redemption happen.[11] Where this point is not fully articulated, not enough is being said about God. It is essential to emphasize the universal reach of God's becoming incarnate and the extent of the doctrinal claim being made. The scandal of particularity—that God became human at a specific point in history—is, however, made too scandalously particular if the equally scandalous generosity of God's self-involvement in the created order is played down. That continuing interaction is wholly consistent with a strong doctrine of creation. It is also a direct corollary of a trinitarian doctrine of God (the Holy Spirit continues the action of the creator God, as known in and through Christ). But unless these further theological ideas are underpinned christologically by a strong doctrine of incarnation (God in Christ came and continues to be present in flesh in the world), then Christian thought and practice will not be either as universal in scope or as materialist as it needs to be.[12] God's continuing action in the world is not just a *consequence* of God's action in Jesus Christ. It *is* the continuing action of God *in Christ*.[13]

The Dispersed Body of Christ

One theologian who saw the full implications of what early Christians were doing in the way they interpreted Jesus as the Christ was David Friedrich Strauss (1808–1874). Though his insights were never fully accepted, and he paid dearly within his academic career for even publishing his reflections, his work offers two major contributions to our present task. Interestingly, although banished for the seemingly unorthodox nature of his views, the extract of his we use below features regularly in standard Christian theology textbooks and readers. It is, in other words, clearly seen in the history of mainstream, orthodox Christian theology that Strauss has explained something important. What is that?

First, following the philosopher Hegel, Strauss insists on the importance of the divine Spirit's becoming material.[14] What Christians perceive as a result of encountering Jesus and acknowledging him as the Christ is *what God has always been and always will be like*. It may indeed be true to say that God has learned something new by being incarnate in Christ.[15] Yet the incarnation indicates who God is and the way in which God relates to the world *as* embodied Spirit. God seeks embodiment. It is only thus that the created order can be redeemed. This insight draws out the impact of God's incarnation beyond the lifetime of Jesus of Nazareth (theologically essential and explains what the early fathers needed to do in formulating early Christian doctrine), and also confirms the divine stamp of approval on the material order. "All flesh" (KJV) may well be "like grass" (Ps. 103:15; Isa. 40:6; 1 Pet. 1:24), and "flesh" is used as a negative term in Paul's theology (e.g., Rom 7:5, 14; Gal. 6:8). But such references must not lead Christian theology to devalue the body, for bodies are of God, created by God for good purposes, even though they decay and can be misused. The resurrection of the body is to be understood as the supreme affirmation of the body's value.

The second and even more far-reaching insight contained in Strauss's work is the recognition that the doctrine of incarnation says something about humanity as a whole. In Strauss's words:

> This is the key to the whole of Christology, that, as subject of the predicate which the church assigns to Christ, we place, instead of an individual, an idea; but an idea which has an existence in reality, not in the mind only. . . . In an individual,

a God-man, the properties and functions which the church ascribes to Christ contradict themselves; in the idea of the race, they perfectly agree. Humanity is the union of the two natures—God becomes man, the infinite manifesting itself in the finite, and the finite spirit remembering its infinitude.[16]

A number of observations need to be made here. Strauss speaks of an "idea." Christ becomes an "idea" for Strauss. Once Jesus of Nazareth was no longer physically present in the world, a new way had to be found for understanding "Christ." It is, though, unhelpful to speak of Christ as "idea," even though Strauss also wants to claim that the presence of Christ "has an existence in reality, not in the mind only." In other words, Strauss recognizes that the continuing presence of Christ must be understood concretely, and that it is theologically wrong to go on speaking of Christ as incarnate only in a single person. He is desperate to articulate the significance of Jesus the Christ in a way that links him with the whole of humanity.

His mistake is that of *replacing* an insight about God's incarnation in Jesus Christ with a claim for God's incarnation throughout the whole of humanity. Rather, his suggestions could press more positively for the continuity of God's presence in Christ (Jesus) with the nature of that divine presence after the death and resurrection. However, by not being too ecclesiologically preoccupied, Strauss is clear that a commitment to incarnation must extend to the whole of humankind.

We therefore learn from Strauss nevertheless. We want to accentuate Strauss's correct insight into what can perhaps be called the dispersal of Christ throughout humanity. Christ lives only in diaspora, yet is really present in embodied form, celebrated in flesh, and incorporated in social bodies. It is this insight, we claim, that people's musical enjoyment at its best is tapping into. *How* that celebration and incorporation is to be fully and appropriately recognized and marked takes us well beyond this book. But that it is a theological, and specifically a christological, matter has been shown by the argument of this book, we believe. Human bodies matter that much.

Articulation of a doctrine of incarnation falls short, then, when it does not have the whole of humanity in view. When the whole of humanity, indeed the whole of creation, is brought into view, it does not mean that God is embodied within it without remainder, or that God can be found in just any place. It means that God *can* appear in the form of Christ wherever God chooses and where creation does not prevent God from being incarnate in this way. Here is the incarnational principle of which we spoke at the start of this section: reflection on Jesus the Christ is vital as the means by which it is possible to discern where God is now present. Talk of Christians as "mini-Christs" can too easily become sloppy as a way of describing the extent to which Christians are to seek to imitate Christ: such talk may end up claiming too much.[17] The incarnational principle suggests something more basic, and something not just confined to Christians:

God seeks presence wherever the God-givenness of creation is acknowledged and wherever therefore the divine value of materiality is celebrated. This insight informs our two further theological explorations (into church and sacraments), which we shall now conduct.

Connectedness/Church: The Indispensability of the Social

The significance of people's being connected through music (itself another notion of embodiment)—be this emotionally with an artist, with one another as fans, or in the context of live performance—came through strongly as an emphasis in our analysis of the way popular music works (part 2). In formal social and social psychological terms, this sense of connectedness links with the concepts of the visible and invisible church. The church exists as both a present, concrete reality (in multiple local forms) and a collection of communities across the world in the present and throughout time. Our *theological* exploration of the concept of church is not, however, focused on this formal similarity between fan communities and church. Though the likeness exists, in itself it means little more than that groups are important. Rather, our theological exploration uses some of the substantive functions of the social groups that popular-music fandom creates to explore what is meant theologically by the concept "church." In the process we are exploring what may be termed the "indispensability of the social" for human flourishing. But we are doing so in a way that seeks to get at the meaning of church via an experiential route, without neglecting the tradition of thinking about the concept of church that Christianity carries with it. We also draw directly on the insights gained about the incarnational principle brought forward from the previous section. Let us express our starting point succinctly: If God in Christ seeks presence in the world today, in embodied form, then where and how, socially, will God be recognized as such? Our answer is not simply "wherever people listening to popular music are having a good time." But we do want to ask: when popular-music fans are having a good time and with their intentional listening are doing so much more than casually hearing, what impact does this have on contemporary understandings of the concept of church?[18]

Ralph Del Colle begins his 2007 chapter on "The Church" with stern warnings about limitations apparent in readings of the sociological reality of the church undertaken by nontheological disciplines. "Ecclesiology," he says, "cannot afford to be distracted by digressions that subvert its theological integrity."[19] He claims that his remarks "are not an opening polemical overture in favor of strictly classical theological interests," for "the doctrine of the church can no more elide over [omit] the church as material object, its historical and sociological reality, than Christology can diminish the importance of the Jesus of history."[20] While we agree with the latter statement, we are not so sure that Del Colle avoids polemics as much as he claims. There is a quest for theological purism here that may be misplaced. We do applaud the linking of ecclesiology with Christology. By extension we also draw on the conclusion reached in our previous section. Not only can Christology not do without exploration of the Jesus of history; likewise, it cannot do without attention to the concrete forms of Christ's presence in ensuing history. Similarly, if those forms of Christ take us well beyond easily identifiable manifestations of God's concrete presence and action (e.g., as church), then the concrete forms of social living that are constitutive of the contemporary body/bodies of Christ may take us, in ecclesiology, well beyond easily identifiable forms of church. Since "church" is "wherever Jesus Christ is,"[21] the historical and sociological realities that need to be addressed in order better to clarify what "church" means are more and more various than may at first be supposed. Ignatius of Antioch cannot have had a Bruce Springsteen concert in mind when he uttered his second-century words. In the present we do not wish to claim that a Springsteen concert is a church in any unqualified sense. Yet at the start of the twenty-first century, we have no option other than to explore ways in which many forms of social groups and gatherings not only function as surrogate churches, but also overlap with explicitly identifiable churches insofar as they are the concrete, physical manifestations of the presence of God in Christ in the world today.[22]

What, then, would be expected of social groups for them to function as churches for those who participate in (belong to) them? And what would exploration of such groups mean for a contemporary doctrine of church? Of the possible hallmarks of church—understood as a contemporary social manifestation of God's presence as known in Christ—three stand out from the perspective of what serious music fandom does to and for people: deep and liberative friendships, truth-seeking thinking, and justice-seeking action.

Friendships

In part 2, we recognized the sheer intensity with which bonds are formed between fans and artists, and among fans themselves. Deep, meaningful friendships are formed among fans, and through these friendships, and in triangular interaction with an artist and his or her music, meaning-making happens. An artist's work becomes the de facto canon of scripture over against which fans undertake their reflection about life and values. The process of meaning-making does not make a fan group into church in any other than a sociological sense. There are no explicitly theological values necessarily involved in fans and listeners' meeting together or discovering common ground. However, when combined with the ethical and political impact of the meaning-making that occurs through such deep friendships, then a fan group can begin to take on some of the function of a church. When a fan community shapes political commitments that, for example, strive to foster justice, peace, and freedom for the fans and for others, then it is even possible to say that such a group seems more church-like than the church itself insofar as it functions as a body of people in and through whom God's will can become evident.

Here is where the second hallmark—truth-seeking—comes into play. A church is a truth-seeking community. It is not a community containing all truth, for no community can be that. There must be eschatological reticence about all claims to truth, even though Christians believe they have enough truth about God to live on, given that Christ has come. But a church is a truth-seeking community in two senses. Linked with the first hallmark (friendships), the element of truth-seeking means that open truthfulness is a feature of the relationships that make up a church.

Truth-Seeking

First, where Christ is, truthfulness exists in human relations. Where truthfulness exists in human relations, then this is evidence of God's presence, awaiting recognition. Second, a church is a truth-seeking community insofar as it binds people in the common cause of the search for truth. This is not an abstract truth but a practical truth, one in which theory and theology are needed to serve truthful action. For Michael Welker, "truth-seeking communities" are guided by the Spirit of God. They "are not groups of people who look around somehow to find some kind of truth. Nor do they claim to possess the full truth and speak it with the expectation that everybody else must simply listen, agree, and obey." They are, though, "willing to formulate truth claims and to express an utmost certainty."[23] For Welker, the truth claims expressed with certainty will be theologically grounded and hence argued, as Martin Luther did, from Scripture and reason. How, though, does such a theological reading of a truth-seeking community square up with, say, the communal truth-seeking evident among a group of U2 fans who share the group's political commitments, or festival-attending music lovers inspired to trade fairly or live frugally as a consequence of their involvement? Again, it is only through a christological lens that such activity is recognized as God's work. But that such truth-seeking is the presence and activity of God, and not merely church-like behavior, is borne out when we attend to the third hallmark of church that is sometimes evident among music fans: justice-seeking.

Justice-Seeking

If truth-seeking seems too abstract or distant from what the enjoyment of music entails, then attention to justice-seeking reveals the more practical way in which fans are often led to consider the ethical and political implications of their musical commitments. This is admittedly tricky territory. The notion of justice-seeking may seem far away from the antics of some music fans at a drunken rave. Yet the kinds of contexts just cited under truth-seeking serve as reminders that music commitments do correlate with political activity. And where justice is sought, there is Christ. Let us take a topical example: Is Lady Gaga's clear attempt to encourage social acceptance of homosexuality in her song "Born This Way," along with the communal way in which this is encouraged (via seeing fans as "little monsters" and as participants in the "Monster Ball"), an example of justice-seeking or of something more sinister? At the local church level in the UK, we have heard examples of Christians describing Lady Gaga and her music as "demonic." She is certainly playful, creative, willfully exploring (as does Madonna) prominent Christian themes from her early life (especially from the Roman Catholic tradition in which she was raised) in her songs and videos. Her attention-seeking, image-changing behavior is cleverly commercial too. At the point of reception—in the midst of much seemingly outlandish behavior by the artist and her followers—a point is being made: God has made people the way they are, of whatever ethnic background, of whatever level of physical ability, and of whatever sexual orientation. Whether this viewpoint is actually shared by all her followers and whether its implications are carried through in the contexts where the song is sung and among her fans—that is another matter. But as a blatantly theological statement in contemporary public life, and as a challenge to society and church alike, the potency of the song and its reception is unquestionable.[24]

Church and Kingdom

To claim Lady Gaga fans as a form of church is to go too far, although she herself has claimed that her concerts are a religious experience.[25] However, it is a legitimate and timely exercise to ask how the church, as reality and concept, might be challenged to pay more attention to what is already happening in social contexts where the making of deep friendships, truth-seeking, and justice-seeking are evident. One objection to such an approach is that this is to confuse the church and the kingdom of God. It is the kingdom of God—the eschatologically shaped way of understanding what God intends ultimately for the world, as the world appears here and now—that is our way of trying to describe what the world should be like. And all we see are glimpses of this. The church cannot *be* the kingdom, for no human community can. If any human community anticipates it—even the church—it is only in a sketchy way. The objection carries weight. But it does not overwhelm the fact that it is the church's task to bear witness to the kingdom, both in its own life and in the way it interprets what is happening elsewhere in society.

The relationship and tension between the church and the kingdom of God, then, is evident especially at the point where it is clear that the church is *not* the kingdom of God (though it does constitute a community that seeks truth and justice). And it is itself judged when there are examples throughout society where truth and justice seem to be more keenly sought outside the formal bounds of the church. At this point churchgoers everywhere will be able to acknowledge that they know people who have left churches for places where friendships seemed to be deeper and truth and justice seemed to be more actively sought. Many readers who are churchgoers may have been similarly tempted. Music communities and music fandoms overlap with churches but also sometimes function as rival communities. For there, in the company of other fans, in deep communion with the music and with others, is where the conviction arises that ultimate meaning has been disclosed, discovered, or created.

Can such fan communities sustain such meaning over the long haul? Fan communities may look like church and function as meaning-generating communities insofar as they achieve the three things we have highlighted here. But will they have enough resources to keep on supporting people consistently? The question of how the social reality of church might enhance the experience of music fans who already participate in a fulfilling community takes us well beyond this book. But in creating, in its own ritual practice, gatherings that invite people to share a common experience through which to interpret the rest of life, it thereby fosters its own form of fandom. To the significance of ritual—in popular music and Christianity—we now turn.

Ritual/Sacraments: When Symbols Are More than Just Symbolic

The third theme of systematic theology that we wish to explore may seem to be the most surprising. Yet in the light of what we saw contemporary Christian theologians doing with the arts and popular culture (Brown, Beaudoin, and Smith, in chap. 3), and the discoveries and reflections presented in part 2, discussion of sacraments is now an obvious step to take. We shall approach only the two most widely accepted sacraments—baptism and Holy Communion/ Eucharist/Lord's Supper—by a circuitous route.[26] Their appearance in popular culture is not prominent. However, it is necessary to expound the theology of sacrament and to tell the story of how and why only two (or seven) are normally celebrated across the Christian world.

Chapter 7 of our study, where we examined aspects of the explicitly ritualistic use of popular music, provides a basic framework for what we must look at; our studies of embodiment and emotion provide more concrete detail of the raw material with which we must work to understand popular music's sacramental potential. Popular music really can do more than merely entertain. Because it can generate lasting embodied, emotional experiences in a ritualistic context, it can have an impact on a person's inner life and on one's life choices, which invites critical correlation with the way in which sacraments work. The experience of reception and use of forms of popular music—not *just* the music itself, and not *any* music—can mediate (impart, channel, deliver, convey) something to the listener/user beyond what can be computed from the lyrics sung or notes played. It is this mediation that merits exploration. In the same way that sacraments are held not just to symbolize but also to convey divine grace, so also we are faced with the fact that popular music can do more than just provide temporary enjoyment for its listeners. It can do things *to* and *for* them. They *receive* something. But what is being mediated or conveyed? From what? To whom? What are the conditions of reception?

At an international conference on religion and popular culture in 2011, attended by both cowriters, one of the main speakers made a striking claim: the experience he enjoyed at a concert of popular music was "exactly the same" as he had enjoyed in an act of Christian worship earlier in his life. He did not provide full scientific evidence for this claim, and it would have taken quite an exercise to establish its strict accuracy. But it was what he felt and thought, and it fits with Richard K. Fenn's claim that the sacred is "more likely to appear not according to the schedules of institutionalized religion, nor on specific days and at certain seasons, but in more obscure, diffuse, and unpredictable forms. As everyday life has become open and permeable to outside influences, specialized roles and mundane routines may become increasingly responsive to the demands for personal satisfaction, meaning, and transcendental significance."[27] Yet it was possible for the claim to be made only because the conference speaker had, at one time in his life, participated in Christian worship, inhabited the Christian worldview, and been trained in how to read or interpret human experience in a Christian way. It is questionable how his later experience might have seemed without that earlier Christian experience and interpretation. Would the later music-generated experience even have *been* the same experience? Would he have been able to identify what was happening to him as "the same experience" as what Christians around him report? These are unanswerable questions with respect to that particular speaker. They are difficult questions to address in any context, yet they arise when any consideration is given to trying to compare experiences across different religious traditions, and where experiences labeled "religious" are compared with other human experiences. They arise here for us, given our suggestion that in certain contexts and patterns of use, popular music can function sacramentally and that therefore some of the same things are going on when music is performed and listened to, as when a Christian is baptized or participating in Holy Communion. Such a stark statement needs clarifying and defending.

Defining and Exploring Sacraments

The first thing for us to acknowledge about sacraments is that they entail more than words. Though they involve words, they "employ acts and objects that impinge on all the senses and also on the unconscious."[28] Hence, if we are to work backward from human experiences that appear to achieve similar things that sacraments do, we should expect a range of nonverbal factors to be at work. Building on words from David Brown, cited in chapter 3, we should expect to be able to discern something "of the god . . . as it were, embodied" and being encountered in embodied form at the confluence of affective and aesthetic experience.

What, though, is it that is being embodied or encountered, in order to function sacramentally? In the same way as the speaker who claimed to have "the same experience" in both Christian worship and a popular music concert, does one need to already know (from baptism and Holy Communion) what one is looking for? To some extent, this is true. There are features clearly evident in baptism and Holy Communion that enable the shape and content of a sacramental experience to be recognized. But what are these, and how might these features appear in other forms?

From baptism comes the experiences of cleansing, refreshment, identity, and belonging. Through Holy Communion one enjoys the experiences of solidarity, participation, defiance in the face of suffering, being forgiven and accepted, receiving a gift, and anticipation of ultimate communal well-being.[29] Within the framework of this range of potential human experiences an experience may be deemed sacramental.

It is no surprise that many of the experiences reported and reflected on in part 2 fall within this framework. References to experiencing transcendence are themselves purging experiences, experiences of release, invigoration, and refreshment. The sense of connectedness already examined in this chapter denotes identity, belonging (to others), solidarity, and participation. The tingle factor (see chap. 6) suffuses all of this due to the emotional intensity with which these experiences are felt. The truth- and justice-seeking elements in the experiences that led us to look at the ecclesiological similarities are suggestive of the ultimate well-being that is envisioned and worked toward.

Although direct correlations can be drawn, we cannot conclude that such experiences are the *same as* baptism and Holy Communion in all respects. We are not claiming that the two sacraments are fully matched by the experiences identified. We are saying, however, that popular music can generate sufficient experiences to merit closer scrutiny from a sacramental perspective. In other words, what popular music does is not simply sacramental-like: it *is* sacramental experience. Popular music is a medium through which God can self-communicate to generate encounters with God that are genuine and wholly consistent with what happens in baptism and Holy Communion. Starting from the other end: baptism and Holy Communion are specific practices that use defined symbols ("matter," to use the technical term of sacramental theology) and will always mean more than what is produced by popular cultural practices. The challenge, however, is to establish (1) the value of locating the experiences generated by popular music within the sacramental framework, and (2) the dangers of defining sacramental experience too narrowly in relation to the two (or seven) sacraments.

To establish that popular music can function sacramentally is to acknowledge its potential aesthetic, affective, and spiritual function. Simon Frith did not have theology or religious studies in mind when he declared, "Pop can't be sensibly analysed just in terms of musicology or aesthetics. . . . It is . . . pop—more than any other form of music—that changes if not our lives then certainly the ways in which we feel about them."[30] But he is creating space for the interpretation of popular music's reception as offered here. To work backward from what such music *actually does to and for people* means then inviting a range of ways—including the religious—of grasping what is happening in human experience and interpreting what this experience means: how it connects with a person's values, understanding of life's purpose, and how people choose to act.

A Sacramental Challenge to Popular Music

The specifically Christian sacramental framework offers a number of challenges. We cite two examples. First, if one does feel cleansed, purged, or refreshed, then how does this experience, which music may bring, fit into a pattern of experience that will be needed regularly? To put this another way (more theologically): the experience of refreshment or cleansing can be seen as an expulsion, or handling of unpleasant, negative experiences. Is this a form of forgiveness, or at the very least a therapeutic release from the consequences of one's own known failings, or from a sense of being sinned against? Baptism admits one to a community of people who know that they will need forgiveness regularly and will receive this from God in the context of worship. Far from being a negative view of the human person, it is a sobering, healthy outlook that recognizes the importance of a primary forgiving community to which one belongs, and the constant cleansing that a person needs. Even if transcendence and connectedness through music can match this to some extent, this process of constant refreshment generally is not as tightly or clearly structured as within religious practice.

Second, Holy Communion brings together, in principle and frequently in practice, a community of people of differing social and ethnic backgrounds, levels of education, and sense of personal worth. In concrete form it anticipates an eschatological community where divisions fall because all are equal before God.[31] One of the names for Holy Communion, Eucharist (thanksgiving, thankfulness), declares the reason for this sense of togetherness and eschatological anticipation. It is, in Shawn Copeland's words, a "more comprehensive notion of thanksgiving" than "ordinary attitudes or gestures of thanksgiving."[32] Can the sense of gratitude, joy, togetherness, and generosity that a Eucharist at its best embodies and evokes be reflected in the way communal gatherings and individuals respond to what popular music generates? The answer is determined by whether charity flows from their music use. Here "charity" is used in the sense of "sharing with and for others." To cite Copeland again,

> Humanity can only reveal itself as a site of God's presence when it enters into the final act of being human: sharing with and for others, or charity (*caritas*). . . . Charity is often thought of in terms of kindness, or events of giving. However, the meaning of charity transcends reflection and action, incorporating affect as well. Affect refers to the feelings and emotions that ground human interaction. . . . Theologically, the Christian notion of charity is exemplified in the incarnation.[33]

Music fans are frequently moved by music—individually and in groups—in ways that affect their behavior, both as individuals and toward others. We see this when fans function as truth-seeking and justice-seeking communities. But fan communities are challenged by the concept of the church as a eucharistic community insofar as the latter holds out the hope of being a radically diverse community. Even if the church itself, in some of its many concrete forms (especially in the Western world), may fail to make such a vision come alive, nevertheless Holy Communion/Eucharist/Lord's Supper as a practice aspires to and at times embodies the vision and dramatizes that toward which the church lives.

A moral judgment is being made here, of course. But it is not a judgment made by a succeeding church over against failing fan communities. Rather, it is a moral question being asked of both communities, in the light of a message and a social practice (Holy Communion) that the church carries with it and enacts. In being a eucharistic community, the church also affirms eucharistic or Eucharist-like practice that occurs outside of it; recognizes those who give thanks, express joy, and look toward a better future for all; and invites them to use the insights of eucharistic theology and thereby take further the insights that their practice entails.

Popular Music Questions the Sacraments

There is, though, an important question to be asked in the other direction too. If the theology and practice of sacraments can affirm, yet challenge and question the sacrament-like activity of music fans, what do music fans ask of Christian thought and practice? At this point we must briefly touch on the story of how the church ended up with a limited number of sacraments. It was not until Peter Lombard's thinking in the twelfth century and Thomas Aquinas's work in the thirteenth century that the number of sacraments settled down to the now customary seven (in Catholic and Orthodox traditions) and then two (for post–Reformation Protestant traditions).[34] Before this time, baptism and Holy Communion were routinely practiced, and their importance in Christian practice cannot be disputed; yet there was quite a range of other practices through which divine grace was held to be not just symbolized but also actually conveyed. In his list Augustine is thought to have considered as many as thirty different practices as sacraments, including reciting the Nicene Creed and the Lord's Prayer. Other practices widely supported included "the consecration of a Christian king, the distribution of ashes, the sprinkling of holy water, and the rite of Christian burial."[35] Now admittedly this list of practices is overtly religious. But in times when religious practices were less clearly demarcated from daily living, and when people were less able to distinguish between religious and political acts, what now looks like a religious list would have seemed much more like a set of practices closely connected with everyday life. To produce a present list of equivalent practices—if such an imaginative task could even succeed—would require us to draw on practices that would seem quite secular. In musical terms, precisely the kind of things that Daniel Levitin drew to our attention (singing national anthems, using songs and hymns at sporting events) could be seen as equivalents to some earlier contenders to be sacraments.

What popular music actually achieves—at its best, when taken seriously by its fans—should invite us to reflect on the potential dangers of treating sacramental theology and practice too narrowly. It is too easy to allow the two or seven sacraments used within our own traditions to prevent our seeing how God acts in many ways outside of church practices.[36] This was precisely David Brown's concern and the basis of his project, which we summarized in chapter 3. A small number of sacraments and the propensity to devalue that which is "not church" can turn churchgoing into an idolatrous practice (if Christians worship their own habits). When Christians have a negative view of "the world," they may miss the action of God's incarnate Spirit in the world. This, then, is the challenge brought by close attention to positive, life-affirming, politically charged aspects of music fandom. If Christians are not open to God's action beyond church life, then their faith is impoverished.

Here we are not arguing for a formal expansion of the number of sacraments. Yet the findings of this study, when located within contemporary theological thinking about popular culture and the arts with respect to sacramental theology, do require us to argue for a substantial broadening of perception, an expanding generosity of perception about where God in Christ is and what God is doing in human life today. Without this broadened perception, an unduly judgmental view of much popular culture is likely to be adopted, leading churches to become ever more isolated in their social and public role.

Theology in Public Discourse about Music

It could be argued that this is as things should be. In Europe mainstream churches are in numerical decline, and churches that are growing (independent, evangelical, Pentecostal) may be less interested in secular music than members of mainstream churches, while at the same time often using styles of secular music in their worship. In any case, what right do Christians have to join public discussion about secular music? Church leaders and Christian theologians should keep their noses out of the critical discussion happening on the left-hand side of the Magisteria-Ibiza Spectrum (chap. 2). Some claim they have no business there and no authority to speak.

It is precisely this chain of assumptions that we wish to challenge. For one thing, Christians of all persuasions and denominational affiliations are actually listening to very diverse music. Too little empirical study has been undertaken thus far about how Christians think their consumption of secular music influences their faith. With respect to public discussion of popular music, religious commentators need to be involved. But it will not do for Christians to be ill-informed in such discussion. While acknowledging the difficulty of Christians receiving a fair hearing in public discussions of popular culture, this book has sought to demonstrate how this might be done, to present the theological basis on which it can be done, and to argue that it is necessary for Christians to contribute.

We began our third theological discussion in this chapter with the example of the speaker who claimed to have had the same experience in Christian worship as in a popular-music concert. We hope to have shown, both in relation to this example and throughout this book as a whole, that it is not just a matter of adding words to a secular example to demonstrate theological meaning and value, as if the experience itself is left behind. The reality is much more complex. As with a sacrament, words are there; yet meanings are contained within the practice. God speaks and acts in the doing of the act. Like a sacrament, across many secular examples—including popular music—theological meanings may well be contained within music's reception itself. Reflection is still needed to draw out all that the music may be achieving. But the sense that a concert and worship have produced the "same experience" remains an important insight, however difficult it may be to show exactly what that experience means and whether the equivalence can be proved. Nevertheless our attempt to depict—in the Spectrum presented in chapter 2 and adapted in this chapter—how affective space can be shaped culturally and theologically goes some way to showing the common ground between these experiences and the factors that contribute to their production and nature.

Summary Reflection

In this chapter we explored three doctrinal themes: incarnation, church, and sacraments. In effect we have explored three theological principles for interpreting human life: incarnational, ecclesiological, and sacramental. Each theme says something about God (otherwise it would not be a theological principle) yet can be reflected on directly by anyone committed to living according to what the theme says about God. The themes become principles affecting both thought and practice, and in turn they shape and are shaped by so-called secular practice (listening to popular music). Serious music listeners are willing to reflect theologically on their music-listening practice, respect embodiment profoundly (their own and others'), attend closely to the social groups to which they attach themselves or belong, and expect to be encountered by God through a wide range of material media and resources in the course of daily living. This is what it actually means to live theologically according to the three principles we have explored.

These are, we stress, only initial case studies of what is possible in the creative, constructive exchanges that occur between religious/theological traditions and popular culture. Even in terms of Christian theology, we could extend the list much further to include many other themes and subthemes of systematic theology (e.g., revelation, God/Trinity, Holy Spirit, human being, salvation, eschatology). As already stated, to do full justice to the constantly recurring theme of transcendence in relation just to popular music would require an exploration across many such themes.

It is, however, of great significance that even though we explored the *content* of some of Christian theology's themes in this chapter, we quickly turned back to *practice*. Although this reflects our own respective interests in practical theology, the practice of theology, and the practice to which theology leads, it is far from mere utilitarianism. We want to demonstrate here, as throughout the book, the way that theory/theology is always embedded in practice and inextricably linked with practice. Music works in practice and use and is not to be tied down to notes, lyrics, or sounds, but involves all of these *and* the contexts and practices of use; in the same way, theological themes are not to be understood divorced from the practice of living. We can see this broader perspective in our efforts to define how people's affective space is shaped by a wide variety of factors. We have come full circle here. From explorations in affective space (see fig. 2.1 in chap. 2), through recognition of the importance of sacramental theology for theological understandings of popular culture (chap. 3), and via recognition of the decisive nature of both incarnation and church as specific theological lenses through which to appropriate sacramental theology for our task (this chapter)—with all of these excursions, we confront the challenge of a deeply affective moment within Christian practice itself. On the basis of these explorations, we can now rework our original depiction of cultural affective space in theological terms, illustrating how the two forms of affective space are not as far removed from each other as may first be thought (fig. 11.1).[37]

In light of all this, even while themes need to be explored as theological theories, temporarily detached from the stuff of daily life, and in relation to each within the coherence of a system—even so, they cannot remain there and must not be left there. Put the two worlds together—popular music and theological tradition—and two domains of linked theory and practice are set in relation to each other. The interaction is creative because of the overlaps and tensions.

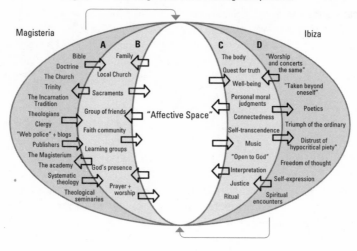

Figure 11.1. The Magisteria-Ibiza Theological Spectrum

We have, then, continued the ongoing program of exchange between specifically Christian theology and popular culture in this chapter. Like William Dyrness, we still wish to claim that there is much constructive, contemporary poetic theology yet to be undertaken. Our own conviction is that such theology is not simply to be undertaken in faith communities and seminaries. It also needs to happen more prominently in broader public life. Otherwise the full significance of what was identified (in chap. 2) already to be happening in the context of popular culture's use will not be addressed. In a brief final programmatic postscript, we shall venture a selection of further suggestions for where our work leads. If music really is shaping people's life commitments, then this is a matter not only of academic interest (though it is that too, across many disciplines). It is also philosophically, ethically, socially, and politically essential to note and act on what is going on.

a programmatic postscript

Practical Consequences for Church, Academy, and Daily Living

The "so what?" question remains. We have argued that offering a theological or religious reading of popular music (from the perspective of the act of listening and use, rather than just the lyrics) has something to be said for it. But while it may prove persuasive for the already-religious, does it really matter much to anyone else? We believe so, precisely because of the material explored in part 2 of our study and the framework (The Magisteria-Ibiza Spectrum) within which, we are claiming, the processing of listening takes place. Many listeners may not be actively expecting their music practices to be a form of "edutainment" (being educated while being entertained, or entertained while being educated). But the cognitive work—the reflection on practice that is going on and can go on around the activity occurring in the affective space that people are inhabiting as they consume popular culture—needs to be considered further in church, academy, and wider society. For it is here that meanings are being made, even if the meaning of meaning itself may vary from listener to listener.

The affective space is clearly not a place for dry study or lifeless thinking. It is a place of passion, of commitment, of emotional intensity. It matters what use people make of this space, what they are doing with what they feel, and what they are thinking through as a result. The religion-likeness of such activity in the affective space is therefore scarcely surprising.

But what follows from all of this in practice? What are churches to do with the insights we have presented, in local church life and in theological education? What are colleges and universities to do when these insights can affect so many different academic disciplines? And what of the everyday life of listeners? In this short, direct postscript—written with heavy use of the imperative form—we simply offer some concrete suggestions for where our study leads.

Church

First, we speak directly to Christian churches, as members, practitioners, and homileticians ourselves of two different traditions, Anglican/Episcopalian and Methodist, though our concerns and comments could equally impact any faith community.

Take church-members' listening habits seriously. This means accepting that people who listen to music will be doing so for all sorts of different reasons, and that the music will potentially influence their faith. Some may listen largely to faith-related music. Others may have a wide range of tastes. Still others might have enthusiasms that are not particularly religious, but that influence who they are. Some may feel uncomfortable about their music preferences. Others may be exasperated that their church involvement gives them so few opportunities to talk about their fandom. This being so, preachers, worship leaders, liturgists, group leaders, priests, campus ministers, and chaplains of all kinds need to be attuned to what role music is playing in the life of the church through its members' nonchurch listening habits, as well as through what is sung or played in church.

Create spaces for listening to and reflecting on music. Those who lead worship or preach may use or refer to music that they know or assume their congregations are listening to. But too often sermons that refer to contemporary popular music give no respect to the role of music listening, and often deal only with lyrics—lyrics that are conducive to what a preacher wants to say anyway. If the way music *actually works* for people—inside and outside of faith communities—is as complex and potentially rich as we are suggesting in this book, then such references do not do enough. Faith communities are places in which listening to music and reflecting on the practice of listening can take place. The challenge is whether faith communities will always feel the need to constrain (censor, control) such listening rather than letting the music just be, permitting listeners to articulate as they wish, both about the music and about their responses to it.

Resist the abuse of music. The positive step of creating space for listening needs to be matched by a commitment to let popular music do its own work. Choosing only music that already says or does what we want it to say or do fails to respect how music works. Even allowing for the reality that a musical meaning results from the interaction between a piece of music (recorded or performed) and a listener heard in a given context, effort has to be made to ensure that it can actually be heard. Faith communities could be at the forefront of ensuring that deep listening happens. Religious people should be able to teach others in society how to be attentive. Too often religious people are among those who hear only what they want to hear, or what their tribe deems acceptable, and then refuse to listen to what is uncomfortable or different.

Christian Theological Education

Formal Christian theological education happens in a variety of settings. In North America, institutions training people for lay and ordained ministry (seminaries) may be more independent in the programs they offer yet are still subject to rigorous academic scrutiny from external bodies. In the UK and other parts of Europe, formal Christian theological education often takes place in state universities or in programs approved by state universities, even when serving the needs of churches. In whatever contexts formal theological education happens, however, this book raises questions for the content of theological curricula.

Our own experience—as students, lecturers, course designers, members of governing bodies, external examiners, and assessors—suggests that the ecclesiastical demands of church-related theological education often produce insular programs. From the 1960s through the 1990s, the many theological movements that can be brought under the heading of "contextualized" or "experiential" theologies (e.g., liberation, feminist, Black, womanist, *Mujerista*) drew attention to the radically concrete form that theology must take to connect with the practice of living. These movements challenged theological programs' insularity. Though they have profoundly influenced Christian thinking and practice across the world, this is not always evident from some of the current theological curricula in the West. Many seminary courses may have added a module on "Contextualization" or "The Social Context of Theology" (even asking a sociologist of religion to teach it), or added elective modules on "Latin American Liberation Theology" or "Black Theology." Where these have disappeared, at best this means that such insights and concerns have genuinely influenced and been appropriately integrated into traditional, mainstream topics (biblical study, church history, systematic theology). At worst, the concern for contextualization in theology was a passing phase, and there is relief that seminary courses are back to the "true business" of teaching Bible and doctrine in a more "pure" form.

This book will have none of this. We have attempted to show, in part 3 especially, that we are much concerned with the so-called traditional subject matter of theology. But we are not simply dealing with an ostensibly pure form of theology that needs to be articulated in the midst of a complex world. The complex world, as exemplified in the messy practices of popular music, is tangled up with the very subject matter of theology itself. This being so, there are some stark imperatives for theological curricula in seminaries.

Explore the social contexts of listening. Asking basic questions such as where and among whom we (all those doing the studying) are doing our theology remains crucial. This means undertaking essential contextualizing work. But it must be done without assuming or implying that this is simply learning about the society into which the gospel comes—as if it drops from the sky. A commitment to incarnation commits us to an incarnational methodology. Examination of popular music as part of a theology course can itself be a channel through which the necessary work of contextualization comes alive.

Critically examine what work on theology, arts, and popular culture has already been done. Some of the insights in this book are new and fresh. But the content builds on the work of others across millennia (in the case of reflection on the relationship between religion and the arts) and decades (in the case of theology and popular culture in the modern period). It is vital for theology programs that a selection of such work be introduced and critically appraised. Rather than letting this be only a specialist's interest (e.g., for campus ministers, chaplains, youth ministers, or enthusiasts), such material is best introduced in the context of a theological course (doctrine or systematics) as a way of showing how a doctrine works in real life. A living faith can never let doctrine be a dry subject. Hence exploration of doctrinal themes in relation to popular music (or other forms of popular culture or the arts) enables both the living quality of doctrine *and* the points of connection between doctrine and ordinary, everyday human practices to become evident.

Critique the notion of "the music itself." One of the major features of our study has been the exploration of listening as a practice. This approach has entailed heavy qualification both of overemphasis on lyrics and of music as existing only as a "text" or in its own right, as if it makes meaning through sounds irrespective of what listeners hear. While we would not say that a piece means nothing until it is heard, we stress above all the interplay of live performance and playing recorded music, with the practice of listening and the experience of the listener. In theological education this is valuable in itself as an insight into how the arts and popular culture work. It also offers a parallel to the way in which theology works. Doctrines and beliefs exist as texts or statements and/or in liturgies. But they are lived by communities and are inhabited by embodied individuals. Approaching theology through the arts and popular culture is educationally enriching both in terms of arts/culture appreciation and in understanding the workings of theology itself.

Ask Christian believers what they think is happening to their faith. We urgently need to form a bridge between academic study of theological ideas and religious beliefs from outside of a seminary context. It is vital that we establish what is actually happening to people of faith as they consume more and more popular culture. Rather than assume that "popular music is bad," we began from the easily defensible premise that it is simply *there*, and Christians and other religious people are listening to it and enjoying it. Some may be influenced constructively and positively, others less so (though who determines what constitutes positive and negative influences is also open to scrutiny). But first of all, we need to know a lot more about what Christians themselves—of many backgrounds and theological persuasions—think is happening to their faith as a result of their devoted fandom or occasional listening. Adherents of other religious traditions may wish to examine the impact of popular culture and music in a similar way. In short, there is some serious empirical research to be done.

Academic Life

Such empirical research would be taken up in the academy (either in research institutes or universities). But it is vital that not only religion scholars and theologians undertake the work. The many disciplines that have contributed to this study (sociology, psychology, anthropology, media and cultural studies, musicology) need to participate.

Study of the interplay between contemporary popular music and theology is not, however, to be confined to study of the already-religious (e.g., sociology of religion, psychology of religion). If our insights into what is happening are informative, then it is vital that disciplines (beyond religious study and theology) do more than just take note of where religion pops up explicitly in public and cultural life. The displacement of the functions of religion into such practices as listening to popular music requires that the tools of the study of religion, and insights from the discipline of theology, all be employed to clarify as fully as possible what is happening at the point of music's reception and use.

Get up to speed on religion and ensure full interdisciplinarity. There is a challenge here to anyone engaged in the academic study of popular music not to neglect its religious dimensions or religious parallels. If popular music's function in contemporary Western society frequently invites comparison with religious practice, then it behooves those in disciplines beyond theology and religious studies to call upon those engaged in the study of religion. The drive to interdisciplinary work must not always be one way. While it is true that theologians, more so than scholars of religion, have not been the most generous in accepting what they may learn from other disciplines (other than from philosophy, languages, and history), knowledge about religion in other disciplines, or willingness to hear what religion scholars have to say, is sometimes woeful. More than occasional interactions at a conference are needed.

Connect with daily life. As we write, there is huge concern that university-level research should have an impact on wider society. This means more than academics offering the odd public lecture to disseminate the findings of their research. Impact denotes a proven effect, change, or benefit beyond the academy. This is telling: it would be a powerful conclusion from research into popular music if it could be demonstrated what this music is already doing in society through dissemination of insights into what some of its most devoted users do with it. It is, in other words, vital that interdisciplinary study of popular music does not remain within the academy.

Everyday Listening.

And what of the ordinary listener, who in so many ways is the focus of our work? A great many popular-music fans will not be interested in our study. But the devoted fans whose practices we have eavesdropped on and reflected on are playing, we are arguing an important role in daily cultural life. It is therefore vital that their habits are examined and the significance of those habits be articulated for wider public recognition. That would be a key aspect of the impact of academic work. It would also value and illuminate the practice of contemporary listening to popular music.

Value everyday conversations about music. Public recognition of the significance of such music use stands the chance, in turn, of encouraging listeners to value more the everyday conversations that occur about music. They are, we contend, the site of much meaning-making, however informal they may be. The post-concert, television-related, "What's currently on your iPod?" conversations that arise around the watercooler, in a cafe, in a bar, online, around meal tables—become the locations of stretching inquiries into what is valued, what is meant, what we think and believe, often riding off the back of what we feel (in the affective space we have identified).

Set up listening and reflection groups. Sometimes informality leads to formality. In the same way as book groups exist in a great many different contexts, as a way to read in a social way, and in order to provide a structure and discipline for reading, so also listening groups can function in a similar way. Religious people may deliberately want to attend groups that are *not* faith-community-related in order to hear what a wider range of people make of music in which they are interested.

Be attentive to bloggers. Comment-leavers on websites sometimes merely invite sympathy. But surfing of websites and regular reading of blogs, even while it eats time, can sometimes be a very stimulating activity. Everyday listening can be enhanced by hearing what others think about songs that prove meaningful to listeners. Paying attention to the comments and insights of ordinary listeners is, in many ways, a democratized form of paying heed to music critics. As an enrichment and a deepening of listening (a participation in the journey of intensification of which we spoke earlier in this book), it can be a profound experience, and depth is ultimately what we have been dealing with throughout.

And finally . . .

All of these programmatic imperatives place a huge onus on those involved in media and cultural life: to recognize the significance of what they do in fresh ways. Entertaining radio and television shows will, we trust, continue to entertain. Documentaries about music and musicians will, we anticipate, still be made. Our study has, though, walked the tightrope between entertainment and education. Religion has always walked this tightrope—even while sometimes being reluctant to own up to the extent to which it has, through its music and religious drama, been a source of popular entertainment. Our hope is that this book successfully invites all students of human culture to recognize that—whether or not we call it education, spiritual development, personal growth, religious experience (or a combination)—the "something else" that can often be discerned or happen as people devote themselves to listening to popular music means that it is frequently more than mere entertainment.

notes

Chapter 1 Music in Context

1. Malcolm Gladwell, writer, *The Observer* newspaper, London, May 2, 2010.
2. North and Hargreaves, *Psychology of Music*, v.
3. Levitin, *The World in Six Songs*, 3.
4. Cobb, *Theology and Popular Culture*, 233.
5. North and Hargreaves, *Psychology of Music*, 227.
6. "Time was when their plebiscite elected Generals, Heads of State, commanders of legions; but now / They've pulled in their horns, there's only two things that concern them: Bread and the Games" (*Satires* 10.77–81; Juvenal, *Sixteen Satires*, 207).
7. Such as, "On the Fetish Character in Music and the Regression of Listening" (1938), in *Culture Industry*, 29–60.
8. Cobb, *Theology and Popular Music*, 47–48. See also Lynch, *Theology and Popular Culture*, chap. 4, "Can Popular Culture Be Bad for Your Health?," esp. 70–77. The most extensive recent consideration of Adorno by a theologian is Brittain, *Adorno and Theology*.
9. The first definition is from Pearsall and Trumble, *Oxford English Reference Dictionary*. Adorno is cited in Cobb, *Theology and Popular Music*, 47.
10. Cobb, *Theology and Popular Music*, 49–50.
11. Middleton, *Studying Popular Music*, 61.
12. Ibid.
13. Ibid., 12–15.
14. Ibid., 13–14.
15. Ibid., 14.
16. Chadwick, *Secularization of the European Mind*; G. Smith, *Short History of Secularism*.
17. Among many relevant studies see, e.g., C. Brown, *Death of Christian Britain*; Bruce, *Religion in the Modern World*; idem, *Secularization*.
18. Middleton, *Studying Popular Music*, 249.
19. We are not claiming that popular music is a form of implicit religion in anything other than a heavily qualified sense.
20. James Carey, *Communication as Culture*, 12.
21. Ibid., 12.
22. B. Taylor, *Entertainment Theology*, 151.
23. James Carey, *Communication as Culture*, 15.
24. Ibid.

25. To express this in terms of the development of Christianity: a ritual view of communication sits more easily with Catholic/Roman Catholic emphases on the drama of eucharistic worship, a transmission view more with Protestant emphases on the communication of a message/the Word.

26. "Neither of these counterposed views of communication necessarily denies what the other affirms. A ritual view does not exclude the processes of information transmission or attitude change. It merely contends that one cannot understand these processes aright except insofar as they are cast within an essentially ritualistic view of communication and social order" (ibid., 17).

27. See, e.g., the work of Barker with Austin, *From Antz to Titanic*; Barker and Mathijs, *Watching the Lord of the Rings*; the journal *Participations*.

28. Middleton, *Reading Pop*, 3. Middleton discusses the weaknesses of such consumptionism (ibid., 7–9).

29. Lynch, *Theology and Popular Culture*, chaps. 6–8.

30. P. Ward, *Participation and Mediation*, 83–84. Ward then applies Longhurst's approach to a study of the Christian song "Shine, Jesus, Shine" (86–91).

31. Vanhoozer, Anderson, and Sleasman, *Everyday Theology*, 48–54.

32. "If . . . we wish to explore whether popular culture serves religious functions in contemporary society, then it is inadequate to base this on theoretical arguments. . . . A fuller insight into significant beliefs, values, and practices of contemporary society can only be achieved by exploring how popular cultural resources are used and experienced in everyday settings" (Lynch, *Theology and Popular Culture*, 164).

33. We shall be drawing, in a limited way, on the data collected from 231 respondents (from the USA and the UK) to a 2009–2010 survey about music use. We expect to process the data fully during 2011–2012.

Chapter 2 Explorations in Affective Space

1. The groundwork for the first part of this chapter was presented in C. Marsh, "Adventures in Affective Space," 6–20.

2. Clarke, Dibben, and Pitts, *Music and Mind in Everyday Life*, 8.

3. C. Marsh and Roberts, "Soundtracks of Acrobatic Selves."

4. We have not found any prior use of the term "affective space" in the way we are using it. The term is used in a quite different way in robotics to denote the space between physical bodies in emotional interaction. After coining the term for our work, we noted some similarity with the term "affinity space" as used by James Gee with respect to informal learning, including video gaming, where learning occurs as a result of groups' forming voluntarily (Gee, *Situated Language and Learning*). This use bears resemblance also to the concept of "community of practice" as developed by Etienne Wenger and Jean Lave in *Situated Learning* and later writings. We have also come across a discussion thread in *The Chronicle of Higher Education* (February 13–14, 2010) devoted to exploration of the term "affective space," though this merely confirms that it is neither widely used nor, as yet, has a clear definition.

5. The Spectrum first saw light on scrap paper over lunch at a restaurant in Coventry, UK, sometime during 2009. Clive Marsh takes credit for the sketch and the basic idea (see n. 1 above), but in this present form, it is a fully collaborative product.

6. Gould, *Rocks of Ages*, 5.

7. Ibid., 88.

8. Polkinghorne, "Interaction of Science and Religion," 44.

9. We use "Ibiza" with apologies to that island and to the Spanish Tourist office: it is no fault of either that late-night activities in small sections of the island have come to symbolize excessive hedonism.

10. Gilmore, *Theater in a Crowded Fire*, 120–21.

11. Ibid., 122.

12. Levitin, *World in Six Songs* (2010).

13. Ibid., 15.

14. Ibid., 20.

15. Ibid., 26.

16. Ibid., 38–39.

17. Ibid., 50.

18. Ibid., 88.

19. Ibid., 87, 88, 93. On sociology and enchantment, see, e.g., Flanagan, *Enchantment of Sociology*; Lyon, *Jesus in Disneyland*.

20. Levitin, *World in Six Songs* (2010), 110.

21. Ibid., 141.

22. Quoted in ibid., 145.

23. Ibid., 186.

24. Ibid.

25. The limits of a worldview approach to meaning-making are brought out well by J. Smith, *Desiring the Kingdom*, whose work we consider in chap. 3.

26. Levitin, *World in Six Songs* (2010), 192.

27. Ibid., 194–95.

28. Ibid., 222.

29. Ibid., 223.

30. Ibid., 262.

31. Ibid., 266.

32. Ibid., 55.

33. Ibid., 215.

34. Ostwalt, *Secular Steeples* (2003), 26.

35. Ostwalt refers to this as the "religious sensibility," which he implies all humans possess (ibid.). We are not wholly convinced that such a clearly definable human instinct or tendency exists. We agree that all humans may have the potential to develop that sense of purpose and enjoyment of life that religions have sought to identify, and to enable people to discover meaning. But it may be that—whether through religion, art, or culture—this discovery needs to be *constructed* and that this requires more than appeals to "religious sensibility" or latent religiosity may suggest.

36. Hoover, *Religion in the Media Age*, 1, 9.

37. Lynch, "Cultural Theory and Cultural Studies," 285, emphasis added.

Chapter 3 Acknowledging a Theological Interest

1. Wright, *Sounds of the Sixties*, 3.

2. Ibid.

3. This influence is noted in the recent (from 2007) musical *Million Dollar Quartet*.

4. Luhr, *Witnessing Suburbia*, 75.

5. C. Taylor, *Secular Age*, 308–9.

6. The lingering conservatism of much of 1960s society in the UK is recorded by Sandbrook, *Never Had It So Good*; idem, *White Heat*.

7. D. Brown, *God and Enchantment*, 2. A discussion of Brown's work appears in MacSwain and Worley, *Theology, Aesthetics and Culture*.

8. D. Brown, *God and Enchantment*, 6.

9. Ibid., 13.

10. D. Brown, *God and Grace of Body*, 4.

11. Ibid., 295.

12. Beaudoin, *Virtual Faith*, 21–36.

13. We take Generation X to mean those born from the early 1960s to the late 1970s, not the Punk Band of the same name; ibid., 28.

14. Ibid., 41–42. These four themes are explored in depth, 51–142. See also B. Taylor, *Entertainment Theology*, 52–53.

15. Beaudoin, *Virtual Faith*, 74–84.

16. Ibid., 84.

17. Ibid., 94.

18. Ibid.

19. Ibid., 147–50.

20. J. Smith, *Desiring the Kingdom*, 24–26. "Liturgical animal" is Smith's term.

21. Ibid., 25.

22. Ibid., 39–73.

23. Ibid., 139–44.

24. Ibid., 139.

25. Ibid., 141.

26. Ibid., 143, emphasis original.

27. Ibid., 75–79, in a discussion of sexuality.

28. C. Taylor, *Secular Age*, 610–11.

29. Ibid., 771.

30. Levitin, *World in Six Songs* (2010), 227.

31. C. Taylor, *Secular Age*, 771.

32. Cf. D. Saliers's view: "The theological import of music is not confined to 'high art' traditions, but comes in the form of folk traditions, which often carry the 'life connection' that theology shaped by the doctrines of creation, *incarnation*, and redemption requires" (*Music and Theology*, 61, emphasis added).

Chapter 4 Pop Music in the Marketplace

1. From a television documentary *Another Green World*, first broadcast on BBC4 [UK] on January 1, 2010, http://www.bbc.co.uk/programmes/b00q9xqk.

2. MacCulloch, *History of Christianity*, 685.

3. For further discussion see Roberts, "Consuming Religion."

4. Ritzer, *Enchanting a Disenchanted World*, x, emphasis original.

5. Lyon, *Jesus in Disneyland*, 122.

6. Ibid., 136.

7. J. Smith, *Desiring the Kingdom*, 19–24, 93–101.

8. Smith (ibid.) recognizes this, we admit, but in our view the enmeshment of religious practices within commercial/economic life is so pronounced that the Christian education or cultural formation he espouses will be more difficult to achieve than he implies.

9. deChant, *Sacred Santa*, 36.

10. Partridge, "Religion and Popular Culture," 492–93.

11. Bono, "Book of Psalms," 139.

12. J. Smith, *Desiring the Kingdom*, 99.

13. Ritzer, *Enchanting a Disenchanted World*, 25–26. On the significance of the megachurch in the context of popular culture's place in the age of secularization, see also Ostwalt, *Secular Steeples*, chap. 2.

14. Prothero, *American Jesus*, 51.

15. The tension between sacred and profane, and public and private, relates to the Magisteria-Ibiza Spectrum we outlined in chap. 2. One respondent to our survey shows the historical roots of this spectrum reflected in the everyday use of music. A male respondent (age 31–40, white, British) remarks: "I usually listen to music myself. I dislike music being played openly from other people's mobile phones/iPods." What may be seen as the comment of a grumpy man can equally be interpreted as a fairly typical comment of someone who has become accustomed to having individual choice of listening music. Technology has enabled this, and the implied power of

individual consumption means that one feels entitled to this. No matter how much restaurants and stores choose music for their customers, there is still evidence that publicly played music can be disliked. But this means that the public, commercial world—in which the music one listens to is produced—is giving way to the private, individual world in which the music is consumed.

16. For a study of praise and worship music from the 1970s onward, see Evans, *Open Up the Doors*.

17. Luhr, *Witnessing Suburbia*, 5.

18. Ibid., 37.

19. Ibid.

20. Ibid., 75.

21. Ibid., 113. See also Moberg, "Christian Metal in Finland."

22. Luhr, *Witnessing Suburbia*, 154. For an analysis of "sacred" ritual in a "secular" public space, see Gilmore's ethnographic study of spirituality at Burning Man, in *Theater in a Crowded Fire*.

23. Assayas, *Bono on Bono*, 146.

24. Bono, "The Book of Psalms," 139–40. See also Bono et al., *U2 by U2*, 167–68.

25. See http://www.youtube.com/watch?v=cOOqvT64mNU&feature=related.

26. See http://www.songmeanings.net/songs/view/36798/.

27. IPod and iPod touch are trademarks of Apple Inc., registered in the USA and other countries.

28. MacCulloch, *History of Christianity*, 182.

29. North and Hargreaves, *Psychology of Music*, 264.

30. There is also much discussion within analysis of contemporary Christian music of the way in which such musical initiatives as Hillsong have themselves become a brand.

31. McGuiness, speech at MIDEM, January 28, 2008. (See bibliography for more information.).

32. Respondent 137, age 31-40, white, British, female.

33. Respondent 171, age 51–60, white, British, male.

34. Respondent[no?], age 31–40, white, British, male.

35. Breihan, "Lily Allen Tangles," http://pitchfork.com/news/36545-lily-allen-tangles-with-radiohead-over-illegal-file-sharing. See also Lily Allen blog, http://www.myspace.com/lilymusic/blog/510114316.**

36. Connor, *Postmodernist Culture*, 210.

37. North and Hargreaves, *Psychology of Music*, 32–37.

38. Ibid., 37–39.

39. For example see http://www.uncut.co.uk/u2/u2-the-joshua-tree-re-mastered-r1987-review.

40. It remains a matter of critical debate as to whether the album *All That You Can't Leave Behind* (2000) found the band seeking to return to *The Joshua Tree* style. On this see, e.g., Scharen, *One Step Closer*.

41. As noted above, a key thinker is Max Weber, particularly his *The Protestant Ethic and the Spirit of Capitalism* (1905). Other trailblazers relating religion and capitalism include Tawney, *Rise of Capitalism*; Demant, *Decline of Capitalism*; Preston, *Persistence of Capitalism*. Further useful texts, representing quite different academic interests from the above four, include Campbell, *Spirit of Modern Consumerism*; Heelas, *Spiritualities of Life*. On the specifically US context, see L. Moore, *Selling God*.

42. In addition to literature cited in chap. 1, nn. 15–16 (above), see also, e.g., Berger, *Sacred Canopy*; Bellah, *Civil Religion*; Markham, *Plurality and Christian Ethics*; Wuthnow, *Christianity in the 21st Century*; D. Martin, *On Secularization*; Milbank, *Theology and Social Theory*; C. Taylor, *Secular Age*.

43. We report music users' self-description of "obsession" or "obsessiveness" in their own practice (C. Marsh and Roberts, "Soundtracks of Acrobatic Selves," 421, 427–28). We shall address the nature of this commitment to music use in chap. 9.

44. A crucial text in discussions of this issue over the past thirty years has been MacIntyre, *After Virtue*. See also Shanks, *Civil Society, Civil Religion*.

45. C. Taylor, *Secular Age*, 449.

46. Ibid., 450.

47. S. Thomas, *Global Resurgence of Religion*.

48. Prothero, *American Jesus*, 299.

49. Stevenson, *David Bowie*, 42.

50. Barber, *Consumed*, 291, emphasis original; cf. Milbank's observation that capitalism "is like science because it is indifferent to anything but power" (*Theology and Social Theory*, 274).

51. Hervieu-Léger, *Chain of Memory*; Davie, *Religion in Modern Europe*.

52. D. Brown, *Tradition & Imagination*, 11–12.

53. Ibid., 30–31, emphasis added.

54. Ibid., 59.

55. D. Brown, *God and Mystery*, 8.

56. Ibid., 60–61.

57. Eco, *Open Work*, 11.

58. D. Brown, *God and Mystery*, 171.

59. S. Connor, *Postmodernist Culture*, 210.

60. D. Brown, *God and Mystery*, 8.

61. B. Taylor, *Entertainment Theology*.

62. D. Cupitt, *The Long-Legged Fly*. For further discussion of water as a theological metaphor in *Waterworld* and Cupitt's image of the long-legged fly, see Roberts, "Water as an Implicit Metaphor."

63. B. Taylor, *Entertainment Theology*, 211, emphasis original.

Chapter 5 Pop Music and the Body

1. Toby Stephens, actor, *The Observer* newspaper, London, July 18, 2010.

2. Al Green, pastor and musician, *The Observer* newspaper, London, June 6, 2010. It is interesting to compare Green's quotation with a comment by world boxing champion Joe Calzaghe on preparing to enter the fight arena: "I prayed before fights. Especially just before I got into the ring. But I'd also have my iPod on. Prodigy and Linkin Park ripping through my ears" (Joe Calzaghe, ex-boxer, *The Observer* newspaper, London, August 8, 2010).

3. Levitin, *World in Six Songs* (2010), 54.

4. Respondent 211, age 21–30, white, British, gender not stated.

5. Respondent 221, age 21–30, white, British, female.

6. Levitin, *World in Six Songs* (2010), 58.

7. Ibid.

8. Ibid., 59.

9. As quoted in Ball, *Music Instinct*, 2–3.

10. Tracy, *Analogical Imagination*, 267.

11. As in such a statement as "All this paper has in it are *raw facts, half-baked ideas, and warmed-over theories*" (Lakoff and Johnson, *Metaphors We Live By*, 46, emphasis original).

12. Milbank, *Theology and Social Theory*, 266.

13. M. Beckford, "Methodists 'Live More than Seven Years Longer.'"

14. We acknowledge that this charge is often made against Christianity, and we acknowledge that the charge has frequently been fair. Yet from the outset we claim that the devaluing and denigration of the body and of matter is a distortion of Christianity and at odds with a religion committed to a creator God, to the incarnation of God in human form.

15. M. Johnson, *The Body in the Mind*, 5.

16. DeNora, *Music in Everyday Life*, 77.

17. Begbie, *Theology, Music, and Time*, 26–27.

18. Respondent 109, age 21–30, white, US, male.

19. Respondent 111, age 21–30, white, other, female.

20. Respondent 85, age 21–30, white, British, female.

21. D. and E. Saliers, *Song to Sing*, 21.

22. Ibid.

23. North and Hargreaves, *Psychology of Music*, 61–63.

24. Levitin, *Your Brain on Music*, 253.

25. D. and E. Saliers, *Song to Sing*, 51.

26. Levitin, *World in Six Songs* (2010), 92.

27. Ibid., 102.

28. DeNora, *Music in Everyday Life*, 109.

29. Ibid., 116.

30. Thornton, *Club Cultures*, 95.

31. D. and E. Saliers, *Song to Sing*, 99.

32. Warner, *Pop Music*, 78.

33. Ibid., 75.

34. Ibid., 88.

35. Frith, "Frankie said," 179.

36. Ibid., 183.

37. Levitin, *World in Six Songs* (2010), 278–79.

38. De Certeau, *Practice of Everyday Life*, 110.

39. Cullen, *Born in the U.S.A.* (2005), 198.

40. Ibid., 199.

41. De Certeau, *Practice of Everyday Life*, 94.

42. Ibid., 106.

43. Ibid., 70, 80, 107.

44. Cavicchi, *Tramps Like Us*, 185–86.

45. See comment by z4ckm0rris, http://www.songmeanings.net/songs/view/128665/.

46. D. Brown, *God and Grace of Body*, 420.

47. Ibid., 192, 197.

48. Ibid., 196.

49. See Cave, "Nick Cave on *The Death of Bunny Munro*."

50. Ibid. Cave is writing the soundtrack to the forthcoming film adaptation of *The Road*.

51. Cave, quoted in "New Nick Cave and the Bad Seeds."

52. D. Brown, *God and Grace of Body*, 185.

53. See comments by ringfingers and crimeofpassion on the SongMeanings website http://www.songmeanings.net/songs/view/2791/ (accessed September 26, 2011).

54. Available on http://www.youtube.com/watch?v=AkvsenvklyM (accessed September 26, 2011).

55. Available on http://www.youtube.com/watch?v=fx2ZmhYHxH4&ob=av2e (accessed September 26, 2011).

56. Cousland, "God, the Bad, and the Ugly," 129.

57. Ibid., 141.

58. Samples from the album cover: "*Today's Lesson* references 'Mr Sandman'—a mythical creature and bringer of dreams; *Night of the Lotus Eaters* alludes to the classical myth about a people who lived in sedated stupor; and *We Call Upon the Author* mentions American poet John Berryman, a writer of dream sequences."

59. Cave, as quoted by Denny, "Carnivals of the Grotesque."

60. Thus *A Refrain in Today's Lesson* suggests a party atmosphere and refers directly to embodiment; *Night of the Lotus Eaters* begins with an embodied description of lost consciousness and concludes with a call for embodied action; and *We Call upon the Author* mixes references to embodied experience in what appears to be a detached stream of consciousness, drawn from something like a dream, a near-death experience, or a highly emotional rant.

61. See comment by morbid morag on http://www.songmeanings.net/songs/view/3530822107858704641/. For further discussion of this track, see Roberts, "Nick Cave and 'Ugly' Bodies."

62. O'Neill, *Communicative Body*, 3.

63. Notable exceptions: S. Moore, *God's Gym*; Sommer, *Bodies of God*.

64. For further discussion see Roberts, "A Body of Consensus?"

65. Sommer, *Bodies of God*, 24.

Chapter 6 The Tingle Factor

1. *The Daily Telegraph* newspaper, August 25, 2011, p. 27.

2. To cite examples from our own empirical research, when reporting on the emotional experience of music: "Music refreshes parts that other media? arts? . . . cannot reach. 'Tingle factor'" (Respondent 6, age over 60, white, British, female). "Spine Tingling," "Transporting to another place" (Respondent 11, age over 60, white, British, male). "Stirring, spine-tingling, relaxing, soothing" (Respondent 131, age under 20, white, other, male).

3. Cited in Gabrielsson, "Strong Experiences with Music," 432.

4. In his own research, it does not appear to occur to Gabrielsson to move away from classical music (or perhaps he knows his research would be taken less seriously if he did).

5. See, e.g., John Carey, *What Good Are the Arts?*, 121–22, 125.

6. Laski published a later study, *Everyday Ecstasy*, in which she states her conclusion clearly at the outset. Against those who believe that ecstatic experiences may have an extrahuman source, Laski states her conviction that the explanation she deems to be true "is that these experiences are purely human, and have no external source" (9). As Carey states (*What Good Are the Arts?*, 124), Laski is deeply suspicious of the impact of ecstatic experiences, thinking them to be harmful. They are all, for Laski, to be judged "in the light of common day" (*Everyday Ecstasy*, 147). Carey is himself skeptical of claims to transcendence anyway (*What Good Are the Arts?*, 126).

7. As well as factors not considered here, such as studying drug use alongside the experience of music.

8. Frith, *Sociology of Rock*, 206; cited in Middleton, *Studying Popular Music*, 247. Middleton also notices how much such aspects have been ignored by musicologists too.

9. Brian Eno, in a television documentary *Another Green World*, first broadcast on BBC4 (UK) on January 21, 2010, http://www.bbc.co.uk/programmes/b00q9xqk.

10. Sendra, review of the album *Med Sud I Eyrum Vid Spilum Endalaust*, by Sigur Rós, released June 24, 2008.

11. From the Sigur Rós album *Med Sud I Eyrum Vid Spilum Endalaust* [*With a Buzz in Our Ears We Play Endlessly*]. The band used English lyrics for the first time on this album ("All Alright").

12. Detweiler and B. Taylor, *Matrix of Meanings*, 140.

13. Ibid., 140–41. Examples of an explicitly nonlyrical approach to songs can be found in the work of The Cocteau Twins and Lisa Gerrard. Singers Elizabeth Fraser and Lisa Gerrard do not use words in the traditional sense. It is also interesting to compare the first two albums by The Clash, where the style of singing adopted by Joe Strummer deliberately leaves the song lyrics ambiguous and open to interpretation.

14. Detweiler and B. Taylor admit that notions of truth become problematic here (ibid., 141). Yet they do helpfully link this recognition with the fact that popular music should not be understood as a medium or art form that simply "transmits" a message. They still talk about pop music getting "a point across," which may be to expect too much. But their observation can be usefully linked with the point made in chap. 1 about the shift from a transmission to a ritual view of communication. The music of Sigur Rós clearly highlights that so much of popular music's impact and function is about how its sounds are received.

15. We are not restricting the use, impact, or concern of the following examples to live settings. Karaoke and personal listening contexts can have similar effects. We are simply observing that in live performance more dimensions of reception are present.

16. The respondent did not complete the personal information, so we do not know his or her age, sex, or ethnicity.

17. In the *Live at Knebworth* version, half of the seven-minute song comprises the sing-along section (*Live at Knebworth 1990*, Eagle DVD 2006, CD 2010).

18. Another example of stadium-sized gatherings is U2, though in a book on theology and pop music, this example is a little too obvious, and we have sought to restrict our U2 references throughout for that reason.

19. Respondent 207, age 31–40, male, self-identified as a "solitary eclectic Pagan."

20. Lynch, *Theology and Popular Culture*, 162–83; cf. other work in this field from Thornton, *Club Cultures*; Till, *Pop Cult*, 131–66.

21. Lynch, *Theology and Popular Culture*, 173–74.

22. On this issue of lyrics as different from poetry, see, e.g., Griffiths, "From Lyric to Anti-lyric"; and Frith, "Why Do Songs Have Words?" (1988), 105–28; repr. (2007), 209–38. We are grateful to Allan F. Moore (editor, *Analyzing Popular Music*) for drawing our attention to these sources.

23. Respondent 184, age 41–50, white, British, female.

24. Available on *All That You Can't Leave Behind* (2000); *The Best of U2, 1990–2000* (2002); and *U218 Singles* (2006).

25. Available on *Home Movies: The Best of Everything but the Girl* (Blanco Y Negro, 1993); *The Platinum Collection* (Rhino, 2006).

26. Artists such as The Alan Parsons Project, Genesis, Pink Floyd, Rick Wakeman, and Yes count as key examples, though the genre would also include The Beatles' "Sergeant Pepper's Lonely Hearts Club Band."

27. Two recent developments in listening practice, linking with performance and community, respectively, are bands choosing to perform an album in track order (e.g., The Psychedelic Furs) and people gathering to listen to an entire album together, remaining silent throughout (e.g., on "Classic Album Sundays," see Silitto, "Are Record Clubs the New Book Clubs?").

28. Hornby, *Juliet, Naked*, 27–28.

29. Zane Lowe's interview with Dave Evans, on BBC Radio 1, at the release of "No Line on the Horizon," March 2009, 7:28–9:00 minutes. http://www.bbc.co.uk/musicevents/u2/video/zanelowe/video3.shtml#emp.

30. We must also accept that sometimes what is referred to (e.g., in lyrics) may seem counter to any positive sense of transcendence that is enjoyed. One respondent to our survey cited Avenged Sevenfold's "A Little Peace of Heaven" as their favorite track. It presents a disturbing "story song" involving a murder, rape, and to-ings and fro-ings between this world and the afterlife; hence its content seems in stark contrast to the "relaxing, happy" emotional responses that the same person (Respondent 115, age 21–30, white, US, female) reported when listening to music.

31. C. Taylor, *Secular Age*, 20.

32. Ibid., 726.

33. Ibid., 727.

34. F. Brown, *Good Taste, Bad Taste, and Christian Taste*, 120–21.

35. We stress that this is not F. Brown's own conclusion.

36. John Carey, *What Good Are the Arts?*, 126.

37. For an exploration of how the language of theology and the practice of music interweave (admittedly with respect to religious music only), see Blackwell, *Sacred in Music*.

38. Of the two direct references to transcendence, one was from a Christian, one from a respondent who did not declare a religious category.

39. Lynch, *Theology and Popular Culture*, 179; cf. Till's discussion of electronic dance music culture (EDMC) and Lynch's approach, where Till argues: "It is clear that EDMC has elements of religion, spirituality and meaning, although Christian influences are often imbued with a sense of transgression" (*Pop Cult*, 142).

40. Lynch, *Theology and Popular Culture*, 181. Gilmore has found a similar phenomenon at Burning Man in the Black Rock Desert: "People go to Burning Man to play with alternative

experiences, identities, and spiritualities. In so doing, they individualistically and idiosyncratically draw on a diverse and limitless pool of global cultural resources and engage in an à la carte mixture of the world's various faith and symbol systems in order to piece together ad hoc and hybrid frameworks" (*Theater in a Crowded Fire*, 66). Some participants see their involvement in this culture as having a religious component; others explicitly disavow any religious element to their experience (ibid., 66–67).

41. In the *Companion's* defense, there are articles about "transcendental analytic," "transcendental arguments," and "transcendentalism" (Honderich, *Oxford Companion to Philosophy*, 878–79). But the absence of "transcendence" per se indicates how what the term tries to identify is deemed to be beyond reason. There is a very short (seventeen-line) entry on "love." By contrast, the *Companion's* article on "music," by Robert Sharpe, helpfully describes and distinguishes expressionist and antiexpressionist theories of music, and concludes that "the jury is even further out on this issue ("What is a piece of music anyway?") than on most philosophical questions" (ibid., 599).

Chapter 7 Pop Music, Ritual, and Worship

1. Richard Ashcroft, singer-songwriter, in *The Observer* newspaper, London, July 11, 2010.

2. Respondent 93, no personal details provided.

3. DeNora, *Music in Everyday Life*, 152; Cavicchi, *Tramps Like Us*, 90.

4. In our late stages of writing, we came across Till, *Pop Cult*.

5. "Andrew Graham-Dixon interviews John Lydon 1–3," first broadcast on *The Culture Show* (BBC2, December 3, 2009), http://www.youtube.com/watch?v=jfzwwIpBVDs&feature=related.

6. Ibid.

7. Ibid. Lydon makes similar points in his BBC1 interview of July 7, 2010, http://www.youtube.com/watch?v=gBymAks0YRY&feature=related.

8. Ibid., 5:05–5:16.

9. "Madonna on Religion—Really Interesting," extracted from Michael Parkinson's interview with her, first broadcast November 12, 2005, http://www.youtube.com/watch?v=SkDvFA6mVWs.

10. In U2's most recent 360 Degree tour, e.g., a video of an address by Archbishop Desmond Tutu was used.

11. Cavicchi, *Tramps Like Us*, 90.

12. Ibid., 92, 94.

13. Ibid., 95.

14. Ibid., 133.

15. Ibid., 94, 95.

16. Ibid., 187.

17. Ibid.

18. Ibid., 110.

19. C. Taylor, *Secular Age*, 25.

20. See Dawkins, *Blind Watchmaker*; Eagleton, *Reason, Faith, and Religion*.

21. See Chadwick, *Secularization of the European Mind*; Nicholls, *God and Government*.

22. Cavicchi, *Tramps Like Us*, viii.

23. Davie, *Religion in Modern Europe*; Hervieu-Léger, *Chain of Memory*; C. Taylor, *Secular Age*.

24. It is precisely the potential theological consequences of contemporary music-listening practices that we examine in part 3.

25. In *Pop Cult*, Till argues (much more strongly than we argue) for music's taking over the role of religion (especially Christianity) in the West. We think things are more complex, and traditional (or mainstream) religious belief and practice still has an important role to play, even while itself being subject to challenge and change.

26. Branch, *Rituals of Spontaneity*; C. Taylor, *Secular Age*, 446.

27. On the role of time in music, see, e.g., Begbie, *Theology, Music, and Time*; DeNora, *Music in Everyday Life*; Fuller, *Wonder*; and D. Saliers, *Music and Theology*.

28. Cavicchi, *Tramps Like Us*, 152.

29. Maffesoli, *Time of the Tribes*, 158–59.

30. Ibid., 59.

31. "Which Music Genres Should be Recognised as Religions," a music blog on *The Guardian* website, http://www.guardian.co.uk/music/musicblog/2010/jan/22/music-genres-recognised-religions.

32. Thornton, *Club Cultures*, 3, emphasis added. Also D. and E. Saliers: "At some basic level, musical taste is tribal. By this we mean that most people experience special bonding with others who prefer the same songs and music. . . . Membership in a specific musical tribe—often one shaped by ethnicity or economic class—becomes a badge of belonging" (*Song to Sing*, 98–99).

33. Till, *Pop Cult*, 7–8.

34. Drawing on the insights of the sociologist Margaret Archer, we have examined the ways in which music users explore their "selves" in response to popular music; see C. Marsh and Roberts, "Soundtracks of Acrobatic Selves."

35. C. Taylor, *Sources of Self*, 131.

36. MacIntyre, *After Virtue*, 36–37.

37. Respondent 152, no personal details provided.

38. Giddens, *Modernity and Self-Identity*, 215.

39. DeNora, *Music in Everyday Life*, 16. Again there is an echo of this in Cavicchi's attention to the way in which narratives about their fandom function for Springsteen fans and contribute to the shaping of their life stories (*Tramps Like Us*, 19, 42–43, 155).

40. Fenn, "Religion and the Secular."

41. Flanagan, *Enchantment of Sociology*, 158.

42. Jurgenssen, "All the Good Band Names Are Taken," *Wall Street Journal*, February 17, 2010.

43. North and Hargreaves, *Psychology of Music*, 264.

44. Ibid., 267.

45. D. Marsh, *Bruce Springsteen: Two Hearts*, 277.

46. Seeger, http://www.youtube.com/watch?v=uw9C8cOBkDw and Springsteen, http://www.youtube.com/watch?v=2YOfBr_efIs (accessed August 22, 2011).

47. See http://www.youtube.com/watch?v=3YLuwd3iqkg (accessed August 22, 2011).

48. One comment left by smittyhooker2 about an earlier track from that performance states boldly: "GOD AT WORK !!!!!!!!" at http://www.youtube.com/watch?v=C12EhfrgNzg (accessed August 22, 2011).

49. Underhill, *Worship*, 3.

50. Targoff, *Common Prayer*, 37.

51. As noted in Branch, *Rituals of Spontaneity*, 59.

52. Ibid., 209.

53. DeNora, *Music in Everyday Life*, 152.

54. Gilmore, *Theater in a Crowded Fire*.

55. Ibid., 70.

56. Ibid., 65.

57. Driver, *Liberating Rites*; DeNora, *Music in Everyday Life*; G. Hughes, *Worship as Meaning*.

58. Driver, *Liberating Rites*, 152. Levitin comments that ceremonial ritual, "as a uniquely human invention, commemorates important events. These can be events of our human life cycle such as birth, marriage, and death, or events in our environmental life cycle such as the seasons, the rains, daybreak, and nightfall. Rituals tie us to the event itself, and to the cycle of history in which many similar events have previously occurred and will continue to occur" (*World in Six Songs* [2010], 191).

59. Quoted in Driver, *Liberating Rites*, 153.

60. Ibid.

61. Till also comments on how the modern period has reduced the social contexts for celebrating and marking significant moments in life; he suggests that electronic dance music culture (EDMC) is one way in which young people in particular have met that need (*Pop Cult*, 163, 175, 177).

62. DeNora, *Music in Everyday Life*, 32.

63. Ibid., 151.

64. Ibid., 74.

65. Ibid., 162. See also Cavicchi's reporting of a Springsteen fan's commenting: "It's almost like a drug! You can just sit in your room and listen to this music, and you're not really dealing with the real world anymore. Then again, maybe it helps you deal with real life" (*Tramps Like Us*, 102). See Till's account of actual drug use by music fans as part of their participation in EDMC (*Pop Cult*, 146–48).

66. G. Hughes, *Worship as Meaning*, 278–83.

67. Ibid., 151.

68. Ibid., 215.

69. Ibid., 295.

70. Ibid., 299.

71. Fuller, *Wonder*, 118.

72. On the role of sense-making life narratives, see n. 40 above.

73. De Certeau, *Practice of Everyday Life*, 31.

74. One of the most useful, expansive recent treatments of the history and practice of Christian worship is Wainwright and Tucker, *Oxford History of Christian Worship*.

75. Gilmore, *Theater in a Crowded Fire*, 99, emphasis added.

76. Ibid., 120–21, 132.

77. Till, *Pop Cult*, 145. See also Lynch, *Theology and Popular Culture*, 179. Resolution of the issue of what happens when participants in practices that "look very much like religion" or seem to function in religious ways yet resist such interpretations lies beyond the scope of this book. But recognizing the issue does highlight the key challenge of all academic work in the interpretation of human behavior (and poses the challenge of whether conclusive answers can ever be reached): what is *really* going on?

Chapter 8 What's on Your iPod?

1. Tracy, *Analogical Imagination*, 115–16. Tracy's is an outstanding, if at times difficult, exploration of the concept of the "classic" as applied to the workings of theology. He is critical of the way in which "technoeconomic" factors have led to the devaluing of the classic in the direction of taste or emotion (e.g., see ibid., 109–10).

2. John Carey, *What Good Are the Arts?*, 252.

3. A Bruce Springsteen fan cited in Cavicchi, *Tramps Like Us*, 187.

4. Major studies on such developments include Du Gay et al., *Story of the Sony Walkman*; Bull, *Sounding Out the City*.

5. For a summary of developments in music technology, see Frith, "Industrialization of Music" (2006), 231–38.

6. On the use and usefulness of "soundtrack" as an image of how popular culture is generally being used, see C. Marsh, "Theology as 'Soundtrack.'" See also C. Marsh and Roberts, "Soundtracks of Acrobatic Selves."

7. Respondent 86, age 21–30, white, British, female.

8. Respondent 182, under 20, white, British, male.

9. Respondent 71, age 31–40, white, British, male.

10. Respondents 82 (age 41–50, white, British, female) and 75 (age over 60, white, British, gender not specified).

11. To quote Cavicchi, wrestling with the music of Springsteen and his fans' interpretations and use of the music: "The discovery of meaning is not simply academic. Fans are consciously engaged

with the ways in which Springsteen's music works to shape their experiences and perceptions. . . . As I talked with fans, I found profound disagreements over the meanings of songs, which really precluded any sort of isolated, single 'message' in Springsteen's work. . . . Springsteen fans clearly see Springsteen's music as communicating meaning, but what is that meaning? And where does the meaning come from if it does not come from lyrics alone? How do we explain meaning in terms of the consensus and difference I found among fans? Unfortunately, much of the scholarship on musical meaning is of little help in answering such questions because it focuses solely on the 'syntax' or symbolic qualities of musical forms" (*Tramps Like Us*, 109, 112–13). Thankfully, since Cavicchi wrote those words, DeNora has been examining how meanings take shape in relation to music. Her remarks are consistent with Cavicchi's discoveries and with our own views about how music "works": "If meaning is not 'in' the music but rather distributed in the environments where musical response occurs, then music offers a resource for meaning-making. This understanding of musical meaning neither collapses music into sociology nor sociology into musicology. Instead it describes a perspective devoted to how actors may find, in musical structures, various 'things' (meanings, values, imageries)" (*Music-in-Action*, xiv).

12. See the account in S. Turner, *Hard Day's Write*, 83–84.

13. Ibid., 84.

14. Ibid., 179–80.

15. We accept, though, that this may not apply in all areas of cultural life. The 2008 Wimbledon tennis final between Roger Federer and Rafael Nadal was able instantly to be hailed as a "classic" because of its length and quality of play. A further time-related factor is, however, brought into consideration because it was instantly compared with past finals in this and other tournaments. With music, such comparisons cannot be made as easily or as quickly: resonance, impact, and response all need longer to take effect.

16. Detweiler and B. Taylor, *Matrix of Meanings*, 18, 21. See also John Carey's observation: "Another thing we should do . . . is to switch the aim of research in the arts to finding out not what critics think about this or that artwork—which is necessarily only of limited and personal interest—but how art has affected and changed other people's lives. . . . Critics . . . have very seldom recorded how people feel about art, what they like, whether it has altered the way they think and behave. The history of audiences and readerships is largely blank" (*What Good Are the Arts?*, 167).

17. In relation to the Magisteria-Ibiza Spectrum (chap. 2), many aspects are important here: music-loving friends; an interest group to which we belong; a radio station to which we listen (section B of the diagram); music critics, newspapers, and magazines we read; websites logged as "Favorites" (section A).

18. For the sake of clarification, we must also acknowledge there is a further and quite different musical definition of the term "canon": a piece of music that uses repetition.

19. See also the attempt to broaden the concept to identify and articulate the range of authoritative resources that function "canonically" in Christianity (Abraham, Vickers, and Kirk, *Canonical Theism*).

20. Bloom, *Western Canon*; he lists recommended canonical works on 531–67.

21. Ibid., 35.

22. Shuker, *Understanding Popular Music Culture*, 265.

23. Appen and Doehring, "Nevermind the Beatles."

24. John Carey, *What Good Are the Arts?*, 260.

25. Most recently by Cavicchi, *Tramps Like Us*; and more tellingly as part of Till's argument that popular-music fans function in groups as cults, in *Pop Cult*.

26. Hence we agree with Cavicchi in being unwilling to conclude that religion-like behavior always really is religion. This is also what makes us uncomfortable with an implicit-religion approach. Despite the value of what such an approach has achieved in inviting reading of secular practices through a religious practice/studies lens, we need to accept the limitations of what we can bring (as Christian, theologically committed scholars of religious and popular cultural

practices). Rather than conclude that popular-music uses really are religion or should be seen as religion, we are noticing their religion-likeness and will, in part 3, see what benefit might be gained (for music users and religious believers) by identifying the tensions and disagreements between popular-music listening and religious practices. In so doing, we shall be more positive than Till in assessing how mainstream/traditional religious (in our example, Christian) practice may contribute to Western culture, even while religious practice has clearly given way in many respects to popular cultural and artistic alternatives.

27. This function of the wide range of available music is confirmed in the music-listening habits reported by those who responded to our music survey. To cite some examples: "Music is like a journal of my life. I often find [that] it affects my mood or vice versa" (respondent 54, age 51–60, European American, US, female); "No matter what mood I'm in, I can find music to go with it" (respondent 113, age 21–30, white, US, female). And as Cavicchi reports, "Many fans described their listening as enabling them to better manage their emotions and moods." Yet he also reports that Springsteen fans use the range of his music for different purposes at different times (thus demonstrating "canonical" use in the sense being explored here): "While most people use different musical styles to manage their moods, . . . fans have located the gamut of their emotions in the music of a single artist" (*Tramps Like Us*, 127).

28. The opening lines of Led Zeppelin's "Stairway to Heaven."

29. See n. 17 above for examples of the influences that shape our music choices.

30. We do accept that while we are arguing for more than a mere parallel between religious and literary canons on one hand, and personal musical collections on the other hand, at this point our work is challengeable: music collections often contain a lot of pieces that may not receive much critical acclaim musically. Even this does not deflect from the basic point, however, for much can come from poor quality music if it interacts with a listener who "gets something out of it." And what should have appeared or does appear in canons is always disputed anyway.

31. The three Dylan albums included in Shuker's canon are "Highway 61 Revisited" (1965), "Blonde on Blonde" (1966), and "Blood on the Tracks" (1975).

32. Hornby, *31 Songs*, 43–44.

33. The concept of "affective alliance" derives from Lawrence Grossberg, whose work we first encountered through P. Ward, "Contemporary Charismatic Worship."

34. In C. Marsh and Roberts, "Soundtracks of Acrobatic Selves," we note the possibility of fan attention to Bono being potentially unhealthy (428).

35. Once more we emphasize that we draw no conclusions about popular music's necessarily *being* religious (as implicit religion). We are working with features of its *actual functioning* as a social practice.

36. DeNora speaks of music as "a place or space for 'work' or meaning and lifeworld making" (*Music in Everyday Life*, 40). See also her earlier article, "How Is Extra-Musical Meaning Possible? Music as a Place and Space for 'Work,'" now available in *Music-in-Action*, 19–29.

37. It must be accepted also that this is not always positive, as it may distract people when undertaking other activities such as walking across a road or driving.

38. Cross and Livingstone, *Oxford Dictionary of the Christian Church*, 1065.

39. Meditation may be aided by particular body postures and might be enabled by particular kinds of music. But those are matters for discussion and should not be a priori assumptions.

40. See http://www.accountancyage.com/aa/profile/1898799/profile-ian-theodoreson-cfo-church-england (accessed August 23, 2011).

41. See http://www.mtelevision.com/news/articles/1628355/lady-gaga-explains-real-meaning-dance-dark.jhtml (accessed August 23, 2011).

Chapter 9 The Discipline of Listening

1. Richard Harries, "We Should Not Fear Religion," *The Observer* newspaper, London, December 19, 2004.

2. In our work we have been very conscious that we have shared the same dilemmas and challenges, but also joys, as those experienced by such writers as Daniel Cavicchi and Matt Hills: we are both scholars and fans. Then "religious commitment" adds a complex third factor. Yet this "complex third" is thankfully recognized in fresh, helpful ways in the academy, beyond the religious (in the West, esp. Christian) domination of theology/religious studies, and beyond the purported secular objectivity that sought to replace it. See, e.g., Ferrer and Sherman, *Participatory Turn*, which contains an outstanding introductory essay by its editors.

3. Markham, *Theology of Engagement*.

4. Ibid., 13–16, 20–21, 191.

5. Ibid., 49, emphasis original.

6. Ibid., 62–70.

7. This was already noticed in our discussion of J. Smith's work in chap. 3.

8. See, e.g., Sommer, *Bodies of God*.

9. See, e.g., Dale Martin, *Corinthian Body*.

10. See, e.g., Beckwith, *Christ's Body*.

11. See, e.g., Rogers, *Sexuality and the Christian Body*.

12. B. Turner, "The Body in Western Society."

13. In chap. 11 we shall theologically consider the question of embodiment.

14. DeNora, *Music in Everyday Life*, 71.

15. Tillich, *Systematic Theology*, 1:238. Despite Tillich's considerable theological engagement with the arts, he nevertheless found it difficult to show similar appreciation for popular culture (Cobb, "Reconsidering the Status of Popular Culture").

16. It is often too easily assumed that Christian theology can only do business with classical music or religious music.

17. The notion of God as verb has been made moot on many fronts in order to emphasize divine dynamism (as, e.g., by the late post-Christian feminist philosopher and theologian Daly in *Beyond God the Father*).

18. Cited in Levitin, *World in Six Songs* (2010), 229.

19. Respondent 120, age 21–30, white other, US, Christian, male.

20. Indeed, Beckwith identifies a dynamic akin to our spectrum in the writings of medieval mystics: "Mystic texts encode a profound conflict about their relationship to authority. They derive their authority, their claim to speak, by claiming originary force: that they are a transcription of the voice of God himself. Yet because they add to that voice, because they supplement it, they also suggest that it might not be the last word it must claim to be" (*Christ's Body*, 20).

21. Thus Markham considers globalization under two headings: assimilation and overhearing (*Theology of Engagement*, 147–58).

22. Ibid., 208–9.

23. Ibid., 209.

24. Although drug use is related to religious experience, as Till states: "Some religious practice aims to achieve altered (or "higher") states of consciousness through various techniques, including the use of chanting, meditation, breathing control, music, and dancing. Drug taking is a short cut that allows those within Western culture who have few skills in this area to achieve such states, in a society that has moved away from rehearsing these practices. Drug taking is popular because mainstream Western religions have often abandoned such practice, and *yet it is a universal and perhaps essential part of human culture*" (*Pop Cults*, 35, emphasis added). In addition, smoking tobacco has its roots in religious practice: "Characteristic of Native American understandings of social reality was the belief that hallucinogenic plants joined the natural and supernatural worlds. These plants were sacred; they were understood to house supernatural beings and to facilitate altered states of consciousness essential to communication with the spirit world." Tobacco was originally one of these hallucinogenic plants (J. Hughes, *Learning to Smoke*, 18).

25. Markham, *Theology of Engagement*, 3.

26. Vanhoozer, Anderson, and Sleasman, *Everyday Theology*, 42.

27. We are adapting and extending the four psychological functions of music that Clarke, Dibben, and Pitts identify in their analysis of the use of music in the funeral of Diana Spencer, Princess of Wales (*Music and Mind*, 2–8). We found it striking that the authors, who do not list religious studies among the many disciplines needed to understand how music works, should begin their book with a close analysis of the use of music in a religious event.

28. Levitin, *World in Six Songs*, passim.

29. Clarke, Dibben, and Pitts, *Music and Mind*, 5.

30. Ibid., 6.

31. Clive Marsh cannot now recall how or when he first came across Alison Krauss, but it was well before the album *O Brother, Where Art Thou?* (2001). Vaughan Roberts cannot remember when or how he came across The White Stripes, though for most of the bands he likes, he is able to point to the date of his "conversion."

32. Cavicchi, *Tramps Like Us*, 114.

33. G. Hughes, *Worship as Meaning*, 295. See our use of G. Hughes's work throughout chap. 7 above.

34. David Brown ends his book with an appeal for "more dialogue with ordinary human experience, not less. . . . Only within such a focus will the grace that the divine has accorded the human body truly then become. As my subtitle indicates it should be, 'a sacrament in ordinary': God experienced in the everyday but always greater than any particular experience or conception of him" (*God and Grace of Body*, 427–28).

35. Schechner speaks of an "efficacy-entertainment dyad" in *Performance Studies*, 79–80. Efficacy and entertainment are "not binary opposites" but are to be seen as "poles of a continuum."

36. Bach may indeed be better musically than Radiohead, but we are not seeking to build a musical or aesthetic argument here. Issues of music *use* involve—and may turn on—matters of affect, ethics, politics, and philosophy rather than just aesthetics.

37. Blake, "Are There Dangers?"

Chapter 10 Three Steps to Heaven?

1. In practice, a radio station's playlist is likely to be more limited in range, since most stations identify a "niche" or a music style and stick to it.

2. Till, *Pop Cult*, 189.

3. MacIntyre, *Whose Justice?*

4. Ibid., 349.

5. Levitin, *World in Six Songs* (2010). See chap. 2 above.

6. Such music, and such use of music, then become the practice of being "gloriously entertained," but at a cost of attentiveness to those in pressing need (e.g., economic, material, or emotional) (G. Ward, *Politics of Discipleship*, 216).

7. Cobb, *Theology and Popular Culture*, 132.

8. Ibid., 142.

9. Ibid., 173–74.

10. Ibid., 175.

11. Ibid., 183. One important challenge to Cobb's insight here, with respect to popular music in the UK, has come recently from the observation that much British popular music is composed and produced by the wealthy, or at least by those who have benefited from private education in early life. Though often affecting to be from the "working classes" or genuinely seeking to step beyond their privileged backgrounds, they have nevertheless developed the confidence to do so, and have the material support and resources to make it in the music world. See, e.g., Tom Bateman, "Has Pop Gone Posh?"

12. Cobb, *Theology and Popular Culture*, 184.

13. Ibid., 192.

14. It is different from the "demotic turn" now reported and analyzed by G. Turner, *Ordinary People and the Media*, which is focused on "reality television."

15. Cobb, *Theology and Popular Culture*, 209.

16. Ibid., 211–12.

17. By which we all too often mean, "Did they happen?" Instead we should by now be able to recognize a narrative's truth without subjecting all narratives to a test of historical facticity. Truth can be contained in fiction and also in narratives that, as far as we know, may or may not be fictional.

18. For a detailed exploration of the role of paradise and sin within Christian history and art, see Brock and Parker, *Saving Paradise*, which affirms the role of embodied ritual in the process of meaning-making: "Sensually rich rituals, full of life, orient us to material and spiritual beauties, embedding us more deeply in love for the world and the many physical dimensions of paradise" (419).

19. Cobb, *Theology and Popular Culture*, 230.

20. Ibid., 233.

21. Ibid., 261.

22. Ibid., 258.

23. Ibid., 231.

24. Ibid., 278–84.

25. This formulation sits well alongside the basic definition of religion offered by Meerten B. ter Borg: "When I speak about religion, I am referring to *powers, meanings or realities that transcend what is ordinarily thought of as human*" ("Religion and Power," 195, emphasis original).

26. In other words, for a person to say, "I'm just having a good time when listening to music, and my sense of being taken out of myself is just a set of chemical processes in my body"—that statement is itself located within a specific, rationalist, scientific worldview. Reflection on life experience is in large part about examining the different frameworks within which we make sense of things. We make use of many things and prefer some to others.

27. For more on this see, e.g., C. Marsh, *Christ in Focus*; and the writings of many feminist theologians, helpfully discussed in Isherwood, *Introducing Feminist Christologies*.

28. G. Ward, *Politics of Discipleship*, 250.

29. Ibid., 280.

30. Such as continued existence, annihilation, the possibility of disembodied spirits, millennialism, and rapture.

31. Heaney, "Eloquence of Music," 204.

32. Ibid.

33. The body "is where Christian arguments get settled or continue for the long term, not with words on paper, but with words embodied in the lives and witness of the faithful" (Rogers, *Sexuality and the Christian Body*, 28). In her discussion of Christ's body within medieval mysticism, Beckwith observes: "Christ's body . . . [was] a highly contested area that is crucially related to the strained social relations of late medieval English society, and an area that touches the very core of self-perception and identity as a means of social control" (*Christ's Body*, 23–24). We pick up the theme of incarnation in chap. 11.

34. We accept that the practice of listening is probably also constitutive of nonserious listeners' identity construction! Our point here, though, is the significance of the *intentional way* in which serious fans seem to address different dimensions of what it means to be human (body and soul/spirit, sociality).

35. The same could also be said of Christianity, although the concept of, and quest for, orthodoxy are clearly much more prominent in Christianity as a religious tradition.

36. Porter, "Implicit Religion in Popular Culture," 277.

37. Helpful here is Wuthnow's distinction between "activity" and "practice": the latter entails developing a set of skills and expending effort, rather than just doing something ("Contemporary Convergence," 361).

38. This relates closely to the notion, in sacramental theology, that a sacrament's effectiveness is not dependent on the worthiness of the one presiding (a priest/minister). A sacrament works *ex opere operato* (i.e., by virtue of the action itself).

39. Partridge, "Religion and Popular Culture," 490.

40. World Council of Churches, *Nature and Mission of the Church*, chap. I, sec. C.

41. Irenaeus, *Against Heresies* 4.20.7.

42. Levitin, *World in Six Songs* (2010), 236.

43. Ibid.

44. Ibid., 241.

45. Ibid., 271.

46. One respondent to our music survey gave us a full description of the way in which music helps her "cope with life" (Respondent 188, under 20, white, British, female). We hope to draw on this more fully in further detailed analysis of the questionnaires.

47. C. Marsh, "Theology as 'Soundtrack.'" We are grateful for the appreciative and constructive use of this article in Nantais, *Rock-a My Soul*, chap. 2.

48. Levitin, *World in Six Songs* (2010), 186.

49. Ibid., 151.

50. In his practical and historical discussion of how the body is important in both corporate and private prayer, Guiver states that "standing, kneeling, sitting; prostrations, signs of the cross, icon corners, music and singing, candles, beads, bells and well-loved books—all have their role in the prayer of the people of God. They may not all come so naturally to us today, but our response has to be to evolve new interpretations of this tradition, rather than simply abandon it, and claim the word can do without flesh" (*Company of Voices*, 150).

51. Dyrness, *Poetic Theology*, 283.

Chapter 11 Embodied Social Rituals

1. Crisp, "Incarnation," 160.

2. Hastings, "Incarnation," 322.

3. Cf. Dyrness's observation: "Christians cannot be united with Christ and celebrate the joy of his resurrection without being thrust back into the struggle of the cross. . . . Here is where our aesthetic theology seems to meet its greatest challenge, but perhaps also where it realizes its greatest potential. How can one look into this darkness and speak of beauty?" (*Poetic Theology*, 305).

4. In this respect "Incarnation" by Hastings is much better since it does address these issues.

5. Crisp, "Incarnation," 160.

6. To cite just one example: http://www.faithfitnessfun.com/3912/30-days-of-self-love-do-we -idolize-our-bodies/.

7. This is akin to what Bosch, in his groundbreaking volume on mission, calls "God's 'yes' and 'no' to the world" (Bosch, *Transforming Mission*, 10–11).

8. As a twentieth-century example of opposition, see "drug prophet" Timothy Leary's reference to "the Judeo-Christian power monolith, which has imposed a guilty, inhibited, grim, anti-body, anti-life repression on Western civilization" (cited in McLeod, *Religious Crisis of the 1960s*, 131). In the early Christian centuries, debates about whether the Gospel of John betrays elements of gnosticism, or opposition to gnosticism, lingering Manichean concerns in the thought of Augustine, and the persistence of neo-Platonism throughout medieval Christianity and into the Reformation are all examples of how Christianity wrestled in its thinking about the body.

9. Ibid., 198.

10. In *Sounds of the Sixties*, Wright argues that in the UK greater acceptance and accommodation to popular music was practiced than is often assumed.

11. Most famously encapsulated in the statement of Gregory of Nazianzus (329–89 CE): "What has not been assumed has not been healed" (cited in McGrath, *Christian Theology Reader*, 270).

12. William Temple's claim that Christianity "is the most avowedly materialist of all the great religions" (*Nature, Man and God*, 478) is important here. His claim is rooted in the doctrine of incarnation.

13. This could even be a point at which Protestants, despite their christocentrism, may have underplayed the importance of the christological concentration of their thought and practice for recognition of the body's significance; see, e.g., the section on creation in Dyrness, *Poetic Theology*, 299, recognizing "the centrality of the body in our dealings with God."

14. Extracts from Strauss's *The Life of Jesus Critically Examined* (1835) appear in Placher, *Readings in Christian Theology*, 2:136–39; and in Kerr, *Readings in Christian Thought*, 223–26.

15. Fiddes, *Past Event and Present Salvation*.

16. Placher, *Readings in Christian Theology*, 138.

17. See, e.g., how Scott Hoezee uses the phrase "mini-Christs" (October 17, 2005), http://cep.calvinseminary.edu/thisWeek/viewArticle.php?aID=33.

18. The material to follow builds on C. Marsh, *Christ in Practice*. See also Copeland, paraphrasing Marianne Sawicki: "Jesus turns up in bodies other than his own" ("Body, Race, and Being," 115).

19. Del Colle, "The Church," 249.

20. Ibid., 250. By contrast Hardy argues that church practice precedes doctrine: "Even in the time of Jesus, and certainly afterward, the Church was not first an idea or a doctrine but a *practice* of commonality in faith and mission" (Hardy, *Finding the Church*, 29, emphasis original).

21. Ignatius, *To the Smyrnaeans* 8.2.

22. For a suggested list of hallmarks of Christ's presence, see Marsh, *Christ in Practice*, chap. 2, which provides ten such hallmarks.

23. Welker, "The Holy Spirit," 242.

24. As an example of de facto influence, by May 26, 2011, some 53,670,577 listeners had accessed the audio version of the song on youtube.com.

25. Dan Martin, "Lady Gaga: 'My Tour Is a Religious Experience.'"

26. The seven sacraments are baptism, Holy Communion (Eucharist, Mass), confirmation (or chrismation in Orthodox traditions), ordination, marriage, penance, and anointing/unction.

27. Fenn, "Religion and the Secular," 12–13.

28. O. Thomas and Wondra, *Introduction to Theology*, 275.

29. A good place to begin fuller exploration of both these sacraments: World Council of Churches, *Baptism, Eucharist and Ministry*.

30. Frith, "Pop Music," 107.

31. Yet sacraments can be therapeutic. In his detailed theological reflection on shame, Pattison explains the ambiguous role that liturgy can play for some people: "In the face-to-face relations of liturgy, Christian people learn of their sense of worth and inclusion or the lack of it. The official ideology of liturgy is that it is intended to build up the body of Christ and make manifest God's accepting love. However, there is a considerable ambivalence in the messages that may be implicitly and explicitly communicated in worship. Some of these . . . may communicate to at least some people a sense of rejection, inferiority, unlovableness, powerlessness, worthlessness and defilement" (*Shame*, 258).

32. Copeland, "Body, Race, and Being," 108–9.

33. Ibid., 113–14.

34. See Loades, "Sacrament," 635. The sixteenth-century Reformer Martin Luther often referred to three sacraments—including penance alongside baptism and Holy Communion.

35. Fahey, "Sacraments," 270.

36. We also acknowledge that the Society of Friends (Quakers) and the Salvation Army operate with no sacraments, thereby having a firm base on which to argue that God can act anywhere and be discernible anywhere. Here the issue becomes the extent to which one has the means by which to discern where God acts without the fixed points that sacraments provide.

37. One possible title for this volume was *Ladies and Gentlemen, We Are Floating in Affective Space*—a play on Spiritualized's widely acclaimed 1997 album *Ladies and Gentlemen, We Are Floating in Space*. That title was itself taken from Gaarder's philosophical novel *Sophie's World*: "Only philosophers embark on this perilous expedition to the outermost reaches of language and existence. Some of them fall off, but others cling on desperately and yell at the people nestling deep in the snug softness, stuffing themselves with delicious food and drink. 'Ladies and Gentlemen,' they yell, 'we are floating in space!'" (16).

bibliography

Abraham, William J., Jason E. Vickers, and Natalie B. Van Kirk, eds. *Canonical Theism: A Proposal for Theology and the Church*. Grand Rapids: Eerdmans, 2008.

Adorno, Theodor. *The Culture Industry: Selected Essays on Mass Culture*. New York: Routledge, 1991. Repr., Routledge Classics, 2001.

Anderson, Chris. *The Long Tail: How Endless Choice Is Creating Unlimited Demand*. London: Random House, 2006.

Assayas, Michka. *Bono on Bono: Conversations with Michka Assayas*. London: Hodder & Stoughton, 2005.

Ball, Philip. *The Music Instinct: How Music Works and Why We Can't Do without It*. London: Bodley Head, 2010.

Barabási, Albert-László. *Linked: The New Science of Networks*. Cambridge, MA: Perseus Pub., 2002. Reissued as *Linked: How Everything Is Connected to Everything Else and What It Means for Business, Science, and Everyday Life*. New York: Plume, 2003.

Barber, Benjamin R. *Consumed: How Markets Corrupt Children, Infantilize Adults, and Swallow Citizens Whole*. New York: W. W. Norton, 2007.

Barker, Martin, and Ernest Mathijs, eds. *Watching "The Lord of the Rings": Tolkien's World Audiences*. New York: Peter Lang, 2007.

Barker, Martin, with Thomas Austin. *From Antz to Titanic: Reinventing Film Analysis*. London: Pluto, 2000.

Bateman, Tom. "Has Pop Gone Posh?" BBC Radio, January 28, 2011. http://news.bbc.co.uk/today/hi/today/newsid_9373000/9373158.stm.

Beaudoin, Tom. *Virtual Faith: The Irreverent Spiritual Quest of Generation X*. San Francisco: Jossey-Bass, 1998.

———. *Witness to Dispossession: The Vocation of a Postmodern Theologian*. Maryknoll, NY: Orbis Books, 2008.

Becker, Howard S. *Art Worlds*. Berkeley: University of California Press, 1982.

Beckford, Martin. "Methodists 'Live More than Seven Years Longer than Rest of Population.'" *The Telegraph*, June 25, 2010. http://www.telegraph.co.uk/news/religion/7855002/Methodists-live-more-than-seven-years-longer-than-rest-of-population.html.

Beckford, Robert. *Jesus Dub: Theology, Music and Social Change*. New York: Routledge, 2006.

Beckwith, Sarah. *Christ's Body: Identity, Culture, and Society in Late Medieval Writings*. New York: Routledge, 1996.

Begbie, Jeremy. "Resonances and Challenges: A Response to the Volume." In *Faithful Performances: Enacting Christian Tradition*, edited by Trevor A. Hart and Steven R. Guthrie, 273–80. Burlington, VT: Ashgate, 2007.

———. *Theology, Music, and Time*. New York: Cambridge University Press, 2000.

Bellah, Robert N. "Civil Society in America." *Daedalus* 96 (Winter 1976): 1–21.

———. *Varieties of Civil Religion*. New York: Harper & Row, 1980.

Berger, Peter L. *The Sacred Canopy*. New York: Doubleday, 1967.

Blackwell, Albert L. *The Sacred in Music*. Louisville: Westminster John Knox, 1999.

Blake, John. "Are There Dangers in Being 'Spiritual but Not Religious'?" CNN, June 9, 2010. http://edition.cnn.com/2010/LIVING/personal/06/03/spiritual.but.not.religious/?hpt=C1.

Bloom, Harold. *The Western Canon*. New York: Harcourt, Brace, 1994. Repr., London: Macmillan, 1995.

Bono. "The Book of Psalms." In *Revelations: Personal Responses to the Books of the Bible*, introduced by Richard Holloway, 133–40. New York: Canongate Books, 2005.

Bono, The Edge, Adam Clayton, and Larry Mullen Jr., with Neil McCormick. *U2 by U2*. Pbk. ed. London: HarperCollins, 2008.

Bosch, David J. *Transforming Mission: Paradigm Shifts in the Theology of Mission*. New York: Orbis Books, 1992.

Branch, Lori. *Rituals of Spontaneity: Sentiment and Secularism from Free Prayer to Wordsworth*. Waco: Baylor University Press, 2006.

Breihan, Tom. "Lily Allen Tangles with Radiohead over Illegal File-Sharing." *Pitchfork*, September 22, 2009. http://pitchfork.com/news/36545-lily-allen-tangles-with-radiohead-over-illegal-file-sharing/.

Brittain, Christopher. *Adorno and Theology*. New York: T&T Clark, 2010.

Brock, Rita Nakashima, and Rebecca Ann Parker. *Saving Paradise: How Christianity Traded Love of This World for Crucifixion and Empire*. Boston: Beacon, 2008.

Brown, Callum. *The Death of Christian Britain*. 2nd ed. London: Routledge, 2009.

Brown, David. *Discipleship and Imagination: Christian Tradition and Truth*. Oxford: Oxford University Press, 2000.

————. *God and Enchantment of Place: Reclaiming Human Experience*. Oxford: Oxford University Press, 2004.

————. *God and Grace of Body: Sacrament in Ordinary*. Oxford: Oxford University Press, 2007.

————. *God and Mystery in Words: Experience through Metaphor and Drama*. Oxford: Oxford University Press, 2008.

————. *Tradition and Imagination: Revelation and Change*. Oxford: Oxford University Press, 1999.

Brown, Frank Burch. *Good Taste, Bad Taste, and Christian Taste: Aesthetics in Religious Life*. New York: Oxford University Press, 2000.

Bruce, Steve. *Religion in the Modern World: From Cathedrals to Cults*. New York: Oxford University Press, 1996.

————. *Secularization: In Defence of an Unfashionable Theory*. New York: Oxford University Press, 2011.

Bull, Michael. *Sounding Out the City: Personal Stereos and the Management of Everyday Life*. New York: Berg, 2000.

Campbell, Colin. *The Romantic Ethic and the Spirit of Modern Consumerism*. Oxford: Blackwell, 1987. 3rd ed., London: Alcuin Academics, 2005.

Carey, James W. *Communication as Culture: Essays on Media and Society*. Rev. ed. New York: Routledge, 2009.

Carey, John. *What Good Are the Arts?* London: Faber & Faber, 2005.

Cave, Nick. "Nick Cave on *The Death of Bunny Munro*." HarperCollinsCanada author interview. http://www.harpercollins.ca/author/authorExtra.aspx?authorID=60085663&isbn13=9781554685400&displayType=bookinterview.

————. Quoted in Alex Denny, "Carnivals of the Grotesque: Nick Cave on *Dig, Lazarus, Dig!!!*" *Drowned in Sound*, March 5, 2008. http://drownedinsound.com/in_depth/3011806–carnivals-of-the-grotesque—nick-cave-on-dig-lazarus-dig.

————. Quoted in "New Nick Cave and the Bad Seeds—*Dig, Lazarus, Dig!!!*" *Stereogum*, January 3, 2008. http://stereogum.com/7603/new_nick_cave_the_bad_seeds_dig_lazarus_dig/news/.

————. "The Secret Life of a Love Song." In *Nick Cave: The Complete Lyrics, 1978–2007*. New York: Penguin Books, 2007.

Cavicchi, Daniel. *Tramps Like Us: Music and Meaning among Springsteen Fans*. New York: Oxford University Press, 1998.

Chadwick, Owen. *The Secularization of the European Mind in the Nineteenth Century*. New York: Cambridge University Press, 1975.

Chronicle of Higher Education, The. Discussion of "Affective Space," February 13–14, 2010. http://chronicle.com/forums/index.php?topic=66541.15.

Clarke, Eric, Nicola Dibben, and Stephanie Pitts. *Music and Mind in Everyday Life*. New York: Oxford University Press, 2010.

Cobb, Kelton. *The Blackwell Guide to Theology and Popular Culture*. Malden, MA: Blackwell, 2005.

———. "Reconsidering the Status of Popular Culture in Tillich's Theology of Culture." *Journal of the American Academy of Religion* 68 (1995): 53–84.

Connor, Steven. *Postmodernist Culture: An Introduction to Theories of the Contemporary*. 2nd ed. Cambridge, MA: Blackwell, 1997.

Copeland, Shawn. "Body, Race, and Being." In *Constructive Theology: A Contemporary Approach to Classical Themes*, edited by Serene Jones and Paul Lakeland, 97–116. Minneapolis: Fortress, 2005.

Cousland, J. R. C. "God, the Bad, and the Ugly: The Vi(t)a Negativa of Nick Cave and P. J. Harvey." In *Call Me the Seeker: Listening to Religion in Popular Music*, edited by Michael J. Gilmour, 129–57. New York: Continuum, 2005.

Crisp, Oliver D. "Incarnation." In *The Oxford Handbook of Systematic Theology*, edited by John Webster, Kathryn Tanner, and Iain Torrance, 160–75. Oxford: Oxford University Press, 2007.

Cross, Frank L., and Elizabeth A. Livingstone, eds. *The Oxford Dictionary of the Christian Church*. 3rd ed. Oxford: Oxford University Press, 1997.

Cullen, Jim. *Born in the U.S.A.: Bruce Springsteen and the American Tradition*. 1997. New ed., Middletown, CT: Wesleyan University Press, 2005.

Cupitt, Don. *The Long-Legged Fly: A Theology of Language and Desire*. London: SCM, 1987.

Daly, Mary. *Beyond God the Father*. Boston: Beacon, 1973.

Dark, David. *Everyday Apocalypse: The Sacred Revealed in Radiohead, The Simpsons, and Other Pop Culture Icons*. Grand Rapids: Brazos, 2002.

Davie, Grace. *Religion in Modern Europe: A Memory Mutates*. New York: Oxford University Press, 2000.

Dawkins, Richard. *The Blind Watchmaker*. New York: Longman, 1986.

De Certeau, Michel de. *The Practice of Everyday Life*. Berkeley: University of California Press, 1984.

deChant, Dell. *The Sacred Santa: Religious Dimensions of Consumer Culture*. Cleveland: Pilgrim Press, 2002.

Del Colle, Ralph. "The Church." In *The Oxford Handbook of Systematic Theology*, edited by John Webster, Kathryn Tanner, and Iain Torrance, 249–66. Oxford: Oxford University Press, 2007.

Demant, Vigo Auguste. *Religion and the Decline of Capitalism: The Holland Lectures for 1949*. London: Faber & Faber, 1952.

DeNora, Tia. *Music-in-Action: Selected Essays in Sonic Ecology*. Burlington, VT: Ashgate, 2011.

———. *Music in Everyday Life*. New York: Cambridge University Press, 2000.

Detweiler, Craig, and Barry Taylor. *A Matrix of Meanings: Finding God in Pop Culture*. Grand Rapids: Baker Academic, 2003.

Driver, Tom F. *Liberating Rites: Understanding the Transformative Power of Ritual*. Boulder, CO: Westelevisioniew, 1998. North Charleston, SC: BookSurge, 2006.

Du Gay, Paul, et al. *Doing Cultural Studies: The Story of the Sony Walkman*. Thousand Oaks, CA: Sage, 1997.

Dyrness, William A. *Poetic Theology: God and the Poetics of Everyday Life*. Grand Rapids: Eerdmans, 2011.

Eagleton, Terry. *Reason, Faith, and Religion: Reflections on the God Debate*. Terry Lectures. New Haven: Yale University Press, 2009.

Eco, Umberto. *The Open Work*. London: Hutchinson Radius, 1989.

Evans, Mark. *Open Up the Doors: Music in the Modern Church*. London: Equinox, 2006.

Fahey, Michael A., SJ. "Sacraments." In *The Oxford Handbook of Systematic Theology*, edited by John Webster, Kathryn Tanner, and Iain Torrance, 267–84. Oxford: Oxford University Press, 2007.

Fenn, Richard K. "Religion and the Secular; the Sacred and the Profane: The Scope of the Argument." In *The Blackwell Companion to Sociology of Religion*, edited by Richard K. Fenn, 3–22. Malden, MA: Blackwell, 2001.

Ferrer, Jorge N., and Jacob H. Sherman, eds. *The Participatory Turn: Spirituality, Mysticism, Religious Studies*. New York: State University of New York Press, 2008.

Fiddes, Paul. *Past Event and Present Salvation: The Christian Idea of Atonement*. London: Darton, Longman & Todd, 1989.

Flanagan, Kieran. *The Enchantment of Sociology: A Study of Theology and Culture*. New York: St. Martin's Press, 1996.

Frith, Simon. "Frankie Said: But What Did They Mean?" In *Consumption, Identity, and Style: Marketing, Meanings, and the Package of Pleasure*, edited by Alan Tomlinson, 172–85. New York: Routledge, 1990.

———. "The Industrialization of Music." In *Music for Pleasure: Essays on the Sociology of Pop*, 11–23. Cambridge: Polity Press, 1988. Repr. in *The Popular Music Studies Reader*, edited by A. Bennett, B. Shank, and J. Toynbee, 231–38. New York: Routledge, 2006.

———. "Pop Music." In *The Cambridge Companion to Pop and Rock*, edited by S. Frith, W. Straw, and J. Street, 93–108. Cambridge: Cambridge University Press, 2001. Repr. in *Taking Popular Music Seriously*, 167–82. Burlington, VT: Ashgate, 2007.

———. *The Sociology of Rock*. London: Constable, 1978.

———. "Why Do Songs Have Words?" In *Music for Pleasure: Essays on the Sociology of Pop*, 105–28. Cambridge: Polity Press, 1988. Repr. in *Taking Popular Music Seriously*, 209–38. Burlington, VT: Ashgate, 2007.

Fuller, Robert C. *Wonder: From Emotion to Spirituality*. Chapel Hill: University of North Carolina Press, 2006.

———. "Spirituality in the Flesh: The Role of Discrete Emotions in Religious Life." *Journal of the American Academy of Religion* 75 (2007): 25–51.

Gaarder, Jostein. *Sophie's World: A Novel about the History of Philosophy*. London: Phoenix House, 1995.

Gabrielsson, Alf. "Emotions in Strong Experiences with Music." In *Music and Emotion: Theory and Research*, edited by Patrik N. Juslin and John A. Sloboda, 431–49. New York: Oxford University Press, 2001.

Gee, James. *Situated Language and Learning: A Critique of Traditional Learning*. New York: Routledge, 2004.

Giddens, Anthony. *Modernity and Self-Identity: Self and Society in the Late Modern Age*. Cambridge: Polity Press, 1991.

Gilmore, Lee. *Theater in a Crowded Fire: Ritual and Spirituality at Burning Man*. Berkeley: University of California Press, 2010.

Gilmour, Michael J., ed. *Call Me the Seeker: Listening to Religion in Popular Music*. New York: Continuum, 2005.

———. *Gods and Guitars: Seeking the Sacred in Post-1960s Popular Music*. Waco: Baylor University Press, 2009.

Gould, Stephen Jay. *Rocks of Ages*. New York: Ballantine Books, 1999.

Gray, Jonathan, Cornel Sandvoss, and C. Lee Harrington, eds. *Fandom: Identities and Communities in a Mediated World*. New York: New York University Press, 2007.

Griffiths, Dai. "From Lyric to Anti-lyric: Analyzing the Words in Pop Song." In *Analyzing Popular Music*, edited by Allan F. Moore, 39–59. Cambridge: Cambridge University Press, 2003.

Guiver, George. *Company of Voices: Daily Prayer and the People of God*. London: SPCK, 1988.

Hardy, Dan. *Finding the Church: The Dynamic Truth of Anglicanism*. London: SCM, 2001.

Hastings, Adrian. "Incarnation." In *The Oxford Companion to Christian Thought: Intellectual, Spiritual, and Moral Horizons of Christianity*, edited by Adrian Hastings, Alistair Mason, and Hugh Pyper, 321–24. New York: Oxford University Press, 2000.

Heaney, Maeve Louise. "The Eloquence of Music in Contemporary Culture." *Theology* 114, no. 3 (2011): 198–206.

Heelas, Paul. *Spiritualities of Life: New Age Romanticism and Consumptive Capitalism*. Oxford: Wiley-Blackwell, 2008.

Hervieu-Léger, Danièle. *Religion as a Chain of Memory*. Cambridge: Polity Press, 2000.

Hills, Matt. *Fan Cultures*. London: Routledge, 2002.

Honderich, Ted, ed. *The Oxford Companion to Philosophy*. New York: Oxford University Press, 1995.

Hoover, Stewart. *Religion in the Media Age*. New York: Routledge, 2006.

Hornby, Nick. *Juliet, Naked*. London: Penguin Books, 2010.

———. *31 Songs*. London: Viking, 2003.

Hughes, Graham. *Worship as Meaning: A Liturgical Theology for Late Modernity*. New York: Cambridge University Press, 2003.

Hughes, Jason. *Learning to Smoke: Tobacco Use in the West*. Chicago: University of Chicago Press, 2003.

Isherwood, Lisa. *Introducing Feminist Christologies*. New York: Continuum, 2002.

Johnson, Mark. *The Body in the Mind: The Bodily Basis of Meaning, Imagination, and Reason*. Chicago: University of Chicago Press, 1987.

Johnson, Steven. *Everything Bad Is Good for You: How Popular Culture Is Making Us Smarter*. London: Allen Lane, 2005.

Jones, Serene, and Paul Lakeland, eds. *Constructive Theology: A Contemporary Approach to Classical Themes*. Minneapolis: Fortress, 2005.

Jurgenssen, John. "From ABBA to ZZ Top, All the Good Band Names Are Taken." *Wall Street Journal*, February 17, 2010. http://online.wsj.com/article/SB10001 424052748703357104575045584007339958.html.

Juslin, Patrik N., and John Sloboda, eds. *Handbook of Music and Emotion*. Oxford: Oxford University Press, 2009.

Juvenal. *The Sixteen Satires*. Translated by Peter Green. Harmondsworth: Penguin, 1967.

Kerr, Hugh T., ed. *Readings in Christian Thought*. 2nd ed. Nashville: Abingdon, 1990.

Lakoff, George, and Mark Johnson. *Metaphors We Live By*. Chicago: University of Chicago Press, 1980.

———. *Philosophy in the Flesh: The Embodied Mind and Its Challenge to Western Thought*. New York: Basic Books, 1999.

Laski, Marghanita. *Everyday Ecstasy*. London: Thames & Hudson, 1980.

Lave, Jean, and Etienne Wenger. *Situated Learning: Legitimate Peripheral Participation*. New York: Cambridge University Press, 1991.

Lazarus, Richard, and Bernice Lazarus. *Passion and Reason: Making Sense of Our Emotions*. New York: Oxford University Press, 1994.

Levitin, Daniel. *This Is Your Brain on Music: Understanding a Human Obsession.* London: Atlantic Books, 2007.

———. *The World in Six Songs: How the Musical Brain Created Human Nature.* London: Aurum, 2009. Updated ed., 2010.

Loades, Ann. "Sacrament." In *The Oxford Companion to Christian Thought: Intellectual, Spiritual, and Moral Horizons of Christianity*, edited by Adrian Hastings, Alistair Mason, and Hugh Pyper, 634–37. New York: Oxford University Press, 2000.

Luhr, Eileen. *Witnessing Suburbia: Conservatives and Christian Youth Culture.* Berkeley: University of California Press, 2009.

Lynch, Gordon. "Cultural Theory and Cultural Studies." In *The Routledge Companion to Religion and Film*, edited by John Lyden, 275–91. New York: Routledge, 2009.

———. *Understanding Theology and Popular Culture.* Malden, MA: Blackwell, 2005.

Lyon, David. *Jesus in Disneyland: Religion in Postmodern Times.* Malden, MA: Polity Press, 2000.

MacCulloch, Diarmaid. *A History of Christianity: The First Three Thousand Years.* New York: Allen Lane, 2009.

MacIntyre, Alasdair. *After Virtue: A Study in Moral Theory.* London: Duckworth, 1981.

———. *Whose Justice? Which Rationality?* London: Duckworth, 1988.

Macquarrie, John. *Principles of Christian Theology.* Rev. ed. London: SCM, 1977.

MacSwain, Robert, and Taylor Worley, eds. *Theology, Aesthetics and Culture: Responses to David Brown.* Oxford: Oxford University Press, 2012.

Maffesoli, Michel. *The Time of the Tribes: The Decline of Individualism in Mass Society.* Thousand Oaks, CA: Sage, 1996.

Markham, Ian S. *Plurality and Christian Ethics.* New York: Cambridge University Press, 1994.

———. *A Theology of Engagement.* Malden, MA: Blackwell, 2003.

Marsh, Clive. "Adventures in Affective Space: The Reconstruction of Piety in an Age of Entertainment; The Fernley Hartley Lecture 2010." *Epworth Review* 37, no. 3 (2010): 6–20.

———. *Christ in Focus: Radical Christocentrism in Christian Theology.* London: SCM, 2005.

———. *Christ in Practice: A Christology of Everyday Life.* London: Darton, Longman & Todd, 2006.

———. Review of *One Step Closer: Why U2 Matters to Those Seeking God*, by Christian Scharen, with a response by Christian Scharen. *Conversations in Religion and Theology* 5, no. 2 (2007): 202–11.

———. "Theology as 'Soundtrack': Popular Culture and Narratives of the Self." *Expository Times* 118, no. 11 (2007): 536–41.

Marsh, Clive, and Vaughan S. Roberts. "Soundtracks of Acrobatic Selves: Fan-Site Religion in the Reception and Use of the Music of U2." *Journal of Contemporary Religion* 26 (2011): 417–30.

Marsh, Dave. *Bruce Springsteen: Two Hearts—The Definitive Biography, 1972–2003.* New York: Routledge, 2004.

Martin, Dale B. *The Corinthian Body.* New Haven: Yale University Press, 1995.

Martin, Dan. "Lady Gaga: 'My Tour Is a Religious Experience.'" May 12, 2011. http://www.guardian.co.uk/music/2011/may/13/lady-gaga-exclusive-guardian-interview. On Simon Hattenstone's interview of Lady Gaga printed in *The Guardian*, May 14, 2011.

Martin, David. *On Secularization: Towards a Revised General Theory.* Burlington, VT: Ashgate, 2005.

———. "Personal Reflections in the Mirror of Halévy and Weber." In *The Blackwell Companion to Sociology of Religion*, edited by Richard K. Fenn, 23–38. Malden, MA: Blackwell, 2001.

McCarthy, Kate. "Deliver Me from Nowhere: Bruce Springsteen and the Myth of the American Promised Land." In *God in the Details: American Religion in Popular Culture*, edited by Eric Michael Mazur and Kate McCarthy, 23–46. New York: Routledge, 2001.

McGrath, Alister E., ed. *The Christian Theology Reader.* 3rd ed. Malden, MA: Blackwell, 2007.

McGuiness, Paul. Speech at *Marché International du Disque et de l'Édition Musicale* (MIDEM), on January 28, 2008, at Cannes, France (music trade fair). http://www.billboard.biz/bbbiz/content_display/industry/news/e3i062b16e707aa99916c212e660cbffd3e.

McLeod, Hugh. *The Religious Crisis of the 1960s.* New York: Oxford University Press, 2007.

Middleton, Richard, ed. *Reading Pop: Approaches to Textual Analysis in Popular Music.* New York: Oxford University Press, 2000.

———. *Studying Popular Music.* Philadelphia: Open University Press, 1990.

Milbank, John. *Theology and Social Theory: Beyond Secular Reason.* Cambridge, MA: Blackwell, 1990.

Million Dollar Quartet. Written by Floyd Mutrux and Colin Escott. Musical, from 2007. http://en.wikipedia.org/wiki/Million_Dollar_Quartet#Musical.

Moberg, Marcus. "Christian Metal in Finland: Institutional Religion and Popular Music in the Midst of Religious Change." In *Religion and Popular Music in Europe: New Expressions of Sacred and Secular Identity*, edited by Thomas Bossius, Andreas Häger, and Keith Kahn-Harris, 31–50. New York: I. B. Tauris, 2011.

Moore, Allan F., ed. *Analyzing Popular Music*. New York: Cambridge University Press, 2003.

Moore, Laurence. *Selling God: American Religion in the Marketplace of Culture*. New York: Oxford University Press, 1994.

Moore, Stephen. *God's Gym: Divine Male Bodies of the Bible*. New York: Routledge, 1996.

Morgan, David, ed. *Key Words in Religion, Media and Culture*. New York: Routledge, 2008.

Nantais, Daniel. *Rock-a My Soul: An Invitation to Rock Your Religion*. Collegeville, MN: Liturgical Press, 2011.

Nicholls, David. *God and Government in an "Age of Reason."* New York: Routledge, 1995.

North, Adrian, and David Hargreaves. *The Social and Applied Psychology of Music*. Oxford: Oxford University Press, 2008.

Nussbaum, Martha. *Upheavals of Thought: The Intelligence of Emotions*. Cambridge: Cambridge University Press, 2001.

O'Neill, John. *The Communicative Body: Studies in Communicative Philosophy, Politics, and Sociology*. Evanston, IL: Northwestern University Press, 1989.

Ostwalt, Conrad. *Secular Steeples: Popular Culture and the Religious Imagination*. Harrisburg, PA: Trinity Press International, 2003. 2nd ed., New York: Continuum International Publishing Group, 2012.

Participations: Journal of Audience & Reception Studies. http://www.participations.org/.

Partridge, Christopher. "Religion and Popular Culture." In *Religions in the Modern World: Traditions and Transformations*, edited by Linda Woodhead, Hiroko Kawanami, and Christopher Partridge, 489–521. 2nd ed. New York: Routledge, 2009.

Pattison, Stephen. "Mend the Gap: Christianity and the Emotions." *Contact* 134 (2001): 3–9.

———. *Shame: Theory, Therapy, Theology*. New York: Cambridge University Press, 2000.

Pearsall, Judy, and Bill Trumble. *Oxford English Reference Dictionary*. New York: Oxford University Press, 1995.

Placher, William C., ed. *Readings in the History of Christian Theology*. Vol. 2. Philadelphia: Westminster, 1988.

Polkinghorne, John. "The Continuing Interaction of Science and Religion." *Zygon* 40 (2005): 43–49.

Porter, Jennifer. "Implicit Religion in Popular Culture: The Religious Dimensions of Fan Communities." *Implicit Religion* 12 (2009): 271–80.

Preston, Ronald H. *Religion and the Persistence of Capitalism: The Maurice Lectures for 1977*. London: SCM, 1979.

Prothero, Stephen. *American Jesus: How the Son of God Became a National Icon*. New York: Farrar, Straus & Giroux, 2003.

Ritzer, George. *Enchanting a Disenchanted World: Revolutionizing the Means of Consumption*. Thousand Oaks, CA: Pine Forge, 1999.

Roberts, Vaughan S. "A Body of Consensus? The Church as Embodied Organization." In *Managing the Church? Order and Organization in a Secular Age*, edited by G. R. Evans and Martyn Percy, 153–73. Sheffield: Sheffield Academic Press, 2000.

———. "Consuming Religion: Faith in the Future and the Future of Faith." *Reviews in Religion and Theology* 8, no. 2 (2001): 118–25.

———. "Nick Cave & 'Ugly' Bodies on *Dig!!! Lazarus Dig!!!*" Presented at the conference "Theology, Aesthetics and Culture: Conversations with the Work of David Brown," University of St. Andrews, 2010. http://itiablog.files.word press.com/2010/09/cave_paperfinal.pdf.

———. "Water as an Implicit Metaphor for Organizational Change within the Church." *Implicit Religion* 5, no. 1 (2002): 29–40.

Rogers, Eugene F., Jr. *Sexuality and the Christian Body: Their Way into the Triune God*. Malden, MA: Blackwell, 1999.

Rojek, Chris. *Celebrity*. London: Reaktion Books, 2001.

Ross, Alex. *The Rest Is Noise: Listening to the Twentieth Century*. London: Harper Perennial, 2009.

Sacks, Oliver. *Musicophilia: Tales of Music and the Brain*. London: Picador, 2007.

Saliers, Don E. *Music and Theology*. Nashville: Abingdon, 2007.

Saliers, Don E., and Emily Saliers. *A Song to Sing, A Life to Live: Reflections on Music as Spiritual Practice*. San Francisco: Jossey-Bass, 2005.

Sandbrook, Dominic. *Never Had It So Good: A History of Britain from Suez to the Beatles*. London: Little, Brown, 2005.

———. *White Heat: A History of Britain in the Swinging Sixties*. London: Little, Brown, 2006.

Sandvoss, Cornel. "The Death of the Reader? Literary Theory and the Study of Texts in Popular Culture." In *Fandom: Identities and Communities in a Mediated World*, edited by Jonathan Gray, Cornel Sandvoss, and C. Lee Harrington, 19–32. New York: New York University Press, 2007.

Savage, Sara, Sylvia Collins-Mayo, and Bob Mayo, with Graham Cray. *Making Sense of Generation Y: The World View of 15- to 25-Year-Olds*. London: Church House, 2006.

Scharen, Christian. *One Step Closer: Why U2 Matters to Those Seeking God*. Grand Rapids: Brazos, 2006.

Schechner, Richard. *Performance Studies: An Introduction*. 2nd ed. New York: Routledge, 2006.

Schenden, Greg. "Rock-n-roll Saved My Soul." *New Wineskins: A Journal of the Jesuit School of Theology at Berkeley* 1, no. 2 (Winter 2006): 2–11.

Schleiermacher, Friedrich D. E. *On Religion: Speeches to Its Cultured Despisers*. Translated by Richard Crouter. Cambridge: Cambridge University Press, 1996.

Sendra, Tim. Review of the album *Med Sud I Eyrum Vid Spilum Endalaust* [*With a Buzz in Our Ears We Play Endlessly*], by Sigor Rós, released June 24, 2008. http://www.allmusic.com/album/med-sud-i-eyrum-vid-spilum-endalaust-r1397505/review.

Shanks, Andrew. *Civil Society, Civil Religion*. Cambridge, MA: Blackwell, 1995.

Shuker, Roy. *Understanding Popular Music Culture*. 3rd ed. New York: Routledge, 2008.

Silitto, David. "Are Record Clubs the New Book Clubs?" *BBC News Magazine*, January 18, 2011. http://www.bbc.co.uk/news/magazine-12209143.

Sims, David. "Living a Story and Storying a Life: A Narrative Understanding of the Distributed Self." In *Organization and Identity*, edited by Alison Pullen and Stephen Linstead, 86–104. New York: Routledge, 2005.

Smith, Graeme. *A Short History of Secularism*. London: I. B. Tauris, 2007.

Smith, James K. A. *Desiring the Kingdom: Worship, Worldview, and Cultural Formation*. Grand Rapids: Baker Academic, 2009.

Sommer, Benjamin D. *The Bodies of God and the World of Ancient Israel*. New York: Cambridge University Press, 2009.

Spickard, James V. "For a Sociology of Religious Experience." In *A Future for Religion?* edited by W. H. Swatos Jr., 109–28. London: Sage, 1993.

Stevenson, Nick. *David Bowie: Fame, Sound and Vision*. Cambridge: Polity Press, 2006.

Stockman, Steve. *The Rock Cries Out: Discovering Truth in Unlikely Music*. Lake Mary, FL: Relevant Books, 2004.

———. *Walk On: The Spiritual Journey of U2*. Lake Mary, FL: Relevant Books, 2001.

Storey, John, ed. *Cultural Theory and Popular Culture: A Reader*. 3rd ed. Harlow: Pearson Education, 2006.

Symynkywicz, Jeffrey B. *The Gospel according to Bruce Springsteen: Rock and Redemption, from Asbury Park to Magic*. Louisville: Westminster John Knox, 2008.

Targoff, Ramie. *Common Prayer: The Language of Public Devotion in Early Modern England*. Chicago: University of Chicago Press, 2001.

Tawney, Richard Henry. *Religion and the Rise of Capitalism: A Historical Study*. Holland Memorial Lectures, 1922. New York: Harcourt, Brace, 1926.

Taylor, Barry. *Entertainment Theology: New-Edge Spirituality in a Digital Democracy*. Grand Rapids: Baker Academic, 2008.

Taylor, Charles. *A Secular Age*. Cambridge, MA: Belknap Press of Harvard University Press, 2007.

———. *Sources of Self: The Making of the Modern Identity*. Cambridge: Cambridge University Press, 1989.

Temple, William. *Nature, Man and God*. London: Macmillan, 1951.

Ter Borg, Meerten B. "Religion and Power." In *The Oxford Handbook of the Sociology of Religion*, edited by Peter B. Clarke, 194–209. New York: Oxford University Press, 2009.

Thiemann, Ronald F. "Piety, Narrative, and Christian Identity." *Word & World* 3, no. 2 (1983): 148–59.

Thomas, Owen C., and Ellen K. Wondra. *Introduction to Theology*. 3rd ed. Harrisburg, PA: Morehouse Pub., 2002.

Thomas, Scott M. *The Global Resurgence of Religion and the Transformation of International Relations: The Struggle for the Soul of the Twenty-First Century*. New York: Palgrave MacMillan, 2005.

Thornton, Sarah. *Club Cultures: Music, Media and Subcultural Capital*. Cambridge: Polity Press, 1995.

Till, Rupert. *Pop Cult*. New York: Continuum, 2010.

Tillich, Paul. *Systematic Theology*. Vol. 1. London: SCM, 1978.

Tracy, David Tracy. *The Analogical Imagination: Christian Theology and the Culture of Pluralism*. London: SCM, 1981.

Turner, Bryan S. "The Body in Western Society: Social Theory and Its Perspectives." In *Religion and the Body*, edited by Sarah Coakley, 15–41. New York: Cambridge University Press, 1997.

Turner, Graeme. *Ordinary People and the Media: The Demotic Turn*. London: Sage, 2009.

Turner, Steve. *A Hard Day's Write: The Stories behind Every Beatles Song*. London: Carlton Books, 2005.

Underhill, Evelyn. *Worship*. London: Nisbett, 1941.

Vanhoozer, Kevin J., Charles A. Anderson, and Michael J. Sleasman, eds. *Everyday Theology: How to Read Cultural Texts and Interpret Trends*. Grand Rapids: Baker Academic, 2007.

Von Appen, Ralf, and André Doehring. "Nevermind the Beatles, Here's Exile 61 and Nico: 'The Top 100 Records of all Time'—A Canon of Pop and Rock Albums from a Sociological and an Aesthetic Perspective." *Popular Music* 25 (January 2006): 21–40.

Wainwright, Geoffrey, and Karen B. Westerfield Tucker, eds. *The Oxford History of Christian Worship*. New York: Oxford University Press, 2006.

Ward, Graham. *The Politics of Discipleship: Becoming Postmaterial Citizens.* Grand Rapid: Baker Academic, 2009.

Ward, Pete. *Participation and Mediation: A Practical Theology for the Liquid Church.* London: SCM, 2008.

———. "The Production and Consumption of Contemporary Charismatic Worship in Britain as Investment and Affective Alliance." *Journal of Religion and Popular Culture* 5 (Fall 2003): 1–12. http://www.usask.ca/relst/jrpc/art4-britconsumption.html.

Warner, Timothy. *Pop Music—Technology and Creativity: Trevor Horn and the Digital Revolution.* Burlington, VT: Ashgate, 2003.

Weber, Max. *The Protestant Ethic and the Spirit of Capitalism.* 1905. Translated by Talcott Parsons. New York: Routledge, 2001.

Weick, Karl E. *Sensemaking in Organizations.* Thousand Oaks, CA: Sage, 1995.

Welker, Michael. "The Holy Spirit." In *The Oxford Handbook of Systematic Theology,* edited by John Webster, Kathryn Tanner, and Iain Torrance, 236–48. Oxford: Oxford University Press, 2007.

World Council of Churches. *Baptism, Eucharist and Ministry.* Faith and Order Paper No. 11. Geneva: World Council of Churches, 1982. http://www.oikoumene.org/en/resources/documents/wcc-commissions/faith-and-order-commission/i-unity-the-church-and-its-mission/baptism-eucharist-and-ministry-faith-and-order-paper-no-111–the-lima-text/baptism-eucharist-and-ministry.html#c10471.

———. *The Nature and Mission of the Church.* Faith and Order Paper No. 198. Geneva: World Council of Churches, 2005. http://www.oikoumene.org/en/resources/documents/wcc-commissions/faith-and-order-commission/i-unity-the-church-and-its-mission/the-nature-and-mission-of-the-church-a-stage-on-the-way-to-a-common-statement.html.

Wright, Stephen. *The Sounds of the Sixties and the Church: How British Christians Responded to the Music of the Beatles, Bob Dylan and Jimi Hendrix.* Guildford: Grosvenor House, 2008.

Wuthnow, Robert. *All In Sync: How Music and Art Are Revitalizing American Religion.* Berkeley: University of California Press, 2003.

———. *Christianity in the 21st Century: Reflections on the Challenges Ahead.* New York: Oxford University Press, 1993.

———. "The Contemporary Convergence of Arts and Religion." In *The Oxford Handbook of the Sociology of Religion,* edited by Peter B. Clarke, 360–74. New York: Oxford University Press, 2009.

subject index

abuse, 184
AC/DC, 82
Adele, 139
Adorno, Theodor, 6–7
aesthetics, 117, 177, 206n36
affective space, 16–17, 19, 20, 27, 48, 181, 183, 192n4
affinity space, 192n4
alcohol, 83, 167
Allen, Lily, 50
Alzheimer's disease, 63
ambiguity, 34, 47, 65, 72, 83, 165–68
analogy, 59, 67, 71
Andress, Ursula, 18
Anglicanism, 33, 184
anthropology, xiv, 15, 22, 143, 151, 157, 187
anticlericalism, 96
Arcade Fire, 12, 139
Archer, Margaret, 201n34
Aristotle, 54, 140
Ashcroft, Richard, 91
Assayas, Michka. *See* Bono
assimilation, 125, 126–27
atheism, 136
attachment, 118
attractiveness, 62
audience, 11–13
Augustine, 99, 107, 140, 178–79, 208n8
authenticity, 7
authority, 118–20
autonomy, 30
avant-garde, 6
awareness, 60, 133

Bach, Johann Sebastian, 111, 206n36
baptism, 33, 176, 178
Barber, Benjamin R., 52
Barrie, Chris, 65, 66

Beatles, The, 31, 65, 112, 116, 139
Beaudoin, Tom, 33–35, 36, 37, 38, 42, 124
Beckwith, Sarah, 205n20, 207n33
Beethoven, Ludwig von, 120
Bell, Catherine, 104
bereavement, 92–94
Berger, Peter, 96
Berryman, John, 197n58
Bibb, Eric, 139
Bill Haley and the Comets, 139
Black Eyed Peas, 139
Black Sabbath, 82
Blake, John, 137
Blind Boys of Alabama, the, 139
bloggers, 188
Bloom, Harold, 113, 114, 115
body, 102
    ambiguity of, 165–68
    physical, 57–58
    social, 62–67
    symbolic, 59–60, 67–71
Bon Jovi, 139
Bono, 44, 46, 48
Boone, Pat, 30
Bowie, David, 52, 73
Bragg, Billy, 139
Branch, Lori, 102–3
bricolage, 20
British Broadcasting Corporation (BBC), 77
Brown, David, 32–34, 36–38, 42, 53–55, 71, 72, 124, 134, 176, 179, 193n7, 206n34
Brown, Frank Burch, 86–87, 88
Bruce, Steve, 96
Buddhism, 137
Burning Man, 18–19, 103–4, 107–8, 137, 195n22, 199–200n40
Bush, George W., 73

canon, 113–18, 119, 152, 204n30
capitalism, 45, 50–53, 70
Carey, James, 9, 10, 104
Carey, John, 86, 87, 88, 109
Carpenters, the, 120
Cave, Nick, 34, 59, 60, 67, 71, 72–74
Cavicchi, Daniel, 70, 95, 97–98, 107, 134, 201n39, 202n65, 202–3n11, 203n26, 204n27, 205n2
censorship, 184
chaos, 106
Chernenko, Konstantin, 65
Chomsky, Noam, 24
Christ figures, 145
Christianity, 113, 141, 196n14
Christian rock, 167
Christology, 149, 165, 167, 168, 170–71
church, 146, 150, 152, 156, 160, 170–74, 178, 184–85
   and world, 31–32
city, 69
Clarke, Eric, 15, 132, 133, 206n27
Clash, The, 139, 198n13
class, 115
classical music, 205n16
classics, 111–18
cleansing, 176, 177
club culture, 83, 88–89
Cobb, Kelton, 6, 37, 141, 142–46, 154, 155, 157, 158–60, 163
Cocteau Twins, The, 198n13
Coldplay, 82
comfort, 22, 23, 157
commodity, 41–42
common grace, 130
communality, 81–82
communication, 9–11
communion. See Holy Communion
communion of saints, 150
community, 105–6, 114–18, 156, 158, 178
connectedness, 150–51, 160, 170–74
Connor, Steven, 54
conservatism, 31, 193n6
consumption, 36, 42–45, 195n15
contemporary Christian music, 45
contentment, 83
contextualization, 185
conveyance, 24–25
Copeland, Shawn, 177, 178
country, 8, 110
Cousland, Robert, 72–74
Cream, 18

creation, 80, 167
creativity, 102
Crisp, Oliver, 164–65, 167
critics, 20–21, 188
Cross, Ian, 23
Crowe, Tucker, 84
Cullen, Jim, 68
Cupitt, Don, 55

dance, 54, 61–62, 83, 131
Davis, Grace, 97
De Certeau, Michel, 67–71, 106
deChant, Dell, 43–44, 47
Deep Purple, 82, 139
Del Colle, Ralph, 170–71
denominations, 51
DeNora, Tia, 63, 64, 99, 103, 104, 105–6, 126, 203n11
desire, 35, 38, 43, 167
Detweiler, Craig, 80, 112, 198n14
devotion, 100–103, 118–20
Dibben, Nicola, 15, 132, 133, 206n27
disenchantment, 25
disposable wealth, 29
dissimilarity, 67, 71
distraction, 26
diversity, 18
Dixie Chicks, 151
doctrine, 186
drama, 54
Dr. Dre, 139
Driver, Tom, 104–5, 106
drug use, 83, 105, 129, 167, 202n65, 205n24
Dylan, Bob, 116–18, 139, 204n31
Dyrness, William A., 161, 182, 208n3

Eagles, The, 139
ecclesiology, 170
economics, 50
ecstasy, 78–79, 81
Editors (band), 139
efficacy, 135
Elbow (band), 82
Elliott, Denholm, 18
Ellul, Jacques, 43
embodiment, 129, 149–50, 160–61, 164–70
Eminem, 12, 139
emotion, 57, 58, 61, 91, 132, 143, 204n27
enchantment, 25
energy, 82
engagement, 124–30
Enlightenment, 8, 151

Eno, Brian, 41, 54
entertainment, 143–44, 188–89
Episcopalian Church, 33, 184
escapism, 4, 78–79, 81, 87, 157
eschatology, 145, 148–49, 150
eternity, 145
ethics, 115, 117, 125, 206n36
Eucharist, 153, 174
Eurythmics, The, 139
evangelicalism, 45
Evans, Dave, 85
Everything But the Girl, 84
evolution, 22, 62
excarnation, 38
exchange, 41
exhilaration, 81
expansion, 8
experience, 34, 89, 175
explanation, 9

faith, 35, 51, 68
faith communities, 184
fandom, 127, 131, 134–35, 136, 153, 171–72,
    174
Federer, Roger, 203n15
feel-good factor, 3–4, 60, 131, 148
Fenn, Richard K., 175
festivals, 41
file sharers, 49
film, 27, 54
Flanagan, Kieran, 100
Flynn, Errol, 18
folk, 8, 64
forgiveness, 27, 177
Frankfurt School, 6
Frankie Goes to Hollywood, 60, 65–67
Fraser, Elizabeth, 198n13
freedom, 30, 151–52
friendship, 22, 156, 171–72
Frith, Simon, 64, 66, 177
Fugees, 139
Fuller, Robert C., 106
fun, 27–28, 79

Gaarder, Jostein, 210n37
Galileo, 54
garage, 8
Garland, Judy, 119
Garvey, Guy, 77
Gaye, Marvin, 46
Gee, James, 192n4
general revelation, 130

Generation X, 34, 35, 193n13
Genesis, 84, 139
Gerrard, Lisa, 198n13
Giddens, Anthony, 99
Gilbert, Daniel, 143
Gilmore, Lee, 18, 103, 107, 108
Gladwell, Malcolm, 3
globalization, 103
gnosticism, 25
God, 143, 150
    body of, 74–75
    doctrine of, 147, 168
    grace of, 37, 101
    self-communication of, 34
    self-revelation of, 37
    work of, 32
goth, 46
Gould, Stephen Jay, 17–18
grace, 101
Graham-Dixon, Andrew, 92
Great Awakening, 51
Green, Al, 57, 58, 75, 196n2
Gregorian chant, 48
Gregory of Nazianzus, 208n11
Grimes, Ronald, 104

habits, xv
Hamnett, Katherine, 66
Hardy, Dan, 209n20
Hargreaves, David, 4, 48–49, 50, 55, 62, 100
Harries, Richard, 123
Harvest Crusade, 45–46
Hastings, Adrian, 164
health, 131, 132, 142
Heaney, 149
heavy metal, 8, 45, 64, 118
hedonism, 165, 192n9
Hegel, Georg Wilhelm Friedrich, 168
Heinlein, Robert, 52
Hervieu-Léger, Danielle, 53, 97
high culture, 17
Hills, Matt, 205n2
Hinduism, 137
hip-hop, 8
history, 51
Holy Communion, 33, 153, 174–78
Holy Spirit, 150
homo liturgicus, 35–37
homosexuality, 173
Hoover, Stewart M., 26–27
Horn, Trevor, 66
Hornby, Nick, 84–85, 117

Hughes, Graham, 104, 105, 106, 134
humanity, 143–44, 146, 169
Huxley, Aldous, 4
hybridity, 20
hymns, 63

Ibiza, 18, 21, 107, 192n9
identity, 27, 53, 60, 69, 105, 143, 153, 157, 176
idolatry, 102, 115, 165, 179
Ignatius of Antioch, 171
image of God, 44, 130
incarnation, 33, 34, 38, 65, 130, 149, 160–61,
    164–70, 186, 196n14
individualism, 6, 86
innovation, 50, 54
intensification, 134
intensity, 118
interdisciplinarity, 187
iPod, 48, 49, 50, 113, 119, 188
Iron Maiden, 82

Jackson, Michael, 73, 139
Jay-Z, 34, 139
Jesus Christ, 74, 150
    birth of, 66
    body of, 147–48, 149–50, 168–70, 207n33
    suffering of, 71
Jesus movement, 45
John, Elton, 84, 139
Johnson, Holly, 67
Johnson, Mark, 59, 60
joy, 22, 23, 63, 83, 156
Judaism, 113, 137
justice, 172, 173–74
Juvenal, 5, 66

Kabbalah mysticism, 94, 97
karaoke, 131, 198n15
Killers, The, 139
King, Carole, 139
kingdom, 173–74
Kings of Leon, 139
kitsch, 6
knowledge, 22, 23–24, 157–58
Krauss, Alison, 139, 206n31
Kubrick, Stanley, 119

Lady Gaga, 65, 119, 139, 173
Lakoff, George, 59
Laski, Marghanita, 78, 198n6
Lave, Jean, 192n4
Lazarus, 72, 74

Leary, Timothy, 208n8
Led Zeppelin, 72
Lévinas, Emmanuel, 105
Levitin, Daniel, 4, 21–26, 38, 58, 62, 63, 67,
    141, 155–60, 163, 179, 201n58
Lil Wayne, 127
Linkin Park, 196n2
listening, 137, 142, 151, 186
    everyday, 188
    repeated, 118
    as spiritual practice, 133–36
liturgy, 10, 32–33, 35–36, 68, 92–96, 105,
    209n31
Lombard, Peter, 178
Longhurst, Brian, 12
Lord's Prayer, 66, 179
Lord's Supper, 153, 174
love, 22, 24, 127, 156
Lovecraft, H. P., 52
Luhr, Eileen, 30, 45, 47, 53
Luther, Martin, 172
Lydon, John, 92–94, 97, 106
Lynch, Gordon, 12, 27, 83, 88–89, 199n40
Lyon, David, 43, 47
lyrics, 83–85, 184, 186

MacCulloch, Diarmaid, 42–43
MacIntyre, Alasdair, 99, 140
Madonna, 93–94, 97, 106, 119, 139, 173
Maffesoli, Michel, 98
Magisteria-Ibiza Spectrum, 17–21, 48, 51, 55,
    65, 75, 103n17, 111, 120, 123, 128, 137,
    140, 180, 183, 194n15
Marcus, Greil, 117
Markham, Ian S., 37, 125–26, 128–29, 130, 138
Marley, Bob, 46
Marsh, Clive, 192n5, 206n31
Marsh, Jill, 31
Martin, David, 96
Marx, Karl, 6
mass culture, 7–9
materiality, 36, 164–70
May, Imelda, 139
McCarthy, Cormac, 72
McCartney, Paul, 82, 112
McElderry, Joe, 131
McEntire, Reba, 139
McGuinness, Paul, 49
meaning, 9, 25, 81
meaning-making, 26–27, 136–38, 171, 188,
    193n25
Mearns, William Hughes, 52

meditation, 204n39
megachurch, 45, 194n13
metanarrative, 158
metaphor, 59, 71–74
metaphysics, 5
Methodist Church, 184
MGMT, 139
Michael, George, 66, 139
Middleton, Richard, 6–9, 12
MIDEM, 49
Milbank, John, 60
Miller, Michael, 60
minimalism, 79
Mitchell, Joni, 139
Moby, 60, 61, 139
Monroe, Marilyn, 119
Morley, Paul, 66
motivation, 58
Motorhead, 82
Mozart, Wolfgang Amadeus, 111
Mumford and Sons, 151
music
  collecting, 109–11
  functions of, 130–32
  and worship, 98
musicology, xiv, 177, 187

Nadal, Rafael, 203n15
narcissism, 100, 136
national anthems, 105, 179
neuroscience, 15, 22
Newman, Randy, 139
Newton, Isaac, 54
Nicene Creed, 179
Nine Inch Nails, 52
Nirvana, 52
Nixon, Richard, 65
Norman, Larry, 30
North, Adrian, 4, 48–49, 50, 55, 62, 100
nostalgia, 6
novelty, 50, 54

O'Neill, John, 74
order, 63, 130–31
orthodoxy, 11, 125, 138, 141, 152
Ostwalt, Conrad, 26, 193n35
overhearing, 128–29

Paisley, Brad, 139
Parker, Charlie, 4
participation, 19, 106, 131–32, 140, 176, 202n65

Parton, Dolly, 139
Paul (apostle), 129, 148, 168
philosophy, 115, 120, 125, 140
physical bodies, 57–58
Pinker, Steven, 58
Pink Floyd, 18, 84
Pitchfork (website), 50
Pitts, 132, 133, 206n27
Pitts, Stephanie, 15
Planet Earth (TV show), 81
Plath, Sylvia, 119
playlists, 111–13
pluralism, 51
politics, 3, 5, 43, 115, 117, 206n36
Polkinghorne, John, 18
pop music, 110
  and the body, 57–75
  as commodity, 41–42
  in digital age, 48–50
  and theology, 139–180
  and transcendence, 77–89
Porter, Jennifer, 153
postrock, 79
prayer, 158
predictability, 50
Presley, Elvis, 30, 101, 139
privatization, 51, 103
Proclaimers, The, 139
Prodigy, 196n2
production, 11–13
Protestantism, 113, 192n25
Protestant Reformation, 99
Prothero, Stephen, 52
psychology, 15, 187
Public Image Limited (PiL), 92, 139
punk, 8, 45

Queen, 139

radio, 110, 139
Radiohead, 50, 139, 206n36
Rage against the Machine, 131
Ramsey, JonBenet, 119
rap, 64
Rappaport, Roy, 24
rationality, 8
rave, 83
Reagan, Ronald, 65, 66, 73
rearrangement, 22
reception, 11–13
redemption, 27, 157
reflection, 188

reflexive self, 99–101
refreshment, 176, 177
relationship, 127
religion, 22, 24, 26, 42–45, 115, 158
REM, 139
Renaissance, 48, 53
repetition, 7
representation, 22
repudiation, 140
resistance, 127–28
revival, 95
revolution, 23, 96
Ricoeur, Paul, 106
Ridgeley, Andrew, 66
ritual, 9–11, 61, 96–106, 151–55, 158, 160, 174–80, 201n58
Ritzer, George, 43, 44, 47
Roberts, Vaughan, 206n31
rock, 8, 30, 31, 64, 110
Rogers, Eugene F., 207n33
Rolling Stones, 120, 139
Roman Catholicism, 17, 33, 35, 92–94, 113, 173, 192n25
Rowe, Chris, 46
Roxy Music, 139
Run-DMC, 61

sacrament, 33, 34, 36–37, 87, 146, 153–55, 160, 174–80, 209n26, 209n36
sacramentality, 48
Salier, Don, 61, 64, 194n32, 201n32
Salier, Emily, 61, 64, 201n32
salvation, 144–45, 148, 150, 157
Salvation Army, 209n36
Sandbrook, Dominic, 193n6
Schechner, Richard, 206n35
Schoenberg, Arnold, 120
Second Great Awakening, 44, 51
secularism, 96–106
secularization, 8, 51, 194n13
secular music, 179–80
security, 60
Seeger, Pete, 101
self, 99, 109–11
self-absorption, 87
self-expression, 166
self-identity, 100, 105
self-understanding, 27, 128
sentimentality, 6
sex, 167
Sex Pistols, 92
sexuality, 65, 66, 126, 127, 129

Shakespeare, William, 113
Sharpe, Robert, 200n41
Shuker, Roy, 114, 204n31
Sigur Rós, 79–81, 198n11, 198n14
similarity, 67
Simon, Paul, 139
Simonton, Dean, 50
sin, 144
sing-along, 81, 82, 131
Sisters of Mercy, 82
Smith, James K. A., 35–37, 38, 42, 43, 124, 193n25
Society of Friends (Quakers), 209n36
sociology, xiv, 15, 50, 187
solidarity, 176
Sommer, Benjamin D., 74–75
SongMeanings (website), 70, 73
soteriology, 167
soundtracks, 110–11, 158
Spencer, Diana, 15, 119, 206n27
spirituality, 61, 78, 136–37, 148, 195n22
Spiritualized (band), 139, 210n37
Springsteen, Bruce, 59, 67–71, 82, 95, 98, 101, 134, 151, 171, 201n39, 202n3, 202–3n11, 202n65
Stephens, Toby, 57
Stephenson, Nick, 52
Sting, 139
St. John, Graham, 104
Strauss, David Friedrich, 168–69
Strummer, Joe, 198n13
Stubbs, David, 67
suffering, 34, 176
suspicion, 34
Switchfoot, 139
symbolic bodies, 59–60
symbols, 174–80
systematic theology, 141, 158, 160, 181

Taylor, Barry, 10, 55, 80, 112, 198n14
Taylor, Charles, 30, 38, 51, 86-88, 96–97, 99
technology, 49–50
Ter Borg, Meerten B., 207n25
thanksgiving, 177
Thatcher, Margaret, 66
theological education, 185–87
theology, 5, 124–30, 142–46
Thomas Aquinas, 178
Thornton, Sarah, 64
Till, Rupert, 96, 98, 108, 140, 199n39, 200n25, 202n61, 204n26, 205n24
Tillich, Paul, 126, 205n15

Tingle Factor, The (TV show), 77
Tracy, David, 59, 109, 202n1
tradition, 140, 152
transcendence, xiii, 54, 78, 79, 135–36, 143,
    147–49, 160, 167, 181, 200n41
  importance of, 85–88
  physicality of, 82–83
transmission, 9–11
tribalism, 64, 98
truth, 172, 173–74
Turner, Bryan, 126
Turner, Steve, 112
Turner, Victor, 104
Tutu, Desmond, 200n10

U2, 15, 42, 44, 46–50, 83, 94, 139, 151, 172
Underhill, Evelyn, 102
Undertones, The, 139

values, 131, 132
Vanhoozer, Kevin, 12, 130
Vendler, Helen, 22
Verve, The, 91

Walters, Jennifer, 137
Ward, Graham, 103, 148
Ward, Pete, 12
Warner, 66

Waterboys, The, 52
Waters, Malcolm, 55
Waterworld (film), 55, 196n62
Watson, Doc, 139
wealth, 29, 206n11
Weber, Max, 42, 195n41
Welch, Gillian, 139
Welker, Michael, 172
Wenger, Etienne, 192n4
Wham! (band), 66
White Stripes, The, 139, 206n31
Williams, Rowan, 129
Wonder, Stevie, 139
Wordsworth, William, 103
world, and church, 31–32
World Trade Center, 67–68
worldview, 24, 35, 36, 120, 139, 147, 149, 152,
    175, 193n25
World War II, 8, 166, 167
worship, 10, 33, 36, 44, 98, 102–3, 153, 175,
    177, 179–80, 202n74
Wright, Stephen, 31, 208n10
Wuthnow, Robert, 207n37

yearning, 83

Zappa, Frank, 127
ZTT, 66

music index

Achtung Baby, U2, 50
"All Alright," Sigur Rós, 198n11
All That You Can't Leave Behind, U2, 195n40, 199n24
American Life, Madonna, 93

Basement Tapes, The, Bob Dylan, 117
"Beautiful Day," U2, 83
"Behind the Mask," Michael Jackson, 73
"Bittersweet Symphony," The Verve, 91
Blonde on Blonde, Bob Dylan, 117, 204n31
Blood on the Tracks, Bob Dylan, 117, 204n31
"Blowing in the Wind," Bob Dylan, 116
"Bodyrock," Moby, 60, 61
Bootleg Series, The, Bob Dylan, 117
"Born in the U.S.A.," Bruce Springsteen, 70
"Born This Way," Lady Gaga, 173
Born to Run, Bruce Springsteen, 101
Bringing It All Back Home, Bob Dylan, 117

"Captain Fantastic and the Brown Dirt Cowboy," Elton John, 84
"Countin' on a Miracle," Bruce Springsteen, 69

"Dance in the Dark," Lady Gaga, 119
"Death Disco," Sex Pistols, 92, 93
Dig, Lazarus, Dig!!!, Nick Cave and the Bad Seeds, 59, 60, 67, 71, 72
Disraeli Gears, Cream, 18

"Empty Sky," Bruce Springsteen, 69
"Every Girl," Lil Wayne, 127

Fame Monster, The, Lady Gaga, 119
"Fljotavik," Sigur Rós, 80
"Forever Young," Bob Dylan, 116

"40," U2, 46
Funeral, Arcade Fire, 12
"Further On (Up the Road)," Bruce Springsteen, 70

"Gobbledigook," Sigur Rós, 80
Good As I Been to You, Bob Dylan, 117
"Grounds for Divorce," Elbow, 82

"Hey Jude," The Beatles, 82, 116
"Heysatan," Sigur Rós, 80
Highway 61 Revisited, Bob Dylan, 117, 204n31
Home Movies: The Best of Everything but the Girl, Everything But the Girl, 199n25
"Hoppipolla," Sigur Rós, 81

"Ibiza Bar," Pink Floyd, 18
"I Didn't Know I Was Looking for Love," Everything But the Girl, 84
"Into the Fire," Bruce Springsteen, 69
"I Still Haven't Found What I'm Looking For," U2, 47

"Jacob's Ladder," Pete Seeger, 101
John Wesley Harding, Bob Dylan, 117
Joshua Tree, The, U2, 50, 195n40

"Killing in the Name," Rage against the Machine, 131

Ladies and Gentleman, We Are Floating in Space, Spiritualized, 210n37
"Lamb Lies Down on Broadway, The," Genesis, 84
"Let It Be," The Beatles, 112
"Like a Rolling Stone," Bob Dylan, 117

"Little Peace of Heaven, A," Avenged Sevenfold, 199n30

"Live to Tell," Madonna, 94

"Lonesome Day," Bruce Springsteen, 69

Love and Theft, Bob Dylan, 117

"Man Who Sold the World, The," David Bowie, 52, 73

Med Sud I Eyrum Vid Spilum Endalaust, Sigur Rós, 80, 198n11

Modern Times, Bob Dylan, 116

"Mofo," U2, 47

"Most of the Time," Bob Dylan, 117

"Mother and Father," Madonna, 93

"Mr. Tambourine Man," Bob Dylan, 116

Oh Mercy, Bob Dylan, 117

Play, Moby, 61

"Playboy Mansion, The," U2, 47

Pop, U2, 50

"Power of Love, The," Frankie Goes to Hollywood, 65, 66

"Rebellion," Arcade Fire, 12

"Relax," Frankie Goes to Hollywood, 65

"Religion," Sex Pistols, 92, 93

Rising, The, Bruce Springsteen, 59, 60, 67–71

Soundtrack for the Film More, Pink Floyd, 18

"Straumnes," Sigur Rós, 80

Street Legal Desire, Bob Dylan, 117

"Sunday Bloody Sunday," U2, 47

Takk, Sigur Rós, 80, 81

"Tales of Brave Ulysses," Cream, 18

"Thriller," Michael Jackson, 73

Time Out of Mind, Bob Dylan, 117

"Two Tribes," Frankie Goes to Hollywood, 60, 65, 67

"Viva La Vida," Coldplay, 82

War, U2, 46

"Why Should the Devil Have All the Good Music?" Larry Norman, 30

"Workingman's Blues #2," Bob Dylan, 116

World Gone Wrong, Bob Dylan, 117

"Yesterday," The Beatles, 112

"You Masters of War," Bob Dylan, 116

Zooropa, U2, 50